国外优秀数学著作
原 版 系 列

[尼日利亚] 穆斯塔法·阿金昆米 (Mustapha Akinkunmi) 著

# R统计学概论

Introduction to Statistics Using R

（英文）

哈尔滨工业大学出版社
HARBIN INSTITUTE OF TECHNOLOGY PRESS

# 黑版贸审字 08-2021-027 号

Introduction to Statistics Using R
Copyright © 2019 by Morgan & Claypool Publishers
Part of the Synthesis Lectures on Mathematics and Statistics
Series Editor：Steven G. Krantz
All rights reserved.
The English reprint rights arranged through Rightol Media(本书英文影印版权经由锐拓传媒取得 Email：copyright@rightol.com)


**图书在版编目(CIP)数据**

R 统计学概论＝Introduction to Statistics Using R：英文/(尼日利)穆斯塔法・阿金昆米(Mustapha Akinkunmi)著. —哈尔滨：哈尔滨工业大学出版社,2024.1
ISBN 978-7-5767-0730-4

Ⅰ.①R… Ⅱ.①穆… Ⅲ.①统计分析-统计程序-英文 Ⅳ.①C819

中国国家版本馆 CIP 数据核字(2023)第 046184 号


R TONGJIXUE GAILUN

策划编辑 刘培杰 杜莹雪
责任编辑 聂兆慈 张嘉芮
封面设计 孙茵艾
出版发行 哈尔滨工业大学出版社
社　　址 哈尔滨市南岗区复华四道街 10 号 邮编 150006
传　　真 0451-86414749
网　　址 http://hitpress.hit.edu.cn
印　　刷 哈尔滨博奇印刷有限公司
开　　本 787 mm×1 092 mm 1/16 印张 15.75 字数 263 千字
版　　次 2024 年 1 月第 1 版 2024 年 1 月第 1 次印刷
书　　号 ISBN 978-7-5767-0730-4
定　　价 88.00 元

(如因印装质量问题影响阅读,我社负责调换)

# Contents

# Preface

**Chapter 1: Introduction to Statistical Analysis**

This chapter helps readers that have litle or no knowledge about different scales of measurement in statistics. It also helps readers to understand the concept of data, data gathering, and how the data collected can be presented. In addition, this chapter helps the readers to be able to understand different categories of data grouping and to explore data analysis and visualization.

**Chapter 2: Introduction to R Software**

This chapter focuses on how to download and install R packages on a computer system, gives the reason for using R, and also gives full details of the steps involved in the installation of R. This chapter introduces readers to basic functions in R with illustrative examples. This chapter uncovers basic operations in R, built-in functions (numerical, statistical probability), and other useful functions in R. This chapter gives an overview on how to import packages and how to change directories for reading and writing local flats files. It helps in explaining how to connect to a database using R commands. Data exploration through visualization in R is demonstrated and desired charts are plotted.

**Chapter 3: Descriptive Data**

This chapter provides different kinds of statistical measures to analyze business-related data. The chapter focuses on measures of central tendency and dispersion, and gives the characteristics of the measures of central tendency and dispersion. Practical examples are given for each of these descriptive statistics mentioned in the chapter along with explanatory short R scripts. This chapter also explains the shapes of the distribution with illustrative examples.

**Chapter 4: Basic Probability Concepts**

This part of the book gives meaning to some probability terminologies—experiment, sample space, elementary event, complementary events, mutually exclusive events, mutually inclusive events, Venn diagram, independent, and dependent events. Axioms of probability is treated alongside basic properties of probability. This chapter walks the readers through the additive and multiplicative rules of probability and conditional probability. The chapter shows how to use R to generate and compute probabilities.

### Chapter 5: Discrete Probability Distribution

This chapter explains the concept of a discrete probability distribution, probability mass function, the expected value, and the variance of a discrete probability distribution. It gives examples of discrete probabilities and deals much on the binomial probability distribution. A subsection is dedicated to showing how to derive the expected value and variance for a binomial distribution. This chapter teaches readers how to generate a random sample from a binomial distribution. All examples given in this chapter are also written in R to acquaint readers on the software.

### Chapter 6: Continuous Probability Distribution

Apart from the discrete probability distribution explained in the previous chapter, there is a need for readers to know about the continuous probability distribution. This chapter focuses on the normal distribution among other continuous probability distributions mentioned in the chapter. The readers can vividly differentiate between the discrete and continuous probability distributions. The normal curve is explained with clear examples, and the properties of a normal distribution are stated. In addition, readers will be able to use standard normal score (z-score) to solve business problems. This chapter exposes readers to using normal approximation to solve a binomial problem. Many worked examples, as well as the R codes, are given on normal probability to sensitize readers to its application in businesses.

### Chapter 7: Other Continuous Probability Distributions

This chapter is an extension of Chapter 6. The chapter explains the commonly used distribution which is important in the testing of an hypothesis. These distributions are the student-t, Chi-square, and F distributions, and their properties and uses. This chapter helps the readers to be acquainted to the conditions when each of the aforementioned distributions are used in the testing of an hypothesis. The main objective of this chapter is for the readers to be able to know when each of the distributions can be used and to obtain respective table values for the distributions, even using the R commands.

### Chapter 8: Sampling and Sampling Distribution

This chapter gives an overview of the sampling techniques with their merits and demerits. This chapter classifies sampling into probability and non-probability sampling. The sampling distribution of the mean is established by using simple random sampling with and without replacement on data. This section of the book covers the central limit theorem and its significance with worked examples.

### Chapter 9: Confidence Intervals for Single Population Mean and Proportion

This chapter explains how to construct confidence intervals for mean and proportion with illustrative examples. It sheds more light on how to calculate the sample size when confidence level and margin of error are given. The chapter gives the main factors that determine a margin of error. Readers are expected to construct confidence limit using appropriate test statistics.

### Chapter 10: Hypothesis Testing for Single Population Mean and Proportion
This chapter is all about the decision-making process and it explains how to form and test hypotheses. It prepares readers on the steps to conduct hypothesis testing and interpret the results. This chapter helps the readers to use available data to make a valid conclusion.

### Chapter 11: Regression Analysis and Correlation
The existence of a relationship between two or more variables is taught in this chapter. The readers would understand and differentiate between the regression and correlation analyses. The chapter explains the uses and assumptions of simple and multiple linear regressions. This chapter helps the readers to know the interpretation of the regression model and to know how to use regression analysis in making predictions. The extent of the association between variable is also discussed with the aid of diagrams; this will give the readers intuition into the regression and correlation analyses. Many examples are given to broaden the scope of the readers on the topic.

### Chapter 12: Poisson distribution
This chapter deals with the count data. It gives statistical definition and a real-life example of a Poisson distribution. Different Poisson distribution graphs are demonstrated to show its characteristics as its parameter increases. This chapter derives and shows that mean and variance of a Poisson distribution are the same. The chapter explains the applications of a Poisson distribution in various aspects of life. Furthermore, this section proves how Poisson can be approximated to binomial distribution with some worked examples.

### Chapter 13: Uniform distribution
The main objectives of this chapter is for readers to be able to identify uniform distribution, its uses, and applications. This chapter explains a uniform distribution with aid of a diagram and the condition for using uniform distribution. It shows how to derive the mean and variance of a uniform distribution.

Mustapha Akinkunmi
February 2019

C H A P T E R   1

# Introduction to Statistical Analysis

Statistics is a science that supports us in making better decisions in business, economics, and other disciplines. In addition, it provides the necessary tools needed to summarize data, analyze data, and make meaningful conclusions to achieve a better decision. These better decisions assist us in running a small business, a corporation, or the economy as a whole. This book is a bit different from most statistics books in that it will focus on using data to help you do business and so the focus is not on statistics for statistics stake but rather on what you need to know to really use statistics.

To help in that endeavor, examples will include the use to the R programming language which was created specifically to give statisticians and technicians a tool to create solutions to standard techiques or to create their own solutions.

Statistics is a word that originated from the Italian word *stato* meaning "state" and *statista* is an individual saddled with the tasks of the state. Thus, statistics is the collection of useful information to the statista. Its application commenced in Italy during the 16th century and diffused to other countries around the world. At present, statistics covers a wide range of information in every aspect of human activities. In addition, it is not limited to the collection of numerical information but includes data summarization, presentation, and analysis in meaningful ways.

Statistical analysis is mainly concerned with how to make generalizations from the data. Statistics is a science that deals with information. In order for us to perform statistical analysis on information (data) you have on hand or collect, you may need to transform the data or work with the data to get it in a form where it can be analyzed using statistical techniques. Information can be found in qualitative or quantitative form. In order to explain the difference between these two types of information, let's consider an example. Suppose an individual intends to start a business based on the information in Table 1.1. Which of the variables are quantitative and which are qualitative? The product price is a quantitative variable because it provides information based on quantity—the product price in dollars. The number of similar businesses and the rent for business premises are also quantitative variables. The location used in establishing the business is a qualitative variable since it provides information about a quality (in this case a location, such as Nigeria or South Korea). The presence of basic infrastructures requires a (Yes or No) response, these are also qualitative variables.

Table 1.1: Business feasibility data

| Product price | Number of similar business | Rent for the business premise | Location | Presence of basic infrastructures |
|---|---|---|---|---|
| US$150 | 6 | US$2,000 | Nigeria | No |
| US$100 | 18 | US$3,000 | South Korea | Yes |

A quantitative variable represents a number for which arithmetic operations such as averaging make sense. A qualitative (or categorical) variable is concerned with quality. In a case where a number is applied to separate members of different categories of a qualitative variable, the assigned number is subjective but generally intentional. An aspect of statistics is concerned with measurements—some quantitative and others qualitative. Measurements provide the real numerical values of a variable. Qualitative variables can be represented with numbers as well, but such a representation might be arbitrary but intended to be useful for the purposes at hand. For instance, you can assign numerics to an instance of a qualitative variable such as Nigeria = 1 and South Korea = 0.

## 1.1 SCALES OF MEASUREMENTS

In order to use statistics effectively, it is helpful to view data in a slightly different way so that the data can be analyzed successfully. In performing a statistical test, it is important that all data is converted to the same scale. For instance, if your quantitative data is in meters and feet, you need to choose one and convert any data to that scale. However, in statistics there is another definition of *scales of measurement*. Scales of measurements are commonly classified into four categories, namely: nominal scale, ordinal scale, interval scale, and ratio scale.

1. **Nominal Scale:** In this scale, numbers are simply applied to label groups or classes. For instance, if a dataset consists of male and female, we may assign a number to them such as 1 for male and 2 for female. In this situation, the numbers 1 and 2 only denote the category in which a data point belongs. The nominal scale of measurement is applied to qualitative data such as male, female, geographic classification, race classification, etc.

2. **Ordinal Scale:** This scale allows data elements to be ordered based on their relative size or quality. For instance, buyers can rank three products by assigning them 1, 2, and 3, where 3 is the best and 1 is the worst. The ordinal scale does not provide information on how much better one product is compared to others, only that it is better. This scaling is used for many purposes, for instance grading, either stanine (1–9) or A–F (no E) where a 4.0 is all A's and all F's are 0.0, or rankings on, for instance, Amazon (1–5 stars so that that 5.0 would be a perfect ranking) or restaurants, hotels, and other data sources which may be ranked on a four- or five-star basis. It is therefore quite important in using this data to

know the data range. The availability of this type of data on the Internet makes this a good category for experimenting with real data.

3. **Interval Scale:** Interval scales are numerical scales in which intervals have the same interpretation. For instance, in the case of temperature, we have a centigrade scale in which water freezes at 0° and boils at 100° and a Fahrenheit scale in which 32° is the temperature at which water freezes, but 212° is the temperature at which it boils. These arbitrary decisions can make it difficult to take ratios. For example, it is not correct to say 8 PM is twice as long as 4 PM. However, it is possible to have ratios of intervals. The interval between 0:00 PM (noon) and 8:00 PM which represents a duration of 8 h is twice as long as the interval between 0:00 PM and 4:00 PM, which represents a duration of 4 h. The time 0:00 PM does not imply absence of any time. It is important that you understand your data and make sure it is converted appropriately so that in cases like this, interval scale can be used in statistical tests.

4. **Ratio Scale:** This scale allows us to take ratios of two measurements if the two measurements are in the ratio scale. The zero in the ratio scale is an absolute zero. For instance, money is measured in a ratio scale. A sum of US$1,000 is twice as large US$500. Other examples of the ratio scale include the measurements of weight, volume, area, or length.

## 1.2　DATA, DATA COLLECTION, AND DATA PRESENTATION

A dataset is defined as a set of measurements gathered on some variables. For example, dividend measurements for 10 companies may create a dataset. In this case, the concerned variable is dividend and the scale of measurement is a ratio scale (a dividend for one company may be twice another company's dividend). In the actual observations of the companies' dividends, the dataset might record US$4, US$6, US$5, US$3, US$2, US$7, US$8, US$1, US$10, and US$9.

Different approaches are used to collect data. Sometimes, a dataset might include the whole population of our interest, whereas in other cases, it might constitute a portion from the larger population. In this situation, the data needs to be carefully collected because we want to draw some inferences about the larger population based on the sample. The conclusion made about an entire population by relying on the information in a sample from the population is referred to as a *statistical inference*. This book assigns a great importance to the topic of statistical inference (it is fully explained in Chapter 6). The accuracy of statistical inference depends on how data is drawn from the population of interest. It is also critically important to ensure that every segment of the population is sufficiently and equally captured in the sample. Data collection from surveys or experiments has to be appropriately constructed, as statistical inference is based on them.

Data can also be obtained from published sources such as statistical abstracts of different publications. The published inflation rate for a number of months is a typical example. This data is collected as it is given without any control over how it is obtained. Inflation data for over a certain time is not a random sample of any future inflation rate, thus, making statistical inferences becomes complex and difficult. If the interest data is on the period where data is available, this makes the data consist of the whole population. However, it is greatly important to observe any missing data or incomplete observations.

This section focuses on the processing, summarization, and presentation of data which represents the first stage of statistical analysis. What are the reasons behind more attention on inference and population? Is it sufficient to observe data and interpret it? Data inspection is appropriate when the interest is aimed at particular observations, but meaningful conclusions require statistical analysis. This implies that any business decision based on a sample requires meaningful insights that can be drawn from the statistical analysis. Therefore, the role of statistics in any business entity is both a necessary and sufficient condition for effective and efficient decision-making. For instance, marketing research, that often aims to examine the link between advertising and sales, might obtain a dataset of randomly chosen sales and advertising figures for a given firm. However, much more useful information can be concluded if implications about the fundamental process are considered. Other businesses like banking might have interest in evaluating the diffusion of a particular model of automatic teller machines; a pharmaceutical firm that intends to market its new drug might require proving the drug does not cause negative side effects. These different aims of business entities can be attained through the use of statistical analysis.

Statistics can also have a dark side. The use of statistics takes a significant role in the success of many business activities. Therefore, it is in a company's interest to use statistics to their benefit. So AIG might say that since 2010 their stock has gone up $X\%$, having been bailed out the year before. You see mutual funds brag all the time about their record since a certain date. You can be certain that right before that date something bad happened. Or a company may claim that their survey showed that 55% prefered their brand of tomato soup. How many surveys did they conduct? How many different types of soup did they survey where the soup did poorly in statistical results? Another is that in a test, one aspect of a product can come out well, but other aspects may get bad results. So the company presents the positive results. Sampling is another area where it is easy to cheat as can be the integrity of existing data. There are many other ways to "lie" with statistics and it has become so commonplace that there are books written on that subject. The bottom line is to have a healthy skepticism when you hear statistics promoted in the media.

## 1.3    DATA GROUPINGS

Data is information that captures the qualitative or quantitative features of a variable or a set of variables. Put differently, data can be defined as any set of information that describes a given entity.

## 1.3.1   CATEGORIES OF DATA GROUPINGS

In statistics, data can be categorized into grouped and ungrouped data. Ungrouped data is data in the raw form. For instance, a list of business firms that you know. Grouped data is data that has been organized into groups known as classes. This implies that grouped data is no longer in the raw format.

A *class* can be defined as a group of data values within specific group boundaries. The *frequency distribution table* is the table that shows the different measurement categories and how often each category occurs. Plotting a frequency distribution of grouped data, such a frequency plot is called a *histogram*. A *histogram* is a chart comprised of bars of different heights. The height of each bar depicts the frequency of values in the class represented by the bar. Adjacent bars share sides. It is used only for measured or ordinal data. This is an appropriate way of plotting the frequencies of grouped data. The area of each bar in a histogram corresponds to the frequency. Table 1.2 is a frequency table that shows a random sample of 30 small-scale businesses based on their years of existance.

Table 1.2: Frequency table for grouped data

| Years of Establishment | Number of Businesses |
|:---:|:---:|
| 0-2 | 12 |
| 3 - 5 | 6 |
| 6 - 8 | 8 |
| 9 - 11 | 3 |
| 12 -14 | 1 |

Figure 1.1 shows the histogram representation for the given data in Table 1.2.

A data class refers to a group of data that are similar based on user-defined property. For instance, ages of students can be grouped into classes such as those in their teens, 20s, 30s, etc. Each of these groups is known as a class. Each class has a specific width known as the class interval or class size. The class interval is very crucial in the construction of histograms and frequency diagrams. Class size depends on how the data is grouped. The class interval is usually a whole number.

However, an example of grouped data that have different class interval is presented in Table 1.4. Tables like Table 1.4 are often called frequency tables as they show the frequency that data is represented in a specific class interval.

## 1.3.2   CALCULATION OF CLASS INTERVAL FOR UNGROUPED DATA

In order to obtain a class interval for a given set of raw or ungrouped data, the following steps have to be taken.

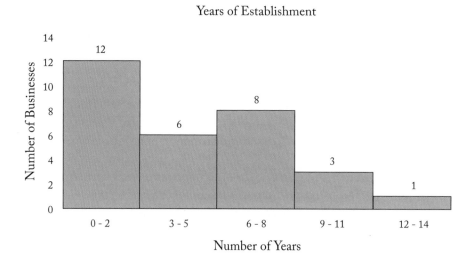

Figure 1.1: Histogram.

Table 1.3: Grouped data with the same class interval

| Daily Income (US$) | Frequency | Class Interval |
|---|---|---|
| 0 - 9 | 5 | 10 |
| 10 - 19 | 8 | 10 |
| 20 - 29 | 12 | 10 |
| 30 - 39 | 17 | 10 |
| 40 - 49 | 3 | 10 |
| 50 - 59 | 4 | 10 |
| 60 - 69 | 7 | 10 |

1. Determine the number of classes you want to have.

2. Subtract the lowest value from the highest value in the dataset.

3. Divide the outcome under Step 2 by the number of classes you have in Step 1.

   The mathematical expression of these steps is below:

   $$Class\ interval = \frac{highest\ value - lowest\ value}{number\ of\ classes}.$$

Table 1.4: Grouped data with different class interval

| Daily Income (US$) | Frequency | Class Interval |
|---|---|---|
| 0 - 9 | 15 | 10 |
| 10 - 19 | 18 | 10 |
| 20 - 29 | 17 | 10 |
| 30 - 49 | 35 | 20 |
| 50 - 79 | 20 | 30 |

For instance, if a market survey is conducted on market prices for 20 non-durable goods with the following prices: US$11, US$5, US$3, US$14, US$1, US$16, US$2, US$12, US$2, US$4, US$3, US$9, US$4, US$8, US$7, US$5, US$8, US$6, US$10, and US$15. The raw data indicate the lowest price is US$1 and the highest price is US$16. In addition, the survey expert decides to have four classes. The class interval is written as follows:

$$Class\,Interval = \frac{highest\,value - lowest\,value}{number\,of\,classes}$$
$$= \frac{16 - 1}{4} = \frac{15}{4}$$
$$Class\,interval = 3.75.$$

The value of the class interval is usually a whole number, but in this case its value is a decimal number. Therefore, the solution to this problem is to round-off to the nearest whole number which is 4. This implies that the raw data can be grouped into 4, as presented in the Table 1.5.

Table 1.5: Class interval generated from ungrouped data

| Number | Frequency |
|---|---|
| 1 - 4 | 7 |
| 5 - 8 | 6 |
| 9 - 12 | 4 |
| 13 - 16 | 3 |

### 1.3.3   CLASS LIMITS AND CLASS BOUNDARIES

*Class limits* are the actual values in the above-mentioned tables. Taking an example of Table 1.5, **1** and **4** are the class limits of the first class. Class limits are divided into two categories: lower class limit and upper class limit. In Table 1.5 for the first class, **1** is the lower class limit while **4** is the upper class limit. Class limits are used in frequency tables.

The lower class boundary is obtained by adding the lower class limit of upper class and upper class limit of the lower class and divide the answer by 2. The upper class boundary is also obtained by adding the upper class limit of lower class and lower class limit of the upper class and divide the answer by 2. Class boundaries reflect the true values of the class interval. In Table 1.5, the first line actually consists of values up to 4.5, which is the upper class boundary there. Class boundaries are also divided into lower and upper class boundaries. *Class boundaries* are not often observed in the frequency tables unless the data in the table is all integers. The class boundaries for the ungrouped data above are shown in Table 1.6 below.

Table 1.6: Class boundaries generated from ungrouped data

| Number | Frequency | Class Boundaries (Lower – Upper) |
|--------|-----------|----------------------------------|
| 1 - 4  | 7         | 0.5 – 4.5                        |
| 5 - 8  | 6         | 4.5 – 8.5                        |
| 9 - 12 | 4         | 8.5 – 12.5                       |
| 13 - 16| 3         | 12.5 – 16.5                      |

A class interval is the range of data in that particular class. The relationship between the class boundaries and the class interval is given as follows:

$$Class\,Interval = Upper\,Class\,Boundary - Lower\,Class\,Boundary.$$

The lower class boundary of one class is the same to the upper class boundary of the previous class for both integers and non-integers. The importance of class limits and class boundaries is highly recognized in the diagrammatical representation of statistical data.

## 1.4    METHODS OF VISUALIZING DATA

1. **Time plot**. A time plot shows the history of several data items during the latest time horizon as lines. The time axis is always horizontal and directed to the right. The plot displays changes in variable of interest over a time period. It is also known as a *line chart*.

2. **Pie charts**. A pie chart simply displays data as a percentage of a given total. This is the most appropriate way of visualizing quantities in relation to percentages of a given total. The entire area of the pie is 100% of the quantity of the concerned matter and the size of each slice is the percentage of the total represented by the category the slice denotes.

3. **Bar charts**. Bar charts are mainly utilized to showcase categorical data without focus on the percentage. Its scale of measurement can be either nominal or ordinal. Bar charts can

be displayed with the use of horizontal or vertical bars. A horizontal bar chart is more appropriate if someone intends to write the name of each category inside the rectangle that represents that category. A vertical bar chart is required to stress the height of different columns as measures of the quantity of the concerned variable.

4. **Frequency polygons**. A frequency polygon displays the same as a histogram, except without rectangles in it. It is only a point, in the midpoint of each interval at a height corresponding to the frequency or a relative frequency of the category of the interval.

5. **Ogives**. An ogive refers to a cumulative frequency or cumulative relative-frequency graph. It commences at 0 and reaches a peak of 1.00 (for a relative-frequency ogive) or to the peak cumulative frequency. The point with height assigned to the cumulative frequency is situated at the right endpoint of each interval.

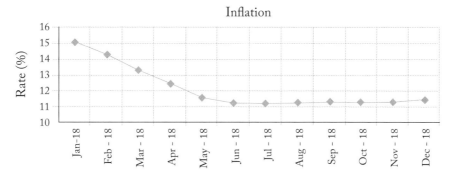

Figure 1.2: Methods of visualizing data: time plot.

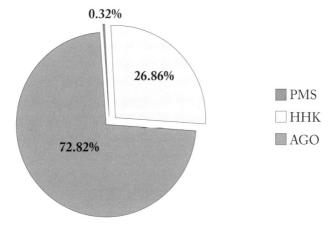

Figure 1.3: Methods of visualizing data: pie chart.

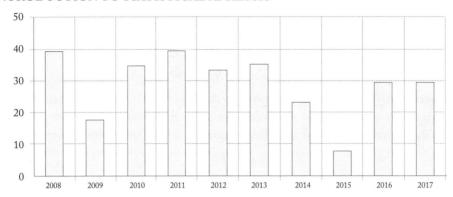

Figure 1.4: Methods of visualizing data: bar chart.

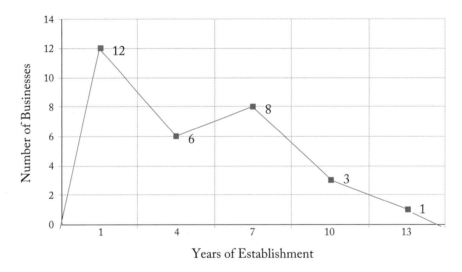

Figure 1.5: Methods of visualizing data: frequency polygon.

**Note:** Charts can often be deceiving. This indicates the disadvantage of merely descriptive methods of analysis and the need for statistical inference. Exploring statistical tests makes the analysis more objective than eyeball analysis and less prone to deception if assumptions of random sampling and others are established.

## 1.5   EXPLORING DATA ANALYSIS (EDA)

EDA is the name ascribed to a broad body of statistical and graphical methods. These approaches present patterns of observing data to determine relationships and trends, identify outliers and influential observations, and quickly describe or summarize datasets. This analysis was initiated

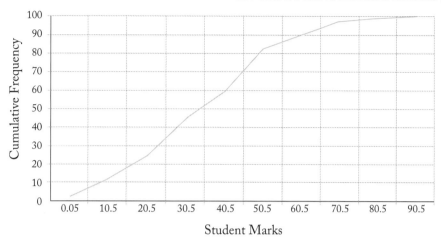

Figure 1.6: Methods of visualizing data: ogive.

from the work of John W. Tukey "Exploratory Data Analysis" in 1977 and has made significant strides in the past five years as software solutions in large data analysis (big data) and in business intelligence (the reporting of characteristics of the data in meaningful ways) has improved dramatically.

## 1.5.1   STEM-AND-LEAF DISPLAYS

This presents a quick way of observing a dataset. It has some attributes of a histogram but prevents the loss of information in a histogram that emanates from organizing data into intervals. Its display adopts the tallying principles as well as the use of the decimal base of a number system. The stem refers to the number without its rightmost digit (the leaf). The stem is written to the left of a vertical line separating the stem from the leaf.

For instance, we have the following numbers: 201, 202, 203, and 205. This can be displayed as:

$$20 \mid 1235.$$

## 1.5.2   BOX PLOTS

A box plot is also known as a box-whisker plot which presents a dataset by determining its central tendency, spread, skewness, and the presence of outliers. The box plot consists of the five summary measures of the distribution of data: median, lower quartile, upper quartile, the smallest observation, and the largest observation (Fig. 1.7). It has two fundamental assumptions. Its first assumption is that the hinges of the box plot are basically the quartiles of the dataset, and the median is a line inside the box. Its second assumption is that its whiskers are constructed by extending a line from the upper quartile to the largest observation, and from the lower quartile to the smallest observation under the condition that the largest and smallest observations lie within a distance of 1.5 times the interquartile range from the appropriate hinge (quartile). Observations that exceed the distance are regarded as suspected outlier.

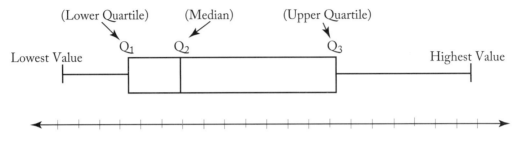

Figure 1.7: Whisker and box plot.

#### 1.5.2.1 Importance of Box Plots

1. They are used to identify the location of a dataset using the median.

2. They are explored to determine the spread of the data through the length of the box, interquartile range, and the length of the whiskers.

3. They provide a means of identifying possible skewness of the distribution of the dataset.

4. They detect suspected outliers in the dataset.

5. They are useful for comparing two or more datasets by drawing box plots for each dataset and displaying the box plots on the same scale.

## 1.6   EXERCISES

**1.1.**   Explain why statistics are necessary.

**1.2.**   Describe the difference between a quantitative variable and qualitative variable.

**1.3.**   List the four scales of measurements discussed in the chapter and discuss each with relevant examples.

**1.4.**   The total liters of petroleum products used for both importation and consumption (truck out) in Nigeria in the second quarter of 2018 is summarized in Table 1.7.

   (a) Represent the liters of petroleum products used for both importation and consumption (truck out) in Nigeria in the second quarter of 2018 in a bar chart.

   (b) Represent the total liters of petroleum products used for both importation and consumption (truck out) in Nigeria in the second quarter of 2018 in a pie chart.

Table 1.7: Total liters of petroleum products (Source: NBS, 2018)

| Months | PMS | AGO | HHK | ATK |
|--------|-----|-----|-----|-----|
| April | 1,781,949,720 | 309,988,876 | 0 | 14,700,325 |
| May | 1,670,390,264 | 387,434,670 | 0 | 64,186,515 |
| June | 1,340,777,749 | 408,153,067 | 43,790,592 | 121,501,304 |
| **Total** | 4,793,117,733 | 1,105,576,613 | 43,790,592 | 200,388,144 |

CHAPTER 2

# Introduction to R Software

R is a programming language designed for statistical analysis and graphics. It is based on S-plus which was developed by Ross Ihaka and Robert Gentleman from the University of Auckland, New Zealand, and R can be used to open multiple datasets. R is an open-source software which can be downloaded at `http://cran.r-project.org/`. Other statistical packages are SPSS, SAS, and Stata but they are not open source. Apart from this, there are large R group users online that can provide real-time answers to questions, and that also contribute to add packages to R. Packages increase the functions that are available for use, thus expanding the users' abilities. The R Development Core Team is responsible for maintaining the source code of R.

**Why turn to R?**
R software provides the following advantages.

1. R is free (meaning open-source software).

2. Any type of data analysis can be executed in R.

3. R includes advanced statistical procedures not yet present in other packages.

4. The most comprehensive and powerful feature for visualizing complex data is available in R.

5. Importing data from a wide variety of sources can be easily done with R.

6. R is able to access data directly from web pages, social media sites, and a wide range of online data services.

7. R software generates an easy and straightforward platform for programming new statistical techniques.

8. It is simple to integrate applications written in other programming languages (such as C++, Java, Python, PHP, Pentaho, SAS, and SPSS) into R.

9. R can operate on any operating system such as Windows, Unix, and Mac OSX. It can also be installed on an iPhone. It is also possible to use R on an Android phone (see `https://selbydavid.com/2017/12/29/r-android/`).

10. R offers a variety of graphic user interfaces (GUIs) if you are not interested in learning a new language.

**Packages in R**

Packages refer to the collections of R functions, data, and compiled code in a well-defined format.

## 2.1  HOW TO DOWNLOAD AND INSTALL R

Many operating systems such as Windows, Macintosh, and Linux can connect with R, since R is a free download; and accommodates many different servers around the world. The software can be downloaded from any of them. All available download links can be found on `http://www.r-project.org/index.html` by viewing the "Get Started" section on the front page and click on "download R." These mirrors are linked with the word "CRAN" which stands for the Comprehensive R Archive Network. The CRAN provides the most recent version of R.

1. By choosing the mirror at the top of your computer screen, a list of the versions of R for each operating system is displayed.

2. Click the R version that is compatible with your operating system.

3. If you decide to have the base version, just click the "download" link that displays on the screen.

**Installation of R**

1. Under the "download" link, there is another link that provides instructions on how to install it. These might be useful if you encounter problems during the installation process.

2. To install R, double-click on the executable file and follow the instruction on the screen. The default settings are perfect. Figure 2.1 shows the first screen that comes up when installing R on a Windows system.

## 2.2  USING R FOR DESCRIPTIVE STATISTICAL AND PLOTS

R can be utilized to develop any statistical analysis. Different types of graphs can be constructed using R statistical software. A range of standard statistical plots such as scatterplots, boxplots, histograms, bar plots, pie charts, and basic 3D plots is provided by R. These basic types of plots can be generated using a single function call in R. The R graphics are able to add several graphical elements together to produce the final outcome. Apart from the conventional statistical plots, R also generates Trellis plots through the package "lattice." Special-purpose plots like lines, text, rectangles, and polygons are available in the R software. Owing to its generality and feasibility, production of graphical images that are above the normal statistical graphics, is possible. This also makes it possible to generate figures that can visualize important concepts or useful insights. The structure of R graphics has four distinct levels, namely: graphics packages, graphics systems, a graphics engine, and graphics device packages (the full application will be discussed in the rest of the book chapters).

## STEPS TO INSTALL R

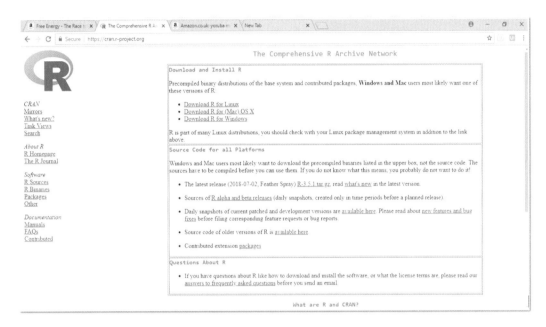

Figure 2.1: Click the appropriate operating system based on your computer.

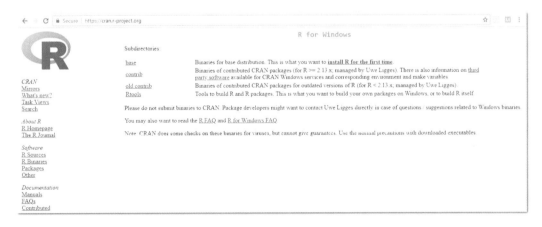

Figure 2.2: Click on "R Sources" to get information on the latest version of R software.

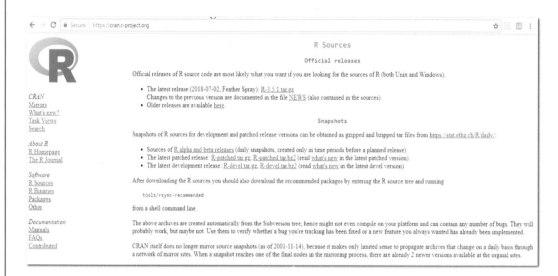

Figure 2.3: Click on "Packages" to get all available packages in R software.

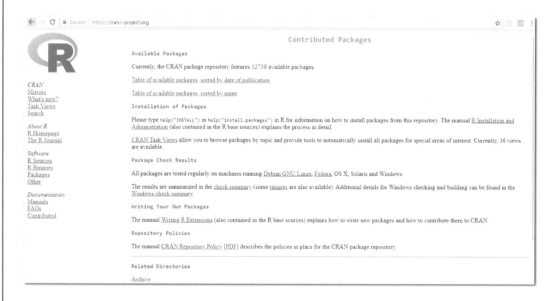

Figure 2.4: Click on "Manuals" to obtain the R user guide.

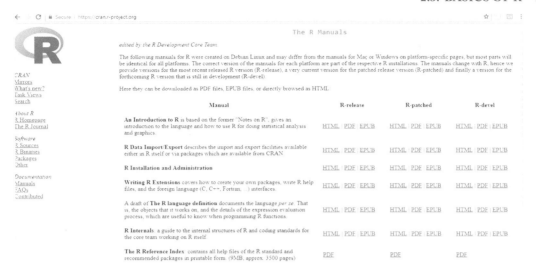

Figure 2.5: R manuals.

## 2.3    BASICS OF R

### 2.3.1    R IS VECTORIZED

Some of the funtions in R are vectorized. This indicates that the functions operate on the elements of a vector by acting on each element one after the other without necessarily undergoing the looping process. Being vectorized allows writing codes in R easy to read, efficient, precise, and concise. The following examples demonstrate vectorization in R.

1.  Multiplication of vector by a constant.

    R language allows multiplying (or dividing) a vector by a constant value. A simplex example is:

    ```
    x<-c(2, 4, 6, 8, 10)
    x*3
    [1]  6 12 18 24 30


    x/3
    [1] 0.6666667 1.3333333 2.0000000 2.6666667 3.3333333
    ```

2.  Addition (or subtraction) of vectors.

    ```
    x<-c(2, 4, 6, 8, 10)
    y<-c(1, 2, 3, 4, 5)
    ```

```
x+y
[1]  3  6  9 12 15
x-y
[1]  1 2 3 4 5
```

3. Multiplication of vectors.

```
x<-c(2, 4, 6, 8, 10)
y<-c(1, 2, 3, 4, 5)
x*y
[1]  2  8 18 32 50
```

4. Logical operations.

```
a<-(x>=4)
a
[1] FALSE  TRUE  TRUE  TRUE  TRUE
```

5. Matrix operations.

```
a <- matrix(1:4, 2, 2)
b <- matrix(0:3, 2, 2)
ab<-a*b
ab
[,1] [,2]
[1,]   0   6
[2,]   2  12
```

## 2.3.2   R DATA TYPES

There are different types of data in R, these include: scalars, vectors, matrices, data frames, lists, coersion, etc.

### 2.3.2.1  Scalar

This is an atomic quantity that can hold only one value at a time. Scalars are the most basic data types that can be used to construct more complex ones. Scalars in R can be numerical, logical, and character (string). The following are examples of the different types of scalars in R.

1. *Numerical*

```
p<-10
q<-12
class(p)
[1] "numeric"
```

```
class(q)
[1] "numeric"
class(p+q)
[1] "numeric"
```

2. *Logical*

```
t<-p<q    # Is p less than q
s<-p>q    # Is p greater than q
t
[1] TRUE
s
[1] FALSE
class(t)
[1] "logical"
class(s)
[1] "logical"
class(NA)
[1] "logical"
```

3. *Character (string)*

```
m<-"10"
n<-"12"
m
[1] "10"
n
[1] "12"
m+n         # this is not the same as p and q in earlier example
Error in m + n : non-numeric argument to binary operator
class(m)
[1] "character"
class(n)
[1] "character"
class(as.numeric(m))
[1] "numeric"
class(as.character(p)) # to coerce this number into number
[1] "character"
class(as.character(p)) # to coerce this number to character
[1] "character"
```

### 2.3.2.2   Vector

A vector is a sequence of data elements of the same basic type.

```
d<-c(1, 2, 3, 4 , 5, (6)   # Numeric vector
class(d)
[1] "numeric"
e<-c("one", "two", "three", "four", "five", "six") # Character vector
class(e)
[1] "character"

f<-c(TRUE, FALSE, TRUE, TRUE, FALSE, TRUE)          # Logical vector
class(f)
[1] "logical"
d;e;f
[1] 1 2 3 4 5 6
[1] "one"    "two"    "three" "four"  "five"  "six"
[1]  TRUE FALSE   TRUE   TRUE FALSE  TRUE
```

### 2.3.2.3   Matrix

A matrix is a collection of data elements arranged in a two-dimensional rectangular form. In the same manner as a vector, the components in a matrix must be of the same basic type. An example of a matrix with 2 rows and 4 columns is created below.

```
# fill the matrix with elements arranged by column in 2 rows
# and 4 columns
mat<-matrix(1:8, nrow=2, ncol=4, byrow= FALSE)
mat
      [,1] [,2] [,3] [,4]
[1,]   1    3    5    7
[2,]   2    4    6    8
```

Alternatively, it is possible to have the elements of the matrix arranged by rows.

```
# fill the matrix with elements arranged by row in 2 rows
# and 4 columns
mat<-matrix(1:8, nrow=2, ncol=4, byrow= TRUE)
mat
      [,1] [,2] [,3] [,4]
[1,]   1    2    3    4
[2,]   5    6    7    8
```

Braces [ ] can be used to reference elements in a matrix; this is similar to referencing elements in vectors.

```
mat[2,3]   # refers to the element in the second row
         # and third column
[1] 7
mat[,4]    # refers to all elements in the fourth column
[1] 4 8
mat[1,]    # refers to all elements in the first row
[1] 1 2 3 4
```

Table 2.1 contains the basic matrix operations and their respective meanings.

Table 2.1: Basic matrix operations

| Function | Meaning |
|---|---|
| t(x) | Transpose of x |
| diag (x) | Diagonal elements of x |
| %*% | Matrix multiplication |
| solve (a,b) | Solves a %*% x = b for x |
| rowsum (x) | Sum of rows for a matrix-like object; RowSums(x) is a faster version |
| rowMeans (x) | Fast version of row means |
| colMeans (x) | Fast version of column means |

#### 2.3.2.4 Data Frame

A data frame is more general than a matrix, in the sense that different columns can have different basic data types. Data frame is one of the most common data type presented for data analysis. Let us consider combining the vectors of numerical, character, and logical vectors to form a data frame. Data frames have a special attribute called (row.names). Data frames are created through **read.table()** or **read.csv()**.

```
d<-c(1, 2, 3, 4 , 5, 6)
e<-c("one", "two", "three", "four", "five", "six")
f<-c(TRUE, FALSE, TRUE, TRUE, FALSE, TRUE)
data<-data.frame(d, e, f)
names(data)<-c("ID", "words", "state")
data
  ID words state
1  1   one  TRUE
2  2   two FALSE
```

```
3   3 three   TRUE
4   4  four   TRUE
5   5  five FALSE
6   6   six   TRUE
```

In addition, components from data frames can be extracted and this is similar to the extraction of components in matrices, but after assigning names to each column makes it more flexible.

```
data$ID
[1] 1 2 3 4 5 6
data[1:2,]
  ID words   state
1  1   one    TRUE
2  2   two   FALSE


data[,3]
[1]  TRUE FALSE  TRUE  TRUE FALSE  TRUE
```

### 2.3.2.5 List

A list is a generic vector containing other objects. There is no restriction on data types or length of the components. It is easier to work with lists that have named components. List is a special type of vector. There are two characteristics of this type of vector—it can contain elements of different classes and each element of a list can have a name.

Consider a list which contains a vector, matrix and data frame.

```
lst<-list(vector=d, matrix=mat, frame=data, count=10)
    lst
    $vector
    [1] 1 2 3 4 5 6

    $matrix
         [,1] [,2] [,3] [,4]
    [1,]    1    3    5    7
    [2,]    2    4    6    8

    $frame
      ID  words    state
    1  1    one     TRUE
    2  2    two    FALSE
    3  3  three     TRUE
    4  4   four     TRUE
```

```
5  5   five     FALSE
6  6    six      TRUE


$count
[1] 10
```

### 2.3.2.6 Factor

Factors are used to represent categorical data and can be ordered or unordered. We can regard a factor as numerical vector when each of the integers contains a label. It is more appropriate using factors with labels than using integers because factors are self-describing (e.g., variable with the values of "Male" and "Female" is better than assigning value to them as 1 and 2).

```
y<-factor(c("yes", "yes", "yes", "no", "no"))
y
[1] yes yes yes no  no
Levels: no yes


table(y)  # tabulate the outcome
y
    no yes
    2   3
```

### 2.3.2.7 Coersion

This occurs when different objects are mixed in a vector; then every element in the vector has the same class.

```
co<-c(50, "big") # character
co
[1] "50" "big"


co<-c(TRUE, (2) # numeric
co
[1] 1 2


co<-c(FALSE, (2) # numeric
co
[1] 0 2
```

### 2.3.2.8  Date and Time

Date is represented by the date class and time is represented by the POSIXct class, a very large integer. POSIXlt class is a list which stores a lot of useful metadata. The function as.Date() to convert strings to dates.

```
x <- as.Date("2018-03-21")
x
[1] "2018-03-21"


# use as.Date() to convert strings to dates
dates <- as.Date(c("2018-03-21", "2018-10-04"))


# number of days between 03/21/2018 and 10/04/2018
days <- dates[2] - dates[1]
days
   Time difference of 197 days
```

Besides, **Sys.Date()** returns today's date, **date()** returns the current date and time, and **strptime()** is used to write times in a different format as characters.

Table 2.2 contains the symbols the can be used with the **format()** function to print dates.

Table 2.2: Symbols to be used with **format()**

| Symbol | Meaning | Example |
|--------|---------|---------|
| %d | Day as a number (0-31) | 31-Jan |
| %a | Abbreviated weekday | Fri |
| %A | Unabbreviated weekday | Friday |
| %m | Month | 00-12 |
| %b | Abbreviated month | Mar |
| %B | Unabbreviated month | March |
| %y | Year without century | 00-99 |
| %Y | Year with century | 2018 |

To print today's date using Sys.Date() function:

```
today <- Sys.Date()  # print today's date
format(today, format="%B %d %Y")
[1] "October 04 2018"


x <- Sys.time()
```

```
x
[1] "2018-10-04 11:35:15 WAT"


p<-as.POSIXlt (x)
names (unclass(p))    # unclass (p) is a list object
[1] "sec"   "min"   "hour"  "mday"  "mon"  "year"  "wday"  "yday"
[9] "isdst"  "zone"   "gmtoff"
p$sec
[1] 15.44309
p$wday
[1] 4
p$mday
[1] 4


timeString<-"October 4, 2018 13:58"
h<-strptime(timeString, "%B %d, %Y %H: %M")
class(h)
[1] "POSIXlt" "POSIXt"
h
[1] "2018-10-04 13:58:00 WAT"
```

### 2.3.3  MISSING VALUES

Missing values are represented by NA (not available). Undefined values are represented by NaN (not a number). NaN is also Na but the converse of this is not true. For example, we have:

```
mv<-c(1, 2, 3, NA , 5)
is.na(mv)  # returns TRUE of mv is missing
[1] FALSE FALSE FALSE  TRUE FALSE
```

In addition, we can exclude missing values from an analysis:

```
mv<-c(1, 2, 3, NA , 5)
mean(mv)  # returns NA
[1] NA
mean(mv, na.rm=T) # returns average of 2.75
                  # by excluding the missing value
[1] 2.75
```

The function na.omit() returns the object with listwise deletion of missing values:

```
# create new dataset without missing data
d<-c(1, 2, 3, NA , 5, 6)
```

```
e<-c("one", "two", "three", "four", "five", "six")
f<-c(TRUE, FALSE, TRUE, TRUE, FALSE, TRUE)
data1<-data.frame(d, e, f)
data1
    d     e     f
1   1   one   TRUE
2   2   two  FALSE
3   3  three  TRUE
4  NA  four   TRUE
5   5  five  FALSE
6   6   six   TRUE
newdata <- na.omit(data1)
newdata    # delete all entries for row 4
           # since it contains the missing value
    d     e     f
1 1   one   TRUE
2 2   two  FALSE
3 3  three  TRUE
5 5  five  FALSE
```

## 2.3.4   DATA CREATION

**c(...)**   : generic function to combine arguments with the default forming a vector; with *recursive* = *TRUE* descends through lists combining all elements into one vector.

**from:to**   : generates a sequence; ":" has operator priority.

```
x<-1:4+1
x
[1] 2 3 4 5

y<-10:14+6
y
[1] 16 17 18 19 20
```

**seq(from, to)**   : generates a sequence by = specifies increment; length = specifies desired length.

seq() function generates a sequence of numbers.

seq(from = 1, to = 1, by = ((to - from)/(length.out - 1)), length.out = NULL, along.with = NULL, ...)

from, to: begin and end number of the sequence

by: step, increment (Default is 1)

length.out: length of the sequence

```
# generate a sequence from -2 to 10, step 2
s<-seq(-2, 10, 2)
s
[1] -2  0  2  4  6  8 10


# generate a sequence with 15 evenly distributed from -2 to 10
s1<-seq(-2, 10, length.out=15)
s1
[1] -2.0000000 -1.1428571 -0.2857143  0.5714286  1.4285714  2.2857143
[7]  3.1428571  4.0000000  4.8571429  5.7142857  6.5714286  7.4285714
[13] 8.2857143  9.1428571  10.0000000
```

**rep(x, times)**   : replicate x times; use each = to repeat "each" element of x each times;

```
rep(c(1, 2, 3, 4, 5), (2)         # repeat 1 2 3 4 5 twice
[1] 1 2 3 4 5 1 2 3 4 5
rep(c(1, 2, 3, 4, 5), each = (2) # repeat each of 1 2 3 4 5 twice
[1] 1 1 2 2 3 3 4 4 5 5


replicate(3, c(1, 3, 6))          # repeat vector 1 3 6 thrice


      [,1] [,2] [,3]
[1,]    1    1    1
[2,]    3    3    3
[3,]    6    6    6
```

**array(x, dim =)**   : array with data x; specify dimensions like dim=c(3, 4, 2); elements of x recycle if c is not long enough. We can give names to the rows, columns, and matrices in the array by using the dimnames parameter.

```
# Create two vectors of different lengths.
vector1 <- c(1,2,3)
vector2 <- c(4,5,6,7,8,9)
column.names <- c("Col1","Col2","Col3")
row.names <- c("Row1","Row2","Row3")
matrix.names <- c("Matrix1","Matrix2")
arr <- array(c(vector1,vector2),dim = c(3,3,2),
             dimnames = list(row.names,column.names,
             matrix.names))
arr
```

```
, , Matrix1

      Col1 Col2 Col3
Row1    1    4    7
Row2    2    5    8
Row3    3    6    9

, , Matrix2

      Col1 Col2 Col3
Row1    1    4    7
Row2    2    5    8
Row3    3    6    9
```

**gl(n, k, length=n*k, labels = 1:n)**   : generates levels (factors) by specifying the pattern of their levels; k is the number of levels, and n is the number of replications.

**expand.grid()**   : a data frame from all combinations of the factors variables.

```
expand.grid(height = seq(1.5, 2.2, 0.05),
            weight = seq(50, 70, 5),sex = c("Male","Female"))

      height weight    sex
1      1.50     50   Male
2      1.55     50   Male
3      1.60     50   Male
4      1.65     50   Male
5      1.70     50   Male
6      1.75     50   Male
7      1.80     50   Male
8      1.85     50   Male
9      1.90     50   Male
10     1.95     50   Male
11     2.00     50   Male
12     2.05     50   Male
13     2.10     50   Male
14     2.15     50   Male
15     2.20     50   Male
16     1.50     55   Male
17     1.55     55   Male
```

| 18 | 1.60 | 55 | Male |
| 19 | 1.65 | 55 | Male |
| 20 | 1.70 | 55 | Male |
| 21 | 1.75 | 55 | Male |
| 22 | 1.80 | 55 | Male |
| 23 | 1.85 | 55 | Male |
| 24 | 1.90 | 55 | Male |
| 25 | 1.95 | 55 | Male |
| 26 | 2.00 | 55 | Male |
| 27 | 2.05 | 55 | Male |
| 28 | 2.10 | 55 | Male |
| 29 | 2.15 | 55 | Male |
| 30 | 2.20 | 55 | Male |
| 31 | 1.50 | 60 | Male |
| 32 | 1.55 | 60 | Male |
| 33 | 1.60 | 60 | Male |
| 34 | 1.65 | 60 | Male |
| 35 | 1.70 | 60 | Male |
| 36 | 1.75 | 60 | Male |
| 37 | 1.80 | 60 | Male |
| 38 | 1.85 | 60 | Male |
| 39 | 1.90 | 60 | Male |
| 40 | 1.95 | 60 | Male |
| 41 | 2.00 | 60 | Male |
| 42 | 2.05 | 60 | Male |
| 43 | 2.10 | 60 | Male |
| 44 | 2.15 | 60 | Male |
| 45 | 2.20 | 60 | Male |
| 46 | 1.50 | 65 | Male |
| 47 | 1.55 | 65 | Male |
| 48 | 1.60 | 65 | Male |
| 49 | 1.65 | 65 | Male |
| 50 | 1.70 | 65 | Male |
| 51 | 1.75 | 65 | Male |
| 52 | 1.80 | 65 | Male |
| 53 | 1.85 | 65 | Male |
| 54 | 1.90 | 65 | Male |
| 55 | 1.95 | 65 | Male |
| 56 | 2.00 | 65 | Male |

| | | | |
|---|---|---|---|
| 57 | 2.05 | 65 | Male |
| 58 | 2.10 | 65 | Male |
| 59 | 2.15 | 65 | Male |
| 60 | 2.20 | 65 | Male |
| 61 | 1.50 | 70 | Male |
| 62 | 1.55 | 70 | Male |
| 63 | 1.60 | 70 | Male |
| 64 | 1.65 | 70 | Male |
| 65 | 1.70 | 70 | Male |
| 66 | 1.75 | 70 | Male |
| 67 | 1.80 | 70 | Male |
| 68 | 1.85 | 70 | Male |
| 69 | 1.90 | 70 | Male |
| 70 | 1.95 | 70 | Male |
| 71 | 2.00 | 70 | Male |
| 72 | 2.05 | 70 | Male |
| 73 | 2.10 | 70 | Male |
| 74 | 2.15 | 70 | Male |
| 75 | 2.20 | 70 | Male |
| 76 | 1.50 | 50 | Female |
| 77 | 1.55 | 50 | Female |
| 78 | 1.60 | 50 | Female |
| 79 | 1.65 | 50 | Female |
| 80 | 1.70 | 50 | Female |
| 81 | 1.75 | 50 | Female |
| 82 | 1.80 | 50 | Female |
| 83 | 1.85 | 50 | Female |
| 84 | 1.90 | 50 | Female |
| 85 | 1.95 | 50 | Female |
| 86 | 2.00 | 50 | Female |
| 87 | 2.05 | 50 | Female |
| 88 | 2.10 | 50 | Female |
| 89 | 2.15 | 50 | Female |
| 90 | 2.20 | 50 | Female |
| 91 | 1.50 | 55 | Female |
| 92 | 1.55 | 55 | Female |
| 93 | 1.60 | 55 | Female |
| 94 | 1.65 | 55 | Female |
| 95 | 1.70 | 55 | Female |

```
96     1.75     55 Female
97     1.80     55 Female
98     1.85     55 Female
99     1.90     55 Female
100    1.95     55 Female
101    2.00     55 Female
102    2.05     55 Female
103    2.10     55 Female
104    2.15     55 Female
105    2.20     55 Female
106    1.50     60 Female
107    1.55     60 Female
108    1.60     60 Female
109    1.65     60 Female
110    1.70     60 Female
111    1.75     60 Female
112    1.80     60 Female
113    1.85     60 Female
114    1.90     60 Female
115    1.95     60 Female
116    2.00     60 Female
117    2.05     60 Female
118    2.10     60 Female
119    2.15     60 Female
120    2.20     60 Female
121    1.50     65 Female
122    1.55     65 Female
123    1.60     65 Female
124    1.65     65 Female
125    1.70     65 Female
126    1.75     65 Female
127    1.80     65 Female
128    1.85     65 Female
129    1.90     65 Female
130    1.95     65 Female
131    2.00     65 Female
132    2.05     65 Female
133    2.10     65 Female
134    2.15     65 Female
```

| 135 | 2.20 | 65 Female |
| 136 | 1.50 | 70 Female |
| 137 | 1.55 | 70 Female |
| 138 | 1.60 | 70 Female |
| 139 | 1.65 | 70 Female |
| 140 | 1.70 | 70 Female |
| 141 | 1.75 | 70 Female |
| 142 | 1.80 | 70 Female |
| 143 | 1.85 | 70 Female |
| 144 | 1.90 | 70 Female |
| 145 | 1.95 | 70 Female |
| 146 | 2.00 | 70 Female |
| 147 | 2.05 | 70 Female |
| 148 | 2.10 | 70 Female |
| 149 | 2.15 | 70 Female |
| 150 | 2.20 | 70 Female |

**rbind** : combines arguments by rows for matrices, data frames, and others.

```
r1<-c(1:10)
r2<-c(1, 3, 5, 7, 9, 11,13,15, 17, 19)
rbind(r1,r2)
    [,1] [,2] [,3] [,4] [,5] [,6] [,7] [,8] [,9] [,10]
r1    1    2    3    4    5    6    7    8    9    10
r2    1    3    5    7    9   11   13   15   17    19
```

**cbind** : combines arguments by rows for matrices, data frames, and others.

```
c1<-c(1:10)
c2<-c(1,3,5,7,9, 11,13,15, 17, 19)
cbind(c1,c2)
       c1 c2
[1,]   1  1
[2,]   2  3
[3,]   3  5
[4,]   4  7
[5,]   5  9
[6,]   6  11
[7,]   7  13
[8,]   8  15
[9,]   9  17
[10,] 10 19
```

## 2.3.5    DATA TYPE CONVERSION

Data type can be changed in R. Adding a character string to a numeric vector converts all the elements in the vector to character. These functions can be used in the conversion of a data type; see Table 2.3.

`is.numeric()`, `is.character()`, `is.vector()`, `is.matrix()`, `is.data.frame()`, `as.numeric()`, `as.character()`, `as.vector()`, `as.matrix()`, `as.data.frame()`.

Table 2.3: Functions

|  | One Long Vector | Matrix |
|---|---|---|
| Vector | c(x,y) | cbind(x,y); rbind(x,y) |
| Matrix | as.vector (mymatrix) |  |
| Data frame |  | as.matrix(myframe) |

## 2.3.6    VARIABLE INFORMATION

1. `is.na(x)`, `is.null(x)`, `is.array(x)`, `is.data.frame(x)`, `is.numeric(x)`, `is.complex(x)`, `is.character(x)` : test for types; or a complete list, use method (is).

2. `length(x)` : number of elements in x.

3. `dim(x)` : retrieve for set the dimension of an object; `dim<-c(3,2)`.

4. `dimnames(x)` : retrieve or set the dimension of an object.

5. `nrow(x)` : number of rows; `NROW(x)` is the same but treats a vector as a one-row matrix.

6. `class(x)` : get or set the class attribute of x; `class(x)<-"myclass"`.

7. `(unclass(x))` : remove the class attribute of x.

8. `attr(x,which)` : get or set the attribute which of x.

9. `attribute(obj)` : get or set the list of attributes obj.

## 2.4    BASIC OPERATIONS IN R

For a list of numbers in memory, basic operations can be performed. These operations can be used to quickly perform a large number of calculations with a single command. It is obvious that if an operation is performed on more than one vector it is often necessary that the vectors all contain the same number of entries. In this section, we will focus on the subsetting, control structures, build-in functions, user written function, packages and the working directory, and R script.

## 2.4.1   SUBSETTING

This is an operator that can be used to extract subsets of R objects, e.g., [ always returns an object of the same class as the original object. With one exception, it can be used to select more than one element. [[ is used to extract elements of a list or a data frame. $ is used to extract elements of a list or data frame by name. The semantics of $ are similar to [[.

In addition, an element of a vector v is assigned an index by its position in the sequence, starting with 1. The basic function for subsetting is [ ]. v[1] is the first element; v[length(v)] is the last. The subsetting function takes input in many forms.

### # Example 1

```
sub<-c("a", "b", "c", "d", "e", "f")
sub[4]
[1] "d"


sub[2:5]
[1] "b" "c" "d" "e"
sub>"c"
[1] FALSE FALSE FALSE   TRUE   TRUE   TRUE


sub[sub>"c"]
[1] "d" "e" "f"
```

### # Example 2

```
sub1<-matrix(1:9,3,3)
sub1
      [,1] [,2] [,3]
[1,]    1    4    7
[2,]    2    5    8
[3,]    3    6    9
sub1[1,3]
[1] 7
sub1[2,]      # entire elements in the second row
[1] 2 5 8
sub1[,1]      # entire elements in the first column
[1] 1 2 3
```

# Example 3

```
sub<-c("a", "b", "c", "d", "e", "f")
v <- c(1, 3, 6)
sub[v]
[1] "a" "c" "e"
v[1:3]
[1] "a" "b" "c"

sub<-c("a", "b", "c", "d", "e", "f")
v <- c(1, 3, 6)
sub[v]
[1] "a" "c" "f"
sub[1:3]
[1] "a" "b" "c"
```

# Example 4

```
sub1<-matrix(1:9,3,3)
sub1[1,3]
[1] 7
sub1[1,2, drop = FALSE]   # return as a matrix of 1 by 1
        [,1]
[1,]    4
sub1[1,2, drop = TRUE]    # return as a single element
[1] 4
sub1[1,, drop = TRUE]     # return as a vector
[1] 1 4 7
```

# Example 5

```
y<-list(w = 1:3, x = 0.5, z ="gender")
y[1]

$w
[1] 1 2 3

y$w
[1] 1 2 3

y$x
```

```
[1] 0.5
```

```
y$z
[1] "gender"
```

## 2.4.2   CONTROL STRUCTURES

Control structures allow one to control the flow of execution of a script typically inside of a function. These control structures cannot be used while working with R interactively. We shall consider some common control structures in this sections. These include: conditional (if-else), for-loop, repeat-loop, and while-loop.

### 2.4.2.1  Conditional

```
if (condition) {
    # do something
} else {
    # do something else
}
```

**# Example 6**

```
x <- 1:20
if (sample(x, (1) <= 10) {
    print("x is less than 10")
  } else {
    print("x is greater than 10")
  }
  [1] "x is greater than 10"
```

### 2.4.2.2  For-Loop

Loops are used in programming to repeat a specific block of code. A loop works on an iterable variable and assigns successive values until the end of a sequence.

**# Example 7**

```
for (i in 1:10) {
    print(i*2)
}

[1] 2
[1] 4
[1] 6
```

```
[1] 8
[1] 10
[1] 12
[1] 14
[1] 16
[1] 18
[1] 20
```

# Example 8

```
x <- c("A", "B", "C", "D")
for (i in seq(x)) {
    print(x[i])
}
[1] "A"
[1] "B"
[1] "C"
[1] "D"
```

Alternatively,

```
for (i in 1:4) print(x[i])
[1] "A"
[1] "B"
[1] "C"
[1] "D"
```

## 2.4.2.3  Repeat-Loop

A repeat-loop is used to iterate over a block of code multiple number of times. There is no condition check in a repeat-loop to exit the loop. There should be an explicit condition within the body of the loop and then use a break statement to terminate the loop.

# Example 9

```
r <- 1
repeat {
print(r)
r = r+1
if (r == 10){
break
}
```

```
}
[1] 1
[1] 2
[1] 3
[1] 4
[1] 5
[1] 6
[1] 7
[1] 8
[1] 9
```

### 2.4.2.4  While-Loop

While loops are used to loop until a specific condition is met.

*# Example 10*

```
w <- 1
while (w < 10) {
print(w)
w = w+1
}

[1] 1
[1] 2
[1] 3
[1] 4
[1] 5
[1] 6
[1] 7
[1] 8
[1] 9
```

### 2.4.3   BUILT-IN FUNCTIONS IN R

There are a lot of functions in R. We will concentrate on the numeric, character, and statistical functions that are commonly used in creating or recoding variables. The tables below show various categories of built-in functions and their descriptions.

### 2.4.3.1 Numerical Functions
See Table 2.4.

Table 2.4: Numerical functions

| Function | Description | Example |
|---|---|---|
| abs(x) | Absolute value | abs(-0.127) <br> [1] 0.127 |
| sqrt(x) | Square root | sqrt(200) <br> [1] 14.14214 |
| ceiling(x) | Numbers are rounded up to the nearest integer | ceiling(100.125) <br> [1] 101 |
| floor(x) | Numbers are rounded down to the nearest integer | floor(100.125) <br> [1] 100 |
| trunc(x) | Truncation | trunc(100.125) <br> [1] 100 |
| round(x, digits=n) | Rounding up | round(100.125, digits=1) <br> [1] 100.1 |
| signif(x, digits=n) | Significant figure | signif(100.125, digits=1) <br> [1] 100 |
| cos(x), sin(x), tan(x) | Trigonometric | cos(90) <br> [1] -0.4480736 |
| log(x) | Natural logarithm | log(90) <br> [1] 4.49981 |
| log10(x) | Common logarithm | log10(90) <br> [1] 1.954243 |
| exp(x) | Exponential | exp(0.125) <br> [1] 1.133148 |

### 2.4.3.2  Character Functions

See Table 2.5.

Table 2.5: Character functions

| Function | Description | Example |
|---|---|---|
| substr(*x*, start=*n1*, stop=*n2*) | Extract or replace substrings in a character vector. | x <- "peter" > substr(x, 2, 4) [1] "ete" |
| grep(*pattern*, *x*, ignore.case = **FALSE**, fixed = **FALSE**) | Search for the pattern in x. If fixed = FALSE then the pattern is a regular expression. If fixed = TRUE then the pattern is a text string. Returns matching indices. | grep("Z", c("X","Y","Z"), fixed=TRUE) [1] 3 |
| sub(*pattern*, *replacement*, *x*, ignore.case = **FALSE**, fixed = **FALSE**) | Find the pattern in x and replace with replacement text. If fixed = FALSE then the pattern is a regular expression. If fixed = T then the pattern is a text string. | sub("\\s",".","Lord God") [1] "Lord.God" |
| strsplit(*x*, *split*) | Split the elements of character vector *x* at *split*. | strsplit("faith", "") [[1]] [1] "f" "a" "i" "t" "h" |
| paste(..., sep="") | Concatenate strings after using *sep* string to seperate them. | paste("child",1:3,sep=" ") [1] "child 1" "child 2" "child 3" |

### 2.4.3.3 Statistical Probability Functions

See Table 2.6.

Table 2.6: Statistical probability functions

| Function | Description | Example |
|---|---|---|
| dnorm($x$) | Normal density function (by default m=0 sd=1) | dnorm(0.5)<br>[1] 0.3520653 |
| pnorm($q$) | Cumulative normal probability for q (area under the normal curve to the left of q) | pnorm(1.96)<br>[1] 0.9750021 |
| qnorm($p$) | Normal quantile. Value at the p percentile of normal distribution | qnorm(.75)  # 75th percentile<br>[1] 0.6744898 |
| rnorm($n$, m=0,sd=1) | n random normal deviates with mean m and standard deviation sd | #50 random normal variates with mean=2.5, sd=0.05<br>x <- rnorm(50, m=2.5, sd=0.05) |
| dbinom(x, *size*, *prob*)<br>pbinom($q$, *size*, *prob*)<br>qbinom($p$, *size*, *prob*)<br>rbinom($n$, *size*, *prob*) | Binomial distribution where size is the sample size and prob is the probability of a head (pi) | # prob of 0 to 5 heads of fair coin out of 10 flips<br>dbinom(0:5,10,0.5)<br><br># prob of 5 or less heads of fair coin out of 10 flips<br>pbinom(5, 10, .5) |
| dpois($x$, *lamda*)<br>ppois($q$, *lamda*)<br>qpois($p$, *lamda*)<br>rpois($n$, *lamda*) | Poisson distribution with m=std=lamda | #probability of 0, 1, or 2 events with lamda=4<br>dpois(0:2, 4)<br>[1] 0.01831564 0.07326256 0.14652511<br><br># probability of at least 3 events with lamda=4<br>1-ppois(2,4)<br>[1] 0.7618967 |
| dunif($x$, min=0, max=1)<br>punif($q$, min=0, max=1)<br>qunif($p$, min=0, max=1)<br>runif($n$, min=0, max=1) | Uniform distribution, follows the same pattern as the normal distribution above | #5 uniform random variates<br>y <- runif(5)<br>y<br>[1] 0.14192169 0.13701585 0.06418781 0.58657717 0.20230663 |

### 2.4.3.4   Other Statistical Functions

See Table 2.7.

Table 2.7: Other statistical functions

| Function | Description | Example |
|---|---|---|
| mean(x, trim=0, na.rm = FALSE) | Mean of object x | # trimmed mean, removing any # missing values and 5% #of highest and lowest scores<br>mx <- mean(x,trim=.05,na.rm=TRUE) |
| sd(x)<br>var(x)<br>mad(x) | Standard deviation of object(x), var (x) for variance, and mad(x) for median absolute deviation. | x<-1:10<br>sd(x)<br>[1] 3.02765<br>var(x)<br>[1] 9.166667<br>mad(x)<br>[1] 3.7065 |
| median(x) | Median | x<-1:10<br>median(x)<br>[1] 5.5 |
| quantile(x, probs) | Quantiles where x is the numeric vector whose quantiles are desired and probs is a numeric vector with probabilities in [0,1] | # 10th and 75th percentiles of x<br>y <- quantile(x, c(0.1,0.75))<br>y<br>10%  75%<br>1.90 7.75 |
| range(x) | Range | range(x)<br>[1]  1 10 |
| sum(x) | Sum | sum(x)<br>[1] 55 |
| diff(x, lag=1) | Lagged differences, with lag indicating which lag to use | diff(x, lag=1)<br>[1] 1 1 1 1 1 1 1 1 1 |
| min(x) | Minimum | min(x)<br>[1] 1 |
| max(x) | Maximum | max(x)<br>[1] 10 |
| scale(x, center=TRUE, scale=TRUE) | Column center or standardize a mat | |

### 2.4.3.5  Other Useful Functions
See Table 2.8.

Table 2.8: Other useful functions

| Function | Description | Example |
|---|---|---|
| seq(*from, to, by*) | Generate a sequence | gen <- seq(1,10,2)<br>gen<br>[1] 1 3 5 7 9 |
| rep(*x*, ntimes) | Repeat *x n* times | r <- rep(1:3, 2)<br>r<br>[1] 1 2 3 1 2 3 |
| cut(*x, n*) | Divide continuous variable in factor with *n* levels | y <- cut(x, 5) |

## 2.4.4  USER-WRITTEN FUNCTIONS

R is so flexible to accomodate the user to add functions and some functions in R are functions of functions.

The structure of a function is given below:

```
my.function <- function(arg1, arg2, ... ){
statements
return(object)
}
```

*# Example 11*

```
my.result <- function(x,npar=TRUE,print=TRUE){
  if (!npar) {
    center <- mean(x); spread <- sd(x)
  } else {
    center <- median(x); spread <- mad(x)
  }
  if (print & !npar) {
    cat("Mean=", center, "\n", "SD=", spread, "\n")
  } else if (print & npar) {
    cat("Median=", center, "\n", "MAD=", spread, "\n")
  }
  result <- list(center=center,spread=spread)
```

```
   return(result)
  }


  # actualizing the function
  set.seed(100)
  rv1 <- rbinom(10, 3, 0.5)
  rv2 <- my.result(rv1)
  Median= 1
   MAD= 0
```

## 2.4.5   IMPORTING, REPORTING, AND WRITING DATA

We will discuss how to import packages and changing directories for reading and writing local flat files, reading and writing local Excel files, connection interfaces, reading XML/HTML files, reading and writing to JSON, connecting to a database, and the textual format.

### 2.4.5.1  Packages

Anything you may think of doing with R, there is a tendency that a package has been written to execute it. The list of packages can be found in the official repository CRAN: `http://cran` `.fhcrc.org/web/packages/`. The installation of any package of your choice is very easy in R, you may use the command: `install.packages("packagename")`.

### 2.4.5.2  Working Directory and R Script

Set the working directory from the menu if using the R-gui (Change dir...) or from the R command line:

```
  setwd("C:\\MyWorkingDirectory ")
  setwd("C:/MyWorkingDirectory ")  # can use forward slash
  setwd(choose.dir())  # open a file browser
  getwd() # returns a string with the current working directory
```

Besides, in order to have access and see a list of the files in the current directory, you can use the R command line:

```
  dir ()    # returns a list of strings of file names
  dir (pattern = ".R$ ") # list of files ending in ".R "
  dir ("C:\\Users")      # show files in directory C:\Users


  Run a script

source("helloworld.R")
```

### 2.4.5.3  Reading and Writing Local Flat Files

Local flat files can be read by using the following: **read.table**, **read.csv**, **readLines**. The acronomy CSV stands for "comma separated values."

For the purpose of illustration, we will be working with the Nigerian exchange rate dataset from the Central Bank of Nigeria website. To procure this dataset, please visit the following link: `https://www.cbn.gov.ng/Functions/export.asp?tablename=exchange`.

Right click and select "save as" to save it to your local directory. The code samples in the remainder of this section assumes that you have set your working directory to the location of the `exchrt.csv` file.

Reading and writing local flat files:

```
exch.rt<-read.csv("G:/BRA Research/BUSINESS STATISTICS IN R/exchrt.csv")
head(exch.rt, 7)
  Rate.Date       Currency Rate.Year Rate.Month Buying.Rate Central.Rate Selling.Rate
1 10/4/2018     US DOLLAR      2018    October     305.4000     305.9000    306.4000
2 10/4/2018 POUNDS STERLING    2018    October     396.6230     397.2723    392.9217
3 10/4/2018          EURO      2018    October     351.1795     351.7544    352.3294
4 10/4/2018    SWISS FRANC     2018    October     307.6458     308.1495    308.6532
5 10/4/2018           YEN      2018    October       2.6766       2.6810      2.6854
6 10/4/2018           CFA      2018    October       0.5178       0.5278      0.5378
7 10/4/2018          WAUA      2018    October     424.2396     424.9341    425.6287

col.head<-readLines("G:/BRA Research/BUSINESS STATISTICS IN R/exchrt.csv", 1)
col.head
[1] "Rate Date,Currency,Rate Year,Rate Month,Buying Rate,Central Rate,Selling Rate"
```

To write local flat files, you can used the functions such as **write.table, write.csv**, and **writeLines**. Meanwhile, it is advisable for someone to take note of the parameters before reading or writing a file.

```
write.table(exch.rt, "new_exchrt.csv")
```

Conversely, the **read.table** is the one of the commonest functions for reading a data. Some of the arguments of **read.table()** are described below:

```
function (file, header = FALSE, sep = "", quote = "\"", dec = ".",
numerals = c("allow.loss", "warn.loss", "no.loss"), row.names,
col.names, as.is = !stringsAsFactors, na.strings = "NA",
    colClasses = NA, nrows = -1, skip = 0, check.names = TRUE,
fill = !blank.lines.skip, strip.white = FALSE,
    blank.lines.skip = TRUE, comment.char = "#", allowEscapes = FALSE,
flush = FALSE, stringsAsFactors = default.stringsAsFactors(),
fileEncoding = "", encoding = "unknown", text, skipNul = FALSE)
```

1. **file** is the name of a file, or a connection.

2. **header** a logical value indicating the variables of the first line.

3. **sep** is a string indicating how the columns are separated.

4. **colClasses** is a character vector indicating the class of each column in the dataset.

5. **nrows** are the number of rows in the dataset.

6. **comment.char** is character string indicating the comment character.

7. **skip** is the number of lines to skip from the beginning.

8. **stringsAsFactors** determines whether character variables be coded as factors.

### 2.4.5.4 Reading and Writing Excel Files

The functions **read.xlsx** or **read.xlsx2** can be used to read an excel file while **write.xlsx** or **write.xlsx2** can also be used write. This is relatively fast but unstable. First, make sure that you install the Excel spreadsheet from the library. We can use the following commands to install the xlsx library:

```
# install the xlsx library
install.packages("xlsx")
```

See Fig. 2.6.

The command in Fig. 2.6 prompted this image and then click OK. Second, we have to load the Excel spreadsheet into the library with the following command lines:

```
# load the library
library(xlsx)
```

Alternatively, you can load library through interface:
Click menu "Packages"
Then select "Load package…"
And then select "xlsx"
Click OK.

### 2.4.5.5 Connection Interfaces

We may not necessarily need to access connection interface directly; it may be made to files or to other channels such as the following.

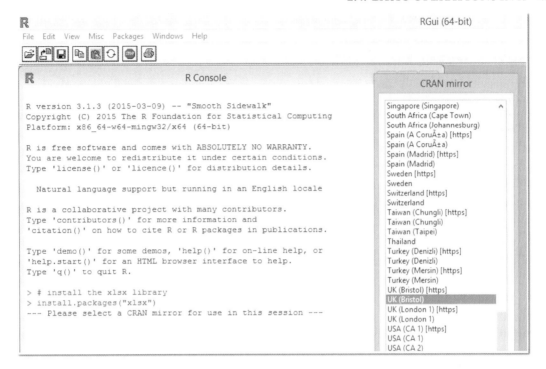

Figure 2.6: Install packages.

1. **file** opens a connection to a file.

2. **gzfile** opens a connection to a file compressed with gzip.

3. **bzfile** opens a connection to a file compressed with bzip2.

4. **url** opens a connection to a web page.

### 2.4.5.6  Connect to a Database

For good data management and efficient warehouse, it is required to store our data in a relational database. A well-designed database architecture improve the robustness on how data can be mined to give a rigourous analysis. To perform statistical computing we will need very advanced and complex Sql queries. R can connect easily to many relational databases like MySql, Oracle, Sql server, among others. One of the advantages of using a database is that the records from the relational database is fetched as a data frame. Hence, it makes data crunch more easily to analyze with the aid of sophisticated packages and functions. R has some packages that connect to R, and these include: `JSONPackages`, `RmySQL`, `RpostresSQL`, `RODBC`, `RMONGO`, etc. In this book, we will use MySql as our reference database for connecting to R.

We can install the "RMySQL" package in the R environment using the following command:

```
install.packages("RMySQL")
library(RMySQL)
```

After installation we will create a connection object in R to connect to the database. It requires the username, password, database name, and host name as input:

```
# Create a connection Object to MySQL database.
# assume our database named "my.database"
# that comes with MySql installation.
mysql.connect = dbConnect(MySQL(), user = 'root', password = '',
                        dbname = ' my.database ', host = 'localhost')


# to list the tables available in this database
dbListTables(mysql.connect)
```

## 2.5    DATA EXPLORATION

This is the initial step that is compulsory to perform before the commencement of the proper analysis. This process involves data visualization (identify summaries, structure, relationships, differences, and abnormalities in the data), descriptive statistics, and inferential statistics.

Oftentimes no elaborate analysis is necessary as all the important conclusions required for a decision are evident from simple visual examination of the data. Other times, data exploration will be used to help guide the data cleaning, feature selection, and sampling process.

Look at the first three rows; we have:

```
head(exch.rt[1:7], 3)
Rate.Date    Currency      Rate.Year Rate.Month Buying.Rate Central.Rate Selling.Rate
1 10/4/2018       US DOLLAR    2018     October     305.4000     305.9000     306.4000
2 10/4/2018 POUNDS STERLING   2018     October     396.6230     397.2723     392.9217
3 10/4/2018            EURO    2018     October     351.1795     351.7544     352.3294
```

For a more specific sample of the data, assuming that we want to view the last three columns of the data frame, and the first-two rows in the columns. The command lines are:

```
# View the last three columns of the data frame,
# and the first two rows in those columns
head(exch.rt[,5:7],2)
  Buying.Rate Central.Rate Selling.Rate
1    305.400     305.9000     306.4000
2    396.623     397.2723     392.9217
```

The **str()** function can be used to summarize the data frame. Let us look at the summary of the exchange rate data.

```
str(exch.rt)
'data.frame':   38728 obs. of  7 variables:
$ Rate.Date    : Factor w/ 4126 levels "1/10/2002","1/10/2003",..:
                 623 623 623 623 623 623 623 623 623 623 ...
$ Currency     : Factor w/ 27 levels "CFA","CFA ","DANISH KRONA",..:
                 21 12 5 19 25 1 23 27 13 18 ...
$ Rate.Year    : int  2018 2018 2018 2018 2018 2018 2018
                 2018 2018 2018 ...
$ Rate.Month   : Factor w/ 15 levels "8","April","August",..:
                 14 14 14 14 14 14 14 14 14 14 ...
$ Buying.Rate  : num  305.4 396.62 351.18 307.65 2.68 ...
$ Central.Rate : num  305.9 397.27 351.75 308.15 2.68 ...
$ Selling.Rate : num  306.4 392.92 352.33 308.65 2.69 ...
```

## 2.5.1   DATA EXPLORATION THROUGH VISUALIZATION

In this section, we shall limit our scope to few number of visual data exploration methods. This includes, a bar chart, pie chart, and box-plot, etc.

### 2.5.1.1  Bar Chart

A bar chart is good at visualizing a categorical data, and it is made up of rectangular bars with heights or lengths proportional to the values that they represent (see Fig. 2.7). The bars can be plotted vertically or horizontally.

```
# Simple bar chart
age <- c(22, 20, 14, 16, 18)
barplot(age, main = "Distribution of Age of Students", xlab = "Age",
  ylab = "Name", names.arg = c("Ade", "Ope", "Olu", "John", "Ayo"),
  col = "green", horiz = TRUE)
```

### 2.5.1.2  Pie Chart

A pie chart depicts the proportions and percentages between categories, by dividing a circle into proportional segments. Each arc length represents a proportion of each category. The full circle represents the total sum of all the data and it is equal to 100%. It gives a reader an insight of the proportional distribution of a dataset. However, a bar chart or dot plot are preferred to a pie chart because of an inability to judge length more accurately.

Pie charts are created with the function **pie(x, labels=)** where x is a non-negative numeric vector indicating the area of each slice and `labels=` notes a character vector of names for the slices (see Fig. 2.8).

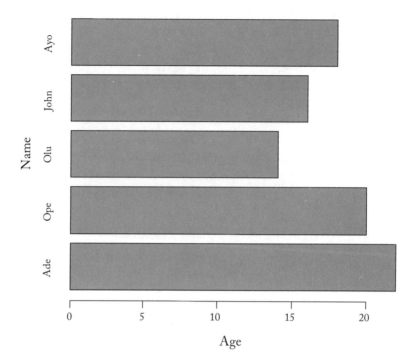

Figure 2.7: Bar chart.

```
# Age distribution of students
age <- c(22, 20, 14, 16, 18)
name <- c("Ade", "Ope", "Olu", "John", "Ayo")
age.pct <- round(age/sum(age)*100)
name <- paste(name, age.pct) # add percents to labels
name <- paste(name,"%",sep="") # ad % to labels
pie(age, labels = name, col=rainbow(length(name)),
    main="Age Distribution")
```

### 2.5.1.3  Box-Plot Distributions

A box plot is very uselful in showing the distribution or pattern between numerical and categorical attributes (see Fig. 2.9). Box plots can be created for individual variables or for variables by group. The format is boxplot(x, data=), where x is a formula and data= denotes the data frame providing the data. A typical example of a formula is y~group where a separate box plot for numeric variable y is generated for each value of group. Add varwidth=TRUE to make box

**Age Distribution**

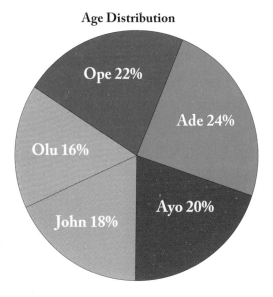

Figure 2.8: Pie chart.

plot widths proportional to the square root of the samples sizes. Add `horizontal=TRUE` to reverse the axis orientation.

```
# simple box plot
age <- c(22, 20, 14, 16, 18)
gender= c("Female", "Male", "Male", "Male", "Female")
mydata<-data.frame(age, gender)
boxplot(age~gender,data=mydata, labels=c("Male","Female"),
        xlab="Gender", ylab="Age", col=c("red","blue"))
```

## 2.6   EXERCISES

**2.1.**   What are the advantages of R software?

**2.2.**   With the aid of examples, explain the term vectorization in R.

**2.3.**   Enumerate different types of data in R.

**2.4.**   What do you understand by control structure in R and list common control structures in R?

**2.5.**   What are the methods to use in visualizing data?

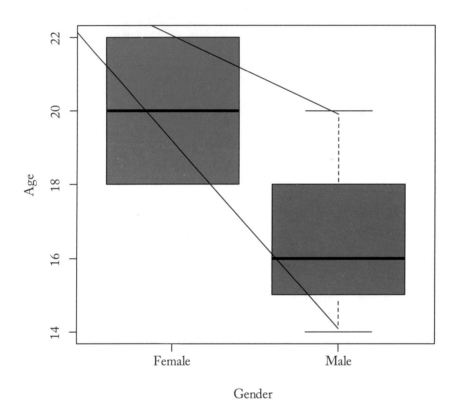

Figure 2.9: Box plot distributions.

# CHAPTER 3

# Descriptive Data

This chapter presents different statistical measures that can be employed to provide descriptive analysis of business-related data. In this chapter we will define the statistical measures of central tendency and dispersion. Explanations of these measures of central tendency and dispersion using example data are provided in this chapter.

## 3.1 CENTRAL TENDENCY

Central tendency concerns the measures that may be used to represent the middle value of a set of data; that is, a value that represents the center of that data. The three common measures of central tendency are mean, median, and mode.

### The Mean

Mean or arithmetic mean: this is the average of a set of observations. It is the aggregate of all observations divided by the number of observations in the data set. For example, observations are denoted by $x_1, x_2, x_3, \ldots, x_n$. The sample mean is represented by $\bar{x}$ which is expressed as follows.

Mean of a sample,

$$\bar{x} = \frac{\sum_{i=1}^{n} x_i}{n} = \frac{x_1 + x_2 + x_3 + \cdots + x_n}{n}, \tag{3.1}$$

where $\sum$ is the summation symbol. The summation covers all of the data points.

As an example, if you have 9 houses on your block and the number of people living in the houses is: 2, 1, 6, 4, 1, 1, 5, 1, and 3 and you want to know the average (mean) number of people living in the house, you simply add the numbers together and get 24 and divide that by 9 to get 2.67 people per house.

If the observation set covers a whole population, the symbol $\mu$ (the Greek letter mu) is used to represent the mean of the entire population. In addition, $N$ is used instead of n to denote the number of elements. The mean of the population is specified as follows.

Mean of a population:

$$\mu = \frac{\sum_{i=1}^{N} x_i}{N}. \tag{3.2}$$

Mean is the most commonly used measure of central tendency. In addition, the mean is relied on information contained in all the observations in the dataset.

**Characteristics of Mean**

- It summarizes all information in the dataset.

- It captures the average of all the observations.

- It is a single point viewed as the point where all observations are concentrated.

- All observations in the dataset would be equal to the mean if each observation has the same size or figure.

- It is sensitive to extreme observations (outliers).

**The Median**

This is a special point because it is located in the center of the data, implying that half the data lies below it and half above it. The median is defined as a measure of the location or centrality of the observations. This is just an observation lying in the middle of the set.

In order to find the median by hand, given a small data set like this one, you need to reorder the dataset in numerical order:

$$1, 1, 1, 1, 2, 3, 4, 5, 6.$$

If you divide the number of data points by two and round up to the next integer, you will find the median. So for our example:

$$9/2 = 4.5.$$

Round up the answer is 5, so the 5th data point is the median, which is 2.

This works nicely if you have an odd number of data points, but if you have an even number, then there would be two middle numbers. To resolve this dilemma, you take those two data points and average them. So let's add a house with 4 people. That means that the middle two numbers would be 2 and 3. So averaging them gives you 2.5 as the median.

**Characteristics of Median**

- It is an observation in the center of the dataset.

- One half of the data lie above this observation.

- One half of the data lie below the observation.

- It is resistant to extreme observations.

## The Mode

The mode denotes the value that has the highest occurrence. Put differently, the mode is the value with most frequency in the dataset. In our example, the mode would be 1 with four occurrences.

### Example 3.1

Calculate the mean, median, and mode of the following observations: 2, 6, 8, 7, 5, 3, 2, and 2.

### Solution

Mean of the observations, $\bar{x} = \frac{2+6+8+7+5+3+2+2}{7} = \frac{35}{8} = 4.4$.

To solve for the mean of the observations in R, the following commands are expressed.

```
x <- c (2,6,8,7,5,3,2,2)
mean(x)
[1] 4.4
```

Median of the observation requires the re-arrangement of the number from smallest to largest: 2, 2, 2, 3, 5, 6, 7, and 8. There are eight observations, so the median is the value in the middle, that is, in the fourth and fifth position. Those values are 3 and 5; so you add the two numbers together and divide the outcome by 2 in order to get the median.

Median is $\frac{3+5}{2} = 4$ because 3 and 5 are the center of the dataset. In R, the command is:

```
median (x)
[1] 4
```

Mode in the observation set is 2 because it appears three times while other values occur once. In R, the command is:

```
mode(x)
[1] 2
```

## 3.2 MEASURE OF DISPERSION

There are different measures of variability or dispersion. These measure the degree of data spread-out from the mean of a dataset. These measures include range, interquartile range, variance, and standard deviation.

(a) Range: this is the difference between the largest observation and the smallest observation. The range in Example 3.1 is largest number—smallest number = $8 - 2 = 6$.

(b) Interquartile range: this can be defined as the difference between the upper quartile ($Q_3$) and lower quartile ($Q_1$). Thus, the interquartile range is a measure of the difference between the higher half of your data and the lower half. To do this, we order the data and separate the lower half of the data from the higher half and calculate the medians of the

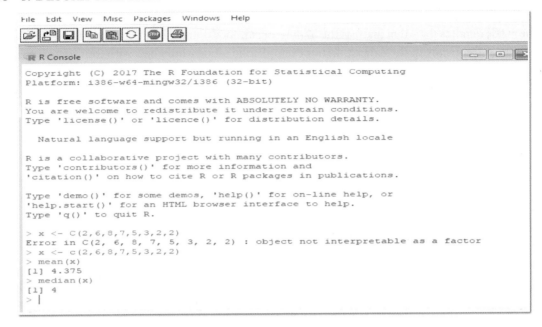

Figure 3.1: The R foundation for statistical computing.

higher half and lower half and then subtract the lower half median from the higher half median to get the interquartile range.

Using data from our first example, 1, 1, 1, 1, 2, 3, 4, 5, 6, we first need to split the data set in two. So we look to the middle and see that the number is odd, so we throw out the median (3.2). Then we find the median of 3, 4, 5, and 6 which is 4.5 and subtract the median of 1, 1, 1, 1 which is 1 to give us 3.5 as the interquartile range. So we see that the spread between the lower half of this data and the higher half is quite significant.

(c) Variance: this is the average squared deviation of the data points from their mean.

(d) Standard deviation: this can be defined as the square root of the variance of the entire dataset. In financial analysis, the standard deviation is explored to capture the volatility as well as the risk associated with financial variables.

(e) The variance, is calculated by calculating the difference from the mean for each data point, then squaring each of them and then adding them all together and then divided by the number of items in the dataset minus one:

$$\frac{\sum_{i=1}^{n} (x_i - \bar{x})^2}{n - 1}.$$

(f) The standard deviation of a sample is the square root of the sample variance while the standard deviation of a population is the square root of the variance of the population. The formulae for these two forms of standard deviation are expressed below:

$$\text{Sample standard deviation: } s = \sqrt{s^2} = \sqrt{\frac{\sum_{i=1}^{n} (x_i - \bar{x})^2}{n-1}}$$

$$\text{Population standard deviation: } \sigma = \sqrt{\sigma^2} = \sqrt{\frac{\sum_{i=1}^{n} (x_i - \mu)^2}{n-1}}.$$

Statisticians prefer working with the variance because its mathematical features make computations easy, whereas applied statisticians like to work with the standard deviation because of its easy interpretation.

Let's calculate the variance and standard deviation of the data in Table 3.1. In order to compute this, a table is used for simplicity (before exploring R software to do everything within a minute).

Table 3.1: Observations for $X$ variables

| x | $x_i - \bar{x}$ | $(x_i - \bar{x})^2$ |
|---|---|---|
| 2 | -2.4 | 9 |
| 2 | -2.4 | 9 |
| 2 | -2.4 | 9 |
| 3 | -1.4 | 4 |
| 5 | 0.6 | 0 |
| 6 | 1.6 | 1 |
| 7 | 2.6 | 4 |
| 8 | 3.6 | 9 |
| **Total** | 0 | 45 |

In reference to the above equation, the variance of the sample equals the sum of the third column in the Table 3.1, 45, divided by $n-1$: $s^2 = \frac{45}{7} = 4.44$. The standard deviation is the square root of the variance: $s = \sqrt{3.44} = 2.335$ or putting in two decimal places, $s = 2.34$.

There is a shortcut formula for the sample variance that is equivalent to the formula above for variance:

$$s^2 = \frac{\sum_{i=1}^{n} x_i^2 - \left(\sum_{i=1}^{n} x_i\right)^2 / n}{n-1}.$$

Solving the standard deviation and variance in Table 3.1 with the aid of R, the commands are:

```
x <- c(2,2,2,3,5,6,7,8)
var(x)
[1]4.44
sd(x)
[1] 2.34
```

## 3.3   SHAPES OF THE DISTRIBUTION—SYMMETRIC AND ASYMMETRIC

(a) *Symmetric distribution*: a dataset or a population is symmetric if one side of the distribution of the observation reflects a mirror image of the other; and if the distribution of the observations has only one mode, then the mode, median, and mean are the same.

(b) *Asymmetric distribution*: this is the kind of distributional pattern in which one side of the distribution is not a mirror image of the other. In addition, in its data distribution, the mean, median, and mode will not all be equal.

Additional attributes of a frequency distribution of a dataset are skewness and kurtosis.

**Skewness:**   measures the degree of asymmetry of a distribution. A right skewness occurs when the distribution stretches to the right more than it does to the left, while a left-skewed distribution is one that stretches asymmetrically to the left. Graphs depicting a symmetric distribution, a right-skewed distribution, a left-skewed distribution, and a symmetrical distribution with two modes, are presented in Fig. 3.2.

For a right-skewed distribution, the mean is to the right of the median, thus lying to the right of the mode. The opposite is observed for left-skewed distribution (see Fig. 3.2). The calculation of skewness is reported by a number that may be positive, negative, or zero. Zero skewness indicates a symmetric distribution. A positive skewness means a right-skewed distribution while a negative skewness denotes a left-skewed distribution. Skewness could be different in terms of their shape even if two distributions have the same mean and variance.

**Kurtosis:**   this measures the peak level of distribution. The larger the kurtosis, the more peaked will be the distribution. Its calculation is reported either as an absolute or a relative value. Absolute kurtosis is usually a positive number. For a normal distribution, the absolute kurtosis is 3. The value of 3 is used as the data point to compute relative kurtosis. Therefore, relative kurtosis is the difference between the absolute kurtosis and 3:

$$\text{Relative kurtosis} = \text{absolute kurtosis} - 3.$$

The relative kurtosis can be either negative, known as platykurtic indicating a flatter distribution than the normal distribution or a positive kurtosis known as leptokurtic showing a more peaked distribution than the normal distribution.

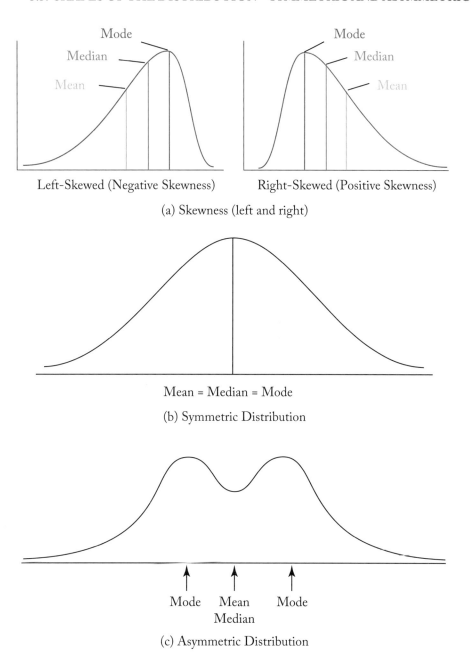

Figure 3.2: (a) Skewness (left and right), (b) symmetric distribution, and (c) asymetric distribution.

## 3.4    EXERCISES

**3.1.**   Create $X$ that includes all even numbers between 0 and 100.

**3.2.**   Calculate the mean, mode, and median of $X$.

**3.3.**   Calculate the dispersion measures (standard deviation and variance) for $X$.

**3.4.**   Explain the characteristics of central tendency measures (mean, mode, and median).

**3.5.**   Explain the two tools discussed here—kurtosis and skewness—for shapes of distribution.

# CHAPTER 4

# Basic Probability Concepts

In this chapter, we shall discuss some basic concepts of probability, and solving the problem of probability using venn diagram. The axioms and rules of probability shall be discussed. We shall extend our discussion to conditional probabilities. Practical examples with R codes will be used for illustration.

## 4.1 EXPERIMENT, OUTCOME, AND SAMPLE SPACE

As we have mentioned before, it is important to understand the definition of certain terms to be able to use them successfully. So the first step in gaining an understanding of probability is to learn the terminology and the rest will be a lot simpler.

### 4.1.1 EXPERIMENT

This is a measurement process that produces quantifiable results. Some typical examples of an experiment are tossing of a die, tossing of a coin, playing of cards, measuring weight of students, and recording growth of plants.

### 4.1.2 OUTCOME

This is a single result from a measurement. Examples of outcomes are getting a sum of 9 in a tossing of two dice, turning up of head in a toss of a coin, selecting a spade in a deck of card, and getting a weight above a threshold (say 50 kg).

### 4.1.3 SAMPLE SPACE

This is the set of all possible outcomes from an experiment and it is denoted as $\mathbb{S}$. The sample space of tossing a die is $\mathbb{S} = \{1, 2, 3, 4, 5, 6\}$; the sample space of tossing a coin is denoted as $\mathbb{S} = \{H, T\}$. In addition, the sample space for the tossing of two dice is

$$\mathbb{S} = \left\{ \begin{array}{llllllll}
\{1,1\}, & \{1,2\}, & \{1,3\}, & \{1,4\}, & \{1,5\}, & \{1,6\}, & \{2,1\}, & \{2,2\}, & \{2,3\}, \\
\{2,4\}, & \{2,5\}, & \{2,6\}, & \{3,1\}, & \{3,2\}, & \{3,3\}, & \{3,4\}, & \{3,5\}, & \{3,6\}, \\
\{4,1\}, & \{4,2\}, & \{4,3\}, & \{4,4\}, & \{4,5\}, & \{4,6\}, & \{5,1\}, & \{5,2\}, & \{5,3\}, \\
\{5,4\}, & \{5,5\}, & \{5,6\}, & \{6,1\}, & \{6,2\}, & \{6,3\}, & \{6,4\}, & \{6,5\}, & \{6,6\}
\end{array} \right\}.$$

## 4.2   ELEMENTARY EVENTS

Any subset of a sample set, empty set, and whole set inclusive is called an *event*. It is an event with a single element taken from a sample space. In set theory, the *elementary event* is a singleton set (a set that contains only one element) and it is denoted as $E$. In addition, elementary event can be written as $E \subset \mathbb{S}$ (where $E$ is a proper subset of the sample space, but not equal to the sample space). Suppose we have n possible outcomes from an experiment say $E_1, E_2, E_3, \ldots, E_n$, then the space of elementary events which is the sample space can be written as: $\mathbb{S} = \{E_1 \cup E_2 \cup E_3 \cup \ldots \cup E_n\}$. That is the sample is the union of all of the events. For instance, when tossing three coins, all possible outcomes are $\{HHH\}, \{HHT\}, \{HTH\}, \{THH\}, \{HTT\}, \{THT\}, \{TTH\}, \{TTT\}$ and when rolling a fair die, all possible outcomes are getting $\{1\}, \{2\}, \{3\}, \{4\}, \{5\}, \{6\}$. Hence, each of the outcomes are elementary events.

## 4.3   COMPLEMENTARY EVENTS

These are events that cannot occur at the same time. Consider an event $A$, having its complement denoted by $A'$ which are mutually exclusive and exhaustive. Hence, the sample space of the experiment can be written as $\mathbb{S} = A \cup A'$ and also $\phi = A \cap A'$. That is, the intersection of $A$ and its complement is the null set. For example, in a tossing of a coin, turning a head and turning tail are complementary events.

## 4.4   MUTUALLY EXCLUSIVE EVENTS

Two events are said to be mutually exclusive if they cannot occur at the same time. A good example of a mutually exclusive event is that in flipping a coin, either a head can appear or a tail, but not the two can appear simultaneously. Let events $A$ and $B$ be mutually exclusive, then $A \cap B = \phi$.

## 4.5   MUTUALLY INCLUSIVE EVENTS

Two events are said to be mutually inclusive, if there are some common outcomes in the two events. Getting a head and a tail in flipping of two coins is an example of mutually inclusive events. Another example is getting an odd number or prime number in a throwing of two dice.

## 4.6   VENN DIAGRAM

Venn diagrams are very useful in visualizing relations between sets. Figures 4.1–4.4 have a diagrammatical representation of sets in a rectangular box.

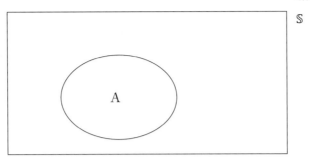

Figure 4.1: Venn diagram, $A \subset \mathbb{S}$.

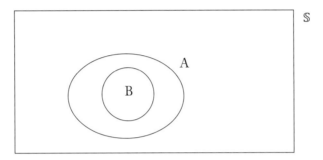

Figure 4.2: Two sets $A$ and $B$, where $B \subset A$.

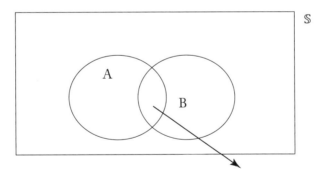

Figure 4.3: Two sets $A$ and $B$, where $A \cap B$.

## 4.7   PROBABILITY

The probability of event $A$ could be defined as the number of ways event $A$ can occur divided by the total number of possible outcomes. It is mathematically defined as:

$$\textbf{Probability (A)} = \frac{number\ of\ outcomes\ favorable\ to\ A}{number\ of\ possible\ outcomes}.$$

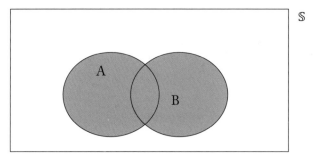

Figure 4.4: Two sets $A$ and $B$, where $A \cup B$ is a shaded area.

$$P(A) = \frac{n(A)}{n(\mathbb{S})}. \tag{4.1}$$

**Example 4.1**
A fair die is rolled once, what is the probability of: (i) Rolling an even number? (ii) Rolling an odd number?

**Solution:**

$$\text{Probability (even number)} = \frac{\textit{number of even number}}{\textit{number of possible outcomes}}.$$

Let $A$ be set of even number, then $A = \{2, 4, 6\}$ and $B$ be a set of odd numbers in a tossing of a die, the $B = \{1, 3, 5\}$ and the sample space, $\mathbb{S} = \{1, 2, 3, 4, 5, 6\}$.

(i)  $P(A) = \frac{3}{6}$.

(ii)  $P(B) = \frac{3}{6}$.

**Example 4.2**
What is the probability that an applicant resume will be treated within a week of submitting application if 5,000 graduates applied for a job and the recruitment firm can only treat 1,000 resumes in a week?

**Solution:**
Probability (treating a resume) = $\frac{1,000}{5,000} = 0.2$.

### 4.7.1   SIMULATION OF A RANDOM SAMPLE IN R

The R command sample is used to simulate drawing a sample. The function *sample* contains three arguments:

$x$   is a vector containing the objects

$size$   the number of samples to be drawn

$replace$   is set TRUE or FALSE depending on whether you want to draw the sample with replacement or not.

**Note:** Sampling with replacement (replace = TRUE) indicates replacing the object before performing another sample selection. On the other hand, sampling without replacement (replace = FALSE) means selection in succession.

**Example 4.3**

Consider an urn containing one blue ball, one green ball, and one yellow ball. To simulate drawing two balls from the urn with replacement and without replacement, we have:

```
# Urn contains one blue, one green and one yellow balls
Urn = c('blue', 'green', 'yellow')
# Sampling with replacement
sample(x = Urn, size =2, replace = TRUE)
[1] "yellow" "yellow"
```

```
# Sampling without replacement
Urn = c('blue', 'green', 'yellow')
sample(x = Urn, size =2, replace = FALSE)
[1] "yellow" "blue"
```

For the two cases, there is no unique answer here as long as they satisfied the condition where they are selected. In the sampling with replacement, our result can be any from the sample space of:

["yellow" "yellow"],  ["yellow" "blue"],  ["blue" "yellow"],  ["blue" "blue"],
[ "blue" "green"],  [ "green" "blue"],  [ "green" "yellow"],  [ "yellow" "green"],
[ "green" "green"]

However, in the case of sampling without replacement, we can have any of these outcomes:

["yellow" "blue"],  ["blue" "yellow"],  [ "blue" "green"],  [ "green" "blue"],
[ "green" "yellow"],  [ "yellow" "green"],

So by putting the yellow ball back in after it was selected the first time, it expands the solution possibilities significantly. In our case it meant picking the yellow ball twice.

**Example 4.4**

Draw four random numbers between 1 and 20 with replacement and without replacement.

```
# Sampling with replacement
sample(x = 1:20, size =4, replace = TRUE)
[1] 17  7  7 10
```

```
# Sampling without replacement
sample(x = 1:20, size =4, replace = FALSE)
[1]  1 17 18 20
```

**Note:** There is no unique answer for both cases in as much the condition of generating the samples is satisfied. It is generated randomly.

**Example 4.5**
Simulate rolling a fair die.

```
# Sample from rolling a fair die
set.seed(25)
sample(x = 1:6, size =1, replace = TRUE)
[1] 3
```

**Note:** Replacement option (TRUE or FALSE) does not hinder the outcome here since the experiment is performed once, i.e., size = 1. A seed is set in the codes in Example 4.5 above; this is done to make the codes reproducible and to ensure the same random numbers will be generated each time the script is executed.

**Example 4.6**
Replicate the experiment in Example 4.5 in 100 times.

```
# Sample replication
set.seed(25)
replicate(100, sample(x = 1:6, size =1, replace = TRUE) )
 [1] 3 5 1 6 1 6 4 3 1 2 2 3 6 4 5 1 4 5 3 5 1 3 1 1 2 2 1 4
     4 2 5 3 2 1 5 3 6 3 1 1 5 2 4 5 4 2 6 5 1 5 1 5 5 3 4
[56] 1 1 4 2 1 1 2 2 5 4 6 3 6 4 2 6 1 1 5 2 3 1 6 2 2 4 3
     4 1 5 5 2 3 5 4 3 2 4 4 1 3 4 6 2 2
```

# 4.8   AXIOMS OF PROBABILITY

The expressions below are the axioms of probability.

- $P(A) \geq 0$, for all $A$   (nonnegativity)
  The probability of $A$ is always greater than or equal to zero (nonegative).

- $P(\mathbb{S}) = 1$   (normalization)
  The probability of the sample space is 1, meaning that probabilities of a sample will be from 0 and 1.

- If event $A$ and event $B$ are disjoint, i.e., $(A \cap B) = \emptyset$, then
  $P(A \cup B) = P(A) + P(B)$   (additivity)
  If event $A$ is disjoint from event $B$, then the probability of both occurring is the same as adding the probability that event $A$ will occur and the probability that event $B$ will occur.

- For an infinite number of points, and $A_1, A_2, \ldots$ are disjoints, then $P\left(\cup_{i=1}^{\infty} A_i\right) = \sum_{i=1}^{\infty} P(A_i)$.

## 4.9    BASIC PROPERTIES OF PROBABILITY

The followings are the basic properties of probability and derived from the axioms of probability.

1. $P(A) = 1 - P(A')$.

2. $P(A) \leq 1$.

3. $P(A) = 0$.

4. $P(A) \leq P(B)$ if only and if $A \subseteq B$; note that they can be equal.

5. $P(A \cup B) = P(A) + P(B) - P(A \cap B)$.

6. $P(A \cup B) \leq P(A) + P(B)$ or, alternatively, $P\left(\cup_{i=1}^{n} A_i\right) = \sum_{i=1}^{n} P(A_i)$.

## 4.10    INDEPENDENT EVENTS AND DEPENDENT EVENTS

Two events $A$ and $B$ said to be independent if occurrence of event $A$ happening does not affect the occurrence of event $B$ to happen. In other words, two events $A$ and $B$ are statistically independent if:

$$P(A \text{ and } B) = P(A) \times P(B).$$

Also, independent events can be of the form:

$$P(A|B) = P(A) \quad \text{and} \quad P(B|A) = P(B).$$

That is, that the probability of $A$ given $B$ is the same as the probability of $A$ happening, because $A$ and $B$ are independent of one another. Similarly, the probability of $B$ given $A$ is the same as the probability of $B$ happening, because they are independent events.

For any finite subset of events $A_{i1}, A_{i2}, A_{i3}, \ldots, A_{in}$ are said to be independent, if:

$$P(A_{i1}, A_{i2}, A_{i3}, \ldots, A_{in}) = P(A_{i1}) P(A_{i2}) P(A_{i3}) \ldots P(A_{in}).$$

A typical example of independent events is flipping a coin twice, the outcome of head (H) or tail (T) facing up in the first toss does not affect the outcome in the second toss.

However, two events $A$ and $B$ said to be **dependent events** if occurrence of event $A$ affects the occurrence of event $B$ or vice versa. The probability that $B$ will occur given that $A$ has occurred is referred as to **conditional probability** of $B$ given $A$, and it can be written as $P(B|A)$.

### Example 4.7

A fruit basket contained 30 pieces of fruit: 8 oranges, 12 apples, and 10 bananas. If two fruits are taken at random after one another:

(a) What is the probability that the first fruit is a banana and the second fruit is an orange if the first fruit is returned in the basket before the second fruit is taken?

(b) What is the probability that the first is an orange and the second is an apple if the fruit is taken without replacement?

### Solution:

Let $A$ represents number of apples.
Let $B$ represents number of bananas.
Let $O$ represents number of oranges.

(a) $P(B \text{ and } O) = P(B).P(O) = \frac{10}{30} \times \frac{8}{30} = 0.088.$

(b) $P(O \text{ and } A) = P(O).P(A|O) = \frac{8}{30} \times \frac{12}{29} = 0.11.$

### Example 4.8

Table 4.1 below shows the outcome of a survey conducted in Enugu State, Nigeria to look at the rate small businesses fail despite the programs of government directed at their survival. Calculate the probability that a restaurant firm is highly prone to chance of occurrence?

Table 4.1: Distribution of firms on their proneness to chance of occurrence

| Proneness | Apparel/Fashion | Restaurant | Technical | Total |
|-----------|-----------------|------------|-----------|-------|
| High prone | 216 | 14 | 20 | 250 |
| Prone | 30 | 10 | 5 | 45 |
| Not prone | 10 | 4 | 6 | 20 |
| Total | 256 | 28 | 31 | 315 |
| Source: Orga and Ogbo (2012) | | | | |

**Solution:**

$$P(restaurant|High\,prone) = \frac{number\ of\ high\ prone\ restaurants}{total\ number\ of\ high\ prone\ firms},$$

$$P(restaurant|High\,prone) = \frac{14}{250} = 0.056.$$

## 4.11   MULTIPLICATION RULE OF PROBABILITY

The multiplication rule states that: the probability of the occurrence of two events is the probability of the intersection of two events and is same as the product (multiplication) of the probability of the occurrence of one event and the probability of the occurrence of the second event:

$$P(A\,and\,B) = P(A \cap B) = P(A) \times P(B). \tag{4.2}$$

If and only if event $A$ and event $B$ are independent:

$$P(A\,and\,B) = P(A \cap B) = P(A) \times P(B|A).$$

Thus, $P(B|A)$ indicates the probability of occurrence of event $B$ given event $A$ has occurred. For an event $A$ and event $B$ are independent.

In general,

$$P(A_1 \cap A_2 \cap \ldots \cap A_n) = P(A_1)\,P(A_2|A_1)\,P(A_3|A_1 \cap A_2) \ldots$$
$$\ldots P(A_n|A_1 \cap A_2 \ldots \cap A_{n-1}). \tag{4.3}$$

## 4.12   CONDITIONAL PROBABILITIES

Let $A$ and $B$ be events in a sample sample, $\mathbb{S}$, where probability of $A$ is not equal to zero, i.e., $P(A) \neq 0$, then the condition probability that event $B$ will occur given that event $A$ has occurred is:

$$P(B|A) = \frac{P(A \cap B)}{P(A)}. \tag{4.4}$$

This is equivalent to:

$$P(A \cap B) = P(B|A) \times P(A). \tag{4.5}$$

Conditional probability permits us to calculate probabilities of events based on partial knowledge of the outcome of a random experiment.

**Example 4.9**

Consider that 10 non-defective bulbs and 2 defective bulbs are contained in a pack. To find the defective bulbs the store manager were randomly selecting the bulbs one-by-one without replacement. What is the probability that he is lucky to find defective bulbs in the first two tests?

**Solution:**
Let $D_1$ be the event that the first selection is defective.
Let $D_2$ be the event that the second selection is defective:

$$P\left(D_1 \cap D_2\right) = P\left(D_1\right) P\left(D_2 | D_1\right) = \frac{2}{10} \times \frac{1}{9} = 0.02.$$

# 4.13  COMPUTATION OF PROBABILITY IN R

**Example 4.10**
Consider rolling two fair dice; calculate the probability of getting a sum of their outcomes when the experiment is performed in 100 times. Hence, plot the obtained results.

**Step 1.** Create a function to roll two fair dice and return their sum as follows.

```
dice.2 <- function () {
  dice <- sample (1:6, size = 2, replace =TRUE)
  return (sum(dice))
}
```

**Step 2.** Replicate the same experiment in 100 times.

```
# replicate the experiment in 100 times
set.seed (1010)
dice.roll<-replicate(100, dice.2())
 dice.roll
 [1] 6  7 11 10  8 11 10  2  8  3  8  4  3  4  9  5  8  5  6  4
     7  9  5  9  3
[26] 11  4  3  8  2  6 12  9  9  6 10  4  4  6  3  8  9  6  8
      5  6  9  8  6 11
[51] 8  4  2  8  7  7  8 10  5 12  9 11 11  5  8  7  6  3  5
     6  7  7  5 12  8
[76] 6  9  7  8 12 12  4 12  5 10  7  3  4  6  2  7  9  6  9
     3  6  2  7 11  6
```

**Step 3.** Tabulate the outcomes of the experiment.

```
# tabulate the outcomes
table (dice.roll)
dice.roll
 2  3  4  5  6   7   8  9  10 11 12
 5  8  9  9  15  11  14 11  5  7  6
```

**Step 4.** Calculate the probabilities.

```
# compute the probabilities of the sum of two dice
prob = table(dice.roll)/length(dice.roll)
prob
dice.roll
   2    3    4    5    6    7    8    9   10   11   12
0.05 0.08 0.09 0.09 0.15 0.11 0.14 0.11 0.05 0.07 0.06
```

The probabilities values produced in R is similar to presenting it as:

| Sum | 2 | 3 | 4 | 5 | 6 | 7 | 8 | 9 | 10 | 11 | 12 |
|---|---|---|---|---|---|---|---|---|---|---|---|
| Prob. | 0.05 | 0.08 | 0.09 | 0.09 | 0.15 | 0.11 | 0.14 | 0.11 | 0.05 | 0.07 | 0.06 |

**Step 5.** Plot of relative frequency.

```
plot (table(dice.roll)/length(dice.roll), xlab = 'Sum of outcomes',
     ylab ='Relative Frequency', main = 'Graph of 100 Rolls of
     two fair Dice')
```

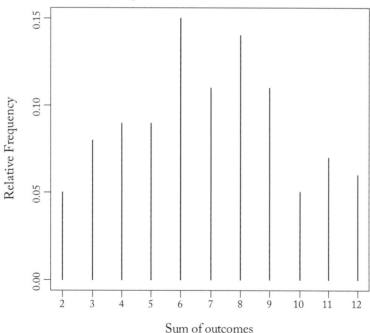

Figure 4.5: Graph of 100 rolls of 2 fair dice.

**Example 4.11**

Consider a bottling company producing three brands of products namely—A, B, and C. The probability of producing A, B, and C are 0.54, 0.36, and 0.10. The probability of a defective product on the assembly line is 0.02 and non-defective product is 0.98. If a random sample of 1,000 brands of the products are produced, what is the probability that the defective product is B?

**Solution:**

```
# set seed number to get the same result always since the
# observation is randomly  generated
set.seed (1001)
Brands <- sample(c("A","B", "C"), 1000,
               prob=c(0.54, 0.36, 0.10), rep=TRUE)
Status <- sample(c("defective","non-defective"), 1000,
               prob=c(0.02,0.98), rep=TRUE)
dataset <- data.frame(Status, Brands)
tabular <-with(dataset, table(Status, Brands))
tabular
```

|  |  | Brands |  |
|---|---|---|---|
| Status | A | B | C |
| defective | 11 | 7 | 0 |
| non-defective | 536 | 357 | 89 |

```
# compute probability of B given that is defective
probB_D <- tabular[1, 2]/sum(tabular[1, ] )
probB_D
[1] 0.3888889
```

## 4.14  EXERCISES

**4.1.**  A fair die is tossed once. Calculate the probability that: (i) exactly 3 comes up, (ii) 3 or 5 come up, and (iii) a prime number comes up.

**4.2.**  Two dice are rolled together once. What is the probability that the sum of the outcome is: (i) 4, (ii) less than 4, (iii) more than 4, and (iv) between 7 and 12 inclusive.

**4.3.**  A card is drawn from a well shuffled pack of 52 cards. Find the probability of:

(a) a king or a queen,

(b) a black card,

(c) a heart or a red king, and

(d) a spade or a jack.

**4.4.** A research firm has 30 staff, which consists of 2 research managers, 5 research associates, 3 administrative staff, and 20 fieldworkers. The managing director of the firm wants to set up a committee of five-man. Find the probability that the committee will consist of:

    (a) 1 research manager, 1 research associate and 3 fieldworkers;

    (b) 1 research manager, 2 research associates and 2 fieldworkers; or

    (c) 2 research managers, 3 research associates.

**4.5.** A firm has 100 employees (65 males and 35 females) and they were asked if they should adopt the paternal leave or not, their responses are summarized in Table 4.2.

Table 4.2: Employees

| Gender | Favor | Oppose | Total |
|--------|-------|--------|-------|
| Male   | 62    | 3      | 65    |
| Female | 20    | 15     | 35    |
| Total  | 82    | 18     | 100   |

    (a) Find the probability that a male opposed to paternal leave policy.

    (b) Find the probability that the person is a female, given that the person is in favor of paternal leave policy.

# CHAPTER 5

# Discrete Probability Distributions

Consider a random variable $(X)$ that takes integers values, $X_1, X_2, \ldots, X_n$ with the corresponding probabilities of $P(X_1), P(X_1), \ldots, P(X_n)$ and the probabilities $P(X)$ such that $\sum_1^n P(X) = 1$ is called a **discrete probability distribution.** The type of the random variable determines the nature of the probability distribution it follows. A discrete random variable usually involves counting which takes an integer value while the continuous random variable involves measuring and it takes both integer and a fractional part or real number. When the probabilities are assigned to random variables, then the collection of such probabilities give rise to a probability distribution. The probability distribution function can be abbreviated as pdf. A discrete probability distribution satisfies two conditions:

$$0 \leq P(X) \leq 1 \tag{5.1}$$

and

$$\sum P(X) = 1. \tag{5.2}$$

## 5.1   PROBABILITY MASS DISTRIBUTION

The probability that a discrete random variable $X$ takes on a particular value $x$, that is, $P(X = x) = f(x)$ is called a probability mass function (pmf) if it satisfies the following:

- $P(X = x) = f(x) > 0$, if $x \in S$.

  All probability must be positive for every element $x$ in the sample space $S$. Hence, if element $x$ is not in the sample space $S$, then $f(x) = 0$.

- $\sum_{x \in S} f(x) = 1$.

  The sum of probabilities for all of the possible $x$ values in the sample space $S$ must equal 1.

- $P(X \in x) = \sum_{x \in A} f(x)$.

  The sum of probabilities of the $x$ values in $A$ is the probability of event $A$.

**Example 5.1**

Experiment: toss a fair coin two times.

Sample space: $S = \{HH, HT, TH, TT\}$.

Random variable $X$ is the number of tosses showing heads.

Thus, $X : S \to \mathbb{R}$

$$X = (HH) = 2$$
$$X = (HT) = (TH) = 1$$
$$X = (TT) = 0$$
$$X = \{0, 1, 2\}.$$

That is, random variable $X$ takes a range of values 0, 1, and 2. Hence, the pmf is given by:

$$P(X = 0) = \frac{1}{4}, \ P(X = 1) = \frac{1}{2}, \quad \text{and} \quad P(X = 2) = \frac{1}{4}.$$

## 5.2    EXPECTED VALUE AND VARIANCE OF A DISCRETE RANDOM VARIABLE

The expected value is a measure of central tendency in a probability distribution and the variance is a measure of dispersion of a probability distribution.

The mean or expected value ($\mu$) for a discrete pdf is computed as:

$$\mu = \sum_{i=1}^{n} X_i P(X_i).$$
(5.3)

The variance ($\sigma^2$) of a discrete pdf is computed as:

$$\sigma^2 = \sum_{i=1}^{n} (X_i - \mu)^2 P(X_i).$$
(5.4)

Also, the standard deviation ($\sigma$) of a discrete pdf is given as:

$$\sigma = \sqrt{\sum_{i=1}^{n} (X_i - \mu)^2 P(X_i)}.$$
(5.5)

Examples of a discrete probability distribution are: rolling a die, flipping of coins, counting of car accidents on highways, producing a defective and non-defective goods, etc.

The following are the common discrete probability distributions used in statistics: Bernoulli distribution, binomial distribution, geometric distribution, hypergeometric distribution, Poisson distribution, negative binomial distribution, and multinomial distribution.

**Example 5.2**

A single tossing of a fair die.

| Roll ($X$) | 1 | 2 | 3 | 4 | 5 | 6 |
|---|---|---|---|---|---|---|
| $P(X)$ | 0.1667 | 0.1667 | 0.1667 | 0.1667 | 0.1667 | 0.1667 |

This has a discrete probability distribution since the random variable ($X$) takes the integers (i.e., 1, 2, 3, 4, 5, and 6) with corresponding probabilities of 0.1667 each. This satisfies that $0 \leq P(X) \leq 1$ and $\sum P(X) = 1$.

**Example 5.3**

Consider a distribution of the family size.

Assuming an analyst obtained the result in the table below in a survey of 1,000 households in Nigeria. Let random variable $X$ be the number of households size with probability of outcome.

| Household size ($X$) | 1 | 2 | 3 | 4 | 5 | 6+ |
|---|---|---|---|---|---|---|
| $P(X)$ | | 2/69 | 4/77 | 3/28 | 29/81 | 1/3 | 3/25 |

This satisfies that $0 \leq P(X) \leq 1$ and $\sum P(X) = 1$.

**Example 5.4**

The number of defectives items per month and the corresponding probabilities in a manufacturing firm are given in the table below.

| Defective($X$) | 0 | 1 | 2 | 3 | 4 | 5 |
|---|---|---|---|---|---|---|
| $P(X)$ | | 1/15 | 1/6 | 3/10 | 1/5 | 2/15 | 2/15 |

Let $X$ be number of defective items in a month, then $0 \leq P(X) \leq 1$ and $\sum P(X) = 1$ are satisfied.

**Example 5.5**

Using the data Example 5.4 above, calculate:

1. expected value of the distribution,

2. standard deviation of distribution, and

3. variance of the distribution.

**Solution:**

| Accident ($X$) | 0 | 1 | 2 | 3 | 4 | 5 |
|---|---|---|---|---|---|---|
| $p(X)$ | 1/15 | 1/6 | 3/10 | 1/5 | 2/15 | 2/15 |
| $Xp(X)$ | 0 | 1/6 | 3/5 | 3/5 | 8/15 | 2/3 |
| $X - \mu$ | -2.57 | -1.57 | -0.57 | 0.43 | 1.43 | 2.43 |
| $(X - \mu)^2$ | 6.59 | 2.45 | 0.32 | 0.19 | 2.05 | 5.92 |
| $p(X)(X - \mu)^2$ | 0.44 | 0.41 | 0.10 | 0.04 | 0.27 | 0.79 |

1.

$$\mu = \sum_{i=1}^{5} X_i P(X_i).$$

Expected value $= 0 + 1/6 + 3/5 + 3/5 + 8/15 + 2/3 = 2.57$.

2. Standard deviation

$$\sigma = \sqrt{\sum_{i=1}^{6} (X_i - \mu)^2 P(X_i)}$$

$$\sigma = \sqrt{0.44 + 0.41 + 0.10 + 0.04 + 0.27 + 0.79} = 1.43.$$

3. Variance $(\sigma^2) = \sum_{i=1}^{n} (X_i - \mu)^2 P(X_i)$.

$$\sigma^2 = 1.43^2 = 2.05.$$

The code below gives how we can use R to get solution to the worked Example 5.5 above.

**Using R Code**
*# to calculate the mean, standard deviation, and variance of the distribution in Example 5.5*

```
set.seed(100)
x <- c(0, 1, 2, 3, 4, 5)
prob <- c(0.067, 0.167, 0.30, 0.20, 0.133, 0.133)
weighted.mean (x, prob)
[1] 2.56
x_miu = x - weighted.mean (x, prob)

# calculate the variance
x_miu2 = x_miu * x_miu
d = prob* x_miu2
var = sum(d)
var
```

[1] 2.045904

```
# calculate the standard deviation
sd = sqrt(var)
[1] 1.430351
```

## 5.3    BINOMIAL PROBABILITY DISTRIBUTION

In this section, we are looking at the one of the commonest discrete probability distributions, its derivations, formula, statistical properties and real life applications using examples. A couple of useful formulas shall be presented in this section to give more understanding about the binomial distribution. The derivation of the mean and variance of a binomial distribution shall be discussed.

Binomial distribution is a discrete probability distribution and it is emanated from the Bernoulli trial, which based on a trial which there are two possible outcomes, say "success" and "failure." The Bernoulli trial can be presented mathematically as:

$$X = \begin{cases} 1 & \text{if the outcome is a sucess} \\ 0 & \text{if the outcome is a failure.} \end{cases} \tag{5.6}$$

Let $p$ represent the probability of success, then $1 - p$ will be probability of failure. The pmf of $X$ can be defined as:

$$f(x) = p^x (1 - p)^{1-x}, \quad x = 0 \quad \text{or} \quad 1. \tag{5.7}$$

However, the binomial probability function is the extension of the Bernoulli distribution when the following properties are met.

- Bernoulli trials are performed in $n$ times.

- Two outcomes, success ($p$) and failure ($q$) are possible in each of the trial.

- The trials are independent.

- The probability of success ($p$) remains the same between the trials.

Let $X$ be the number of successes in the $n$ independent trials, then the pmf of $X$ is given as:

$$f(x) = \binom{n}{x} p^x (1 - p)^{n-x}, \quad x = 0, 1, \ldots, n. \tag{5.8}$$

$\binom{n}{x} = \frac{n!}{(n-x)!x!}$ reads thus: $n$ combination $x$ and $n!$ reads thus: $n$ factorial (e.g., $5! = 5 \times 4 \times 3 \times 2 \times 1$). For example,

$$\binom{5}{2} = \frac{5!}{(5-3)!2!} = 10,$$

where $n$ is the number of trials experiment is performed, $x$ is the number of success recorded, and $p$ is the probability of success.

**Example 5.6**

A farmer supplies eggs in crates to his customers in the neighboring city by motorcycle. An egg gets broken in a crate, due to a bad road system, on his way to the city with the probability of 0.75 if he transports 10 crates of eggs. Assuming that a number of damaged eggs is binomially distributed, what is the probability that three eggs will break before he reaches his destination?

**Solution:**

Given that $n = 10$, $x = 3$, and $p = 0.75$. Then, the pmf of a binomial is given by:

$$f(x) = \binom{n}{x} p^x (1-p)^{n-x}, \quad x = 0, 1, \ldots, n$$

$$f(x = 3) = \binom{10}{3}(0.75)^3 (1 - 0.75)^{10-3}$$

$$f(x = 3) = \frac{10!}{(10-3)!3!}(0.75)^3 (0.25)^7 = 0.0031.$$

## 5.4   EXPECTED VALUE AND VARIANCE OF A BINOMIAL DISTRIBUTION

In this section, we shall derive the expected value or mean of binomial distribution and also show how the variance of binomial distribution is being derived.

### 5.4.1   EXPECTED VALUE (MEAN) OF A BINOMIAL DISTRIBUTION

From the binomial pmf, we have:

$$f(x) = \binom{n}{x} p^x (1-p)^{n-x}, \quad x = 0, 1, \ldots, n.$$

Since the expected value of a discrete distribution is given as:

$$E(x) = \sum_{x=0}^{n} x \cdot f(x).$$

Substituting for $f(x)$, we have:

$$E(x) = \sum_{x=0}^{n} x \cdot \binom{n}{x} p^x (1-p)^{n-x}.$$

Let $q = 1 - p$.

$$E(x) = \sum_{x=0}^{n} x \cdot \binom{n}{x} p^x q^{n-x}.$$

Now, substituting for the binomial coefficient yields

$$E(x) = \sum_{x=0}^{n} x \cdot \frac{n!}{x!(n-x)!} p^x q^{n-x}$$

$$E(x) = \sum_{x=0}^{n} x \cdot \frac{n(n-1)!}{x(x-1)!(n-x)!} p^{x-1} pq^{n-x}.$$

So,

$$E(x) = \sum_{x=0}^{n} x \cdot \frac{n(n-1)!}{x(x-1)!\,(n-x)!} p^{x-1} pq^{n-x}.$$

Pulling out $np$ yields

$$= np \sum_{x=1}^{n} \frac{(n-1)!}{(x-1)!\,(n-x)!} p^{x-1} q^{n-x}$$

and

$$= np \sum_{x-1=0}^{n-1} \binom{n-1}{x-1} p^{x-1} q^{(n-1)-(x-1)}.$$

Since sum of probabilities for all of the possible $x$ values in the sample space $S$ is equal 1, then the result yields

$$E(x) = np. \tag{5.9}$$

Therefore, the expected value (mean) of the binomial probability function is $np$ where $n$ is the number of trials in the experiment and $p$ is the probability of success.

## 5.4.2 VARIANCE OF A BINOMIAL DISTRIBUTION

The variance of a distribution can be compute from the expected value of that distribution:

$$var(x) = E(x^2) - (E(x))^2.$$

Let $x^2 = x(x-1) + x$. Then, substitute for the value of $x^2$

$$var(x) = E(x(x-1) + x) - (E(x))^2.$$

Let's solve $E(x(x-1))$ the same approach we use to derive the mean ($E(x)$) of a binomial distribution. Therefore,

$$E(x(x-1)) = \sum_{x=0}^{n} x(x-1) \cdot \frac{n!}{x!(n-x)!} p^x (1-p)^{n-x}.$$

So,

$$E(x(x-1)) = \sum_{x=0}^{n} x(x-1) \cdot \frac{n(n-1)(n-2)!}{x(x-1)(x-2)!(n-x)!} p^x (1-p)^{n-x}.$$

Let $p^x = p^{x-2+2} = p^2 p^{x-2}$.
Substituting for $p^x$ gives

$$E(x(x-1)) = \sum_{x=0}^{n} x(x-1) \cdot \frac{n(n-1)(n-2)!}{x(x-1)(x-2)!(n-x)!} p^2 p^{x-2} (1-p)^{n-x}.$$

And letting $q = 1 - p$ gives

$$E(x(x-1)) = \sum_{x=0}^{n} x(x-1) \cdot \frac{n(n-1)(n-2)!}{x(x-1)(x-2)!(n-x)!} p^2 p^{x-2} q^{n-x}.$$

Pulling out the constant terms and then evaluate yields

$$E(x(x-1)) = n(n-1) p^2 \sum_{x=0}^{n} \frac{(n-2)!}{(x-2)!(n-x)!} p^{x-2} q^{n-x}.$$

Since $\sum_{x=0}^{n} \frac{(n-2)!}{(x-2)!(n-x)!} p^{x-2} q^{n-x} = 1$. Then, $E(x(x-1)) = n(n-1) p^2$:

$$var(x) = E(x(x-1)) + E(x) - (E(x))^2.$$

Therefore, we can find the variance by substituting for $E(x(x-1))$:

$$var(x) = n(n-1) p^2 + np - (np)^2,$$
$$var(x) = n^2 p^2 - np^2 + np - n^2 p^2,$$
$$var(x) = np - np^2,$$
$$var(x) = np(1-p),$$

or

$$var(x) = npq, \tag{5.10}$$

where $n$ is the number of trials, $p$ is the probability of success, and $q$ is the probability of failure.

Here, we have shown that the variance of a binomial distribution is the product of number of trials $(n)$, the probability of success $(p)$, and the probability of failure $(q)$.

## Example 5.7

A manufacturing company has 100 employees and an employee has a chance of 5% of being absent from work at a particular day. It is assumed that absent of a worker from work would not affect another. The company can continue production at a particular day if no more than 20 worker absent for that day. Calculate the probability that out of the 10 workers randomly selected, 3 workers will be absent from work. Hence, find the expected number of workers that will be absent from work at that particular day.

**Solution:**

1. Number of trials, $n = 10$ workers.

   Possible outcomes: success $(p)$ is the probability that a worker is absent from work and failure $(q)$ is the probability that a worker is not absent from work.

   Probability of success: $P$ (worker is absent from work) $= 0.05$ and it is constant all through the trials.

   The events are independent, i.e., the presence of a worker in the company does not affect another.

   The pmf of binomial is:

   $$f(x) = \binom{n}{x} p^x (1-p)^{n-x}, x = 0, 1, \ldots, n$$

   $$f(x = 3) = \binom{10}{3} (0.05)^3 (1 - 0.05)^{10-3}$$

   $$f(x = 3) = \binom{10}{3} (0.05)^3 (0.95)^7 = 0.0105.$$

2. The expected number of worker to be absent in that day is: $np = 10 \times 0.05 = 0.5$. This interpreted that only one worker is expected to absent on that particular day.

## Example 5.8

An airline operator has 12 airplanes. On a rainy day, the probability that an airplane will fly is 0.65. What is the probability that:

1. an airplane will fly;

2. three airplanes will fly;

3. at most, two airplanes will fly; and

4. at least, two airplanes will fly.

   Hence, calculate the number of airplanes that are expected to fly.

**Solution:**

1. Let $x$ be number of airplane to fly.

   $N = 10$ and $p = 0.65$

   $$f(x = 1) = \binom{10}{1} (0.65)^1 (0.35)^9 = 0.0005.$$

2.

   $$f(x = 3) = \binom{10}{3} (0.65)^3 (0.35)^7 = 0.0212.$$

3.

   $$f(x \leq 2) = (f(x = 0) + f(x = 1) + f(x = 2))$$
   $$f(x \leq 2) = \binom{10}{0} (0.65)^0 (0.35)^{10} + \binom{10}{1} (0.65)^1 (0.35)^9 + \binom{10}{2} (0.65)^2 (0.35)^8$$
   $$= 0.000028 + 0.0005123017 + 0.004281378 = 0.0048.$$

4.

   $$f(x \geq 2) = 1 - (f(x = 0) + f(x = 1) + f(x = 2))$$
   $$= 1 - 0.0048 = 0.9952.$$

5. The expected number airplanes to fly on a rainy day is $np = 10 \times 0.65 = 6.5$. This indicates that only seven airplanes will fly on a rainy day.

**Example 5.9**

A market representative makes a sale on a particular product per day with a probability of 0.25. If he has 30 products to sell that day, find the probability that:

1. no sales are made;

2. five sales are made; and

3. more than four sales are made.

**Solution:**

1. Let $X$ be number of sales made on the product

$$p(x = \text{making sales}) = 0.25$$

$$n = 30$$

$$p(x = 0) = \binom{30}{0}(0.25)^0 (0.75)^{30} = 0.00018.$$

2.

$$p(x = 5) = \binom{30}{5}(0.25)^5 (0.75)^{25} = 0.1047.$$

3.

$$p(x > 4) = 1 - [p(x = 0) + p(x = 1) + p(x = 2) + p(x = 3) + p(x = 4)]$$

$$= 1 - \left\{ \binom{30}{0}(0.25)^0 (0.75)^{30} + \binom{30}{1}(0.25)^1 (0.75)^{29} \right.$$

$$+ \binom{30}{2}(0.25)^2 (0.75)^{28} + \binom{30}{3}(0.25)^3 (0.75)^{27}$$

$$\left. + \binom{30}{4}(0.25)^4 (0.75)^{26} \right\}$$

$$= 1 - \{0.00018 + 0.01786 + 0.008631 + 0.026853 + 0.06042\} = 0.90213.$$

## 5.5    SOLVE PROBLEMS INVOLVING BINOMIAL DISTRIBUTION USING R

In this section, we shall demonstrate how we can use R to generate a random sample from a binomial distribution through simulation and how to calculate probability from a binomial distribution parameters. We shall use most of the examples illustrated in this chapter to compare the results with R outputs.

## 5.5.1   GENERATING A RANDOM SAMPLE FROM A BINOMIAL DISTRIBUTION

We shall use the R function to simulate a binomial random variables with given parameters.

The function rbinom() is used to generate n independent binomial random variables. The general form is rbinom (n, size, prob).

    n      number of random sample
    size   number of trials
    prob  probability of success.

```
# To simulate 100 binomial random number with parameters
  n = 10 and p = 0.75
set.seed(10)
rv=rbinom (100, 10, 0.75)
rv
[1]   10  8  8  6  9  8  8  8  8  6  7  5  6  8  7  5  7  9  9  8  8
       9 10  9  8
[26]   7  8  7  8  7  5  6  7  9  6  7  7  9 10  8  7  7  6  8  6  8
       8 10  4  8
[51]   6  6  6  7  9  8  5  9  8  6  6  5 10  8  7  8  6  8  8  6  7
       4  6  8 10
[76]   6  7  7  9  4  9  8  8  7  9 10  6 10  8  9  8  9  5  8  6  8
       7  6  7  9

# the mean of the random sample
mean(rv)
[1] 7.44

# the standard deviation and variance of the random sample
sd(rv)
[1] 1.465564

var(rv)
[1] 2.147879

# To plot the bar chart of the random samples generated
set.seed(150)
rv=rbinom (100, 10, 0.75)
barplot(table(rv))
```

```
barplot(table(rv), ylab="Frequency", xlab="Random Number",
        main="X~Binomial (10, 0.75)")
```

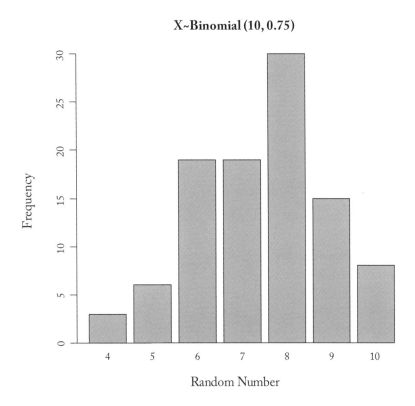

Figure 5.1: $X$-binomial.

## 5.5.2  CALCULATE PROBABILITY FROM A BINOMIAL DISTRIBUTION

In this section, dbinom—is the function to calculate binomial pdf (x, size, prob, log = False).

x        number of successes
size    is the number of independent trials
prob    is the probability of success.

**Example 5.10**
Using the data from Example 5.7 above, use R code to obtain the binomial probability distribution and compare the result.

```
dbinom(3,10,0.05)
[1] 0.01047506
```

This is exactly what we got in Example 5.7.


**Example 5.11**

Use the data on airplane Example 5.8 above, and then use R to obtain the probabilities in Example 5.8 (1–4). Hence, compare the results:

```
# an airplane will fly
dbinom(1,10,0.65)
[1] 0.0005123017

# three (3) airplane will fly
dbinom(3,10,0.65)
[1] 0.02120302

# at most two airplanes will fly
no_air=dbinom(0,10,0.65)
air1=dbinom(1,10,0.65)
air2=dbinom(2,10,0.65)
prob_most2= no_air+ air1+ air2
prob_most2
 [1] 0.004821265

 # at least two airplanes will fly
 prob_least2=1-prob_most2
 prob_least2
 [1] 0.9951787

 # Expected number airplane to fly on a raining day
 p<-0.65
 n<-10
 expected_value<-n*p
 > expected_value
 [1] 6.5
```

Good! We got the same result.

**Example 5.12**

Use the data on product sales in Example 5.9 to solve the example in R and then compare the results:

```
# no sale of the product
dbinom(0,30,0.25)
[1] 0.0001785821


# 5 sales of the products
dbinom(5,30,0.25)
[1] 0.1047285


# more than 4 sales of the products
p0<-dbinom(0,30,0.25)
p0
[1] 0.0001785821


p1<-dbinom(1,30,0.25)
p1
[1] 0.001785821


p2<-dbinom(2,30,0.25)
p2
[1] 0.008631468


p3<-dbinom(3,30,0.25)
p3
[1] 0.02685346


p4<-dbinom(4,30,0.25)
p4
[1] 0.06042027


prob<-1-(p0+p1+p2+p3+p4)
prob
[1] 0.9021304
```

The results in Example 5.9 (1–3) are the same with what we got using R.

## 5.6   EXERCISES

**5.1.**   (a) What is a discrete probability distribution and what is it used for?

(b) State the conditions to be satisfied for a discrete probability distribution.

**5.2.**   (a) If $X$ be a discrete random variable with the probability $p(X)$, what is the expected value and standard deviation of $X$?

(b) The table below shows the cases of malaria recorded in a health center with their respective probabilities.

| Malaria Cases ($X$) | 0 | 1 | 2 | 3 | 4 | 5 | 6 | 7 | 8 |
|---|---|---|---|---|---|---|---|---|---|
| $P(X)$ | | 0.12 | 0.20 | 0.15 | 0.18 | 0.12 | 0.08 | 0.07 | 0.03 | 0.05 |

(a) Calculate the mean of the distribution of the malaria cases.

(b) Calculate the variance of the distribution.

(c) Calculate the standard deviation of the distribution.

**5.3.**   (a) List the names of the discrete probability distribution you know.

(b) State the binomial probability distribution.

(c) Hence, derive the expected value and the variance of a binomial distribution.

**5.4.**   The probability of having typhoid fever after drinking from a well water in a villager is 0.45. If ten villagers drank out of the well, what is the probability that:

(a) one villager will have typhoid fever;

(b) two villagers will have typhoid fever;

(c) at most two villagers will have typhoid fever;

(d) at least two villagers will have typhoid fever; and

(e) hence, calculate the number of villagers that expected to have typhoid fever.

**5.5.**   Let $X$ be a number of times a head appear in a tossing of a die. If a fair die is tossed ten times, what is the probability that: (a) $P(X = 0)$, (b) $P(X \leq 1)$, (c) $P(X > 2)$, or (d) $P(X \leq 3)$?

CHAPTER 6

# Continuous Probability Distributions

In the previous chapter, we discused discrete probability distributions and their properties. In the discrete probability distribution, the random variable takes only integer values or countably infinite number of possible outcomes. However, in the countinous probability distribution, the random variable takes any real value within a specified range. Typical examples of countinous random variables are weight, temperature, height, and some economic indicators (prices, costs, sales, inflation, investments, etc.). A continuous probability distribution demonstrates the complete range of values a continuous random variable can take with their associated probabilities along the range of values. This distribution is very useful in the prediction of the likelihood of an event within a specified range of values. In this section we are discussing continous probability distributions and we will observe that the sum symbol, $\sum$, which is used in derivation of mean and variance of discrete probability distribution has turned to an integral symbol. The integral sign indicates sum of continous random variable over an interval of points. Examples of continous probability distributions are normal distribution, exponential distribution, student-t distribution, chi-sqaure distribution, etc.

Let $X$ be a continuous random variable that can take any real value within a specified range, then the probability over a random variable is called a **continuous probability distribution**. Consider $x$ to be continous, the probability denisty function denoted by $f(x)$ such that the probability of event $a \leq x \leq b$ is represented mathematically as:

$$P(a \leq x \leq b) = \int_a^b f(x)\, dx,$$

where $a$ and $b$ are the limits or points interval.

This implies the probability of a continous variable $x$ within a specified range, say, $a$ and $b$, is the same as taking the integral function of the random variable over its bounded range.

However, the probability is zero if the continous random variable $x$ is not bounded an interval.

That is,

$$P(x = a) = \int_a^a f(x)\, dx = 0,$$

since $b = a$.

**Example 6.1**

The time required by a driver to drive his boss from home to office is a function of $\left(\frac{1}{x^2}\right)$. What is the probability that the driver will get to the office between 5–10 min?

**Solution:**

Let $x$ denotes the time required for the driver to move from home to office.

Given that:

$$f(t) = \frac{1}{x^2}, \quad a = 5 \quad \text{and} \quad b = 10.$$

Then,

$$P(5 \le x \le 10) = \int_5^{10} \left(\frac{1}{x^2}\right) dx.$$

Integrate the Right-hand side (RHS) over the interval,

$$P(5 \le x \le 10) = \left[-\frac{1}{x}\right]_5^{10}.$$

Substitute the value of $x$ and then evaluate the RHS,

$$P(5 \le x \le 10) = \left[-\frac{1}{10}\right] - \left[-\frac{1}{5}\right]$$

$$P(5 \le x \le 10). = 0.10$$

The probability that the driver will reach office from home within 5–10 min is 0.10. This means that he has a low chance of getting to office under this condition.

# 6.1   NORMAL DISTRIBUTION AND STANDARDIZED NORMAL DISTRIBUTION

In this section, we are considering a normal distribution as most important distribution because if you have many independent variables by non-normal distributions, the aggregation of these variables will tend to a normal distribution as the number of observations is large (i.e., central limit theorem). The central limit theorem is discussed in Chapter 7. Normal distribution charicterizations makes it the most widely used distribution in statistics and applied mathematics. It is also useful in measuring moments, kurtosis, skweness, etc. A normal distribution is also known as **Gaussian distribution**, named after after the mathematician Karl Friedrich Gauss.

A normal ditribution is a bell-shaped curve having a mean denoted by $\mu$ and standrd deviation denoted by $\sigma$. The density curve of a normal distribution is symmentrical, centered about its mean and the spread by its standard deviation. The altitude of a normal density curve at a point $y$ is given as:

$$f\left(y; \mu, \sigma^2\right) = \frac{1}{\sigma\sqrt{2\pi}} \exp\left\{-\frac{1}{2}\left(\frac{y-\mu}{\sigma}\right)^2\right\}, \quad -\infty \leq y \leq \infty,$$

where $y$ is a continuous random variable, $\mu$ is the mean, and $\sigma^2$ is the variance of the distribution.

The standard normal curve is a special case of the normal curve when the mean is 0 and standard deviation is 1. A normal distribution can be written in the form $X \sim N(\mu, \sigma^2)$ and reads, thus $X$ is normally distributed with mean, $\mu$, and variance, $\sigma^2$. The total area under the curve is 100%, i.e., all observations fall under the curve. A dataset is said to be normally distributed, if 68% of the observations fall within $\pm 1SD$ of the mean. Also, about 95% of the observations will fall within $\pm 2SD$ and 99.7% of the observations will fall within $\pm 3SD$, as shown in Fig. 6.1.

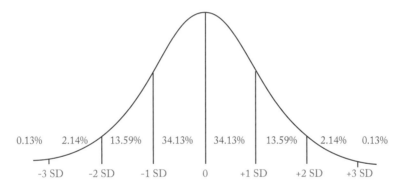

Figure 6.1: Normal curve.

**Properties of a Normal Distribution**
The followings are the properties of a normal distribution.

(a) The mean, median, and mode have the same value.

(b) The curve is symmetric.

(c) The total area under the curve is 1.

(d) The curve is denser in the center and less dense in the tails.

(e) Normal distribution has two parameters: mean ($\mu$) and variance ($\sigma^2$).

(f) About 68% of the area of a normal distribution is within one standard deviation of the mean.

(g) About 95% of the area of a normal distribution is within two standard deviations of the mean.

(h) About 99% of the area of a normal distribution is within three standard deviations of the mean.

## 6.2  STANDARD NORMAL SCORE ($Z$-SCORE)

The standard normal score is the standardized value of a normally distributed random variable and it is usually referred as $z$-score. Standard normal score is useful in the area of statistics because it enables us to find the probability of a score occurring within a normal distribution and also used to make a comparison between two scores that comes from different normal distributions. A random variable is standardized by substracting the mean of the distribution from standardized value, and then divides it by the standard deviation of the distribution. The $z$-score of a random variable can be written mathematically as:

$$z = \frac{X - \mu}{\sigma} \sim N(0, 1).$$

Thus, $z$ is normally distributed with a mean of 0 and standard deviation of 1.

In the above equation $X$ is the random variable to being standardize, $\mu$ is the mean of the distribution and $\sigma$ is the standard deviation of the distribution. Thus, once the random variable is standardized, it is approximately normal with mean of 0 and standard deviation of 1 which is same as standard normal.

**Example 6.2**

A class of 30 students sat for examinations on mathematics, the class mean score is 65 and the standard deviation is 12.5. Assuming that the scores is normally distributed, what is the percentage of students scoring above 70 in the mathematics examination?

**Solution:**

Given that: $n = 30$, $\mu = 65$, and $\sigma = 12.5$. $P(x > 70) =$?

Standardize the students' scores:

$$P(x > 70) = P\left(\frac{x - 65}{12.5} > \frac{70 - 65}{12.5}\right).$$

Let $z = \frac{x-65}{12.5}$:

$$P(x > 70) = P(z > 0.4).$$

Since sum of probability is 1, thus the left side of normal curve can be written as

$$P(x > 70) = 1 - P(z \leq 0.4).$$

Look at the probability corresponding to $z \leq 0.4$ from the standard normal table. That is, $\Phi(0.4) = 0.6554$.

$$P(x > 70) = 1 - \Phi(0.4) = 1 - 0.6554 = 0.3446.$$

Thus, 34% of the students that sat for the mathematics examination scored above 70.

**Example 6.3**
A plastic production machine produces plastics with the mean of 80 and standard deviation of 5 in a minute. Assuming that the production of plastics followed a normal distribution, calculate:

(a) the probability that the machine will produce between 78 and 85; and

(b) the probability that the machine will produce less than 90.

**Solution:**
Given that: $\mu = 80$ and $\sigma = 5$.
First, standardize the production.
Let $z = \frac{X-80}{5}$.

(a) $P(78 \leq x \leq 85) = P\left(\frac{78-80}{5} \leq \frac{X-80}{5} \leq \frac{85-80}{5}\right)$.
   Subtitute for $z = \frac{X-80}{5}$

$$P(78 \leq x \leq 85) = P\left(\frac{78-80}{5} \leq z \leq \frac{85-80}{5}\right) = P(-0.4 \leq z \leq 1).$$

Look for the probability corresponding to $-0.4 \leq z$ and $z \leq 1$ from the standard normal table and substract small value from high value:

$$= \Phi(1) - \Phi(-0.4) = 0.8413 - (1 - 0.6554) = 0.4967.$$

This means that the probability that the machine will produce between 78–85 plastics with a minute is 0.5.

(b) Standardize the production variable:

$$P(x < 90) = P\left(\frac{x-80}{5} < \frac{90-80}{5}\right) = \Phi(2) = 0.9772$$

$$P(x < 90) = P\left(z < \frac{90-80}{5}\right) = \Phi(2) = 0.9772.$$

This indicates that the probability that the machine will produce less than 90 plastics is 0.98; this implies it is almost sure for the machine to produce 90 plastics within a minute.

**Example 6.4**

Suppose that a Corporate Affairs Commission official knows that the monthly registration of new companies followed a normal distributed withaverage of 50 new registrations per month and variance of 16 new registrations. Find the probability that: (a) new registered companies will less than 35, (b) new registered companies will be 45, and (c) new registered companies fall between 35 and 45 new companies.

**Solution:**

Let $x$ be the number of registered companies.

$x$ is normally distributed with mean (50) and variance (16). That is, $x \sim N(50, 16)$.

Since the standard deviation is the square root of variance then,

(a) $P(x < 35) = P\left(\frac{x-50}{4} < \frac{35-50}{4}\right)$

$$P(x < 35) = P(z < -3.75) = 1 - \Phi(3.75) = 0.99991.$$

This means that it is very that less than 35 companies will register within a month period.

(b) $P(x = 45) = P\left(\frac{x-50}{4} = \frac{45-50}{4}\right) = 1 - \Phi(1.25) = 1 - (0.89435) = 0.1056.$

The result shows that there is low possibility of getting exactly 45 companies to register within a month.

(c) $P(35 \leq x \leq 45) = P\left(\frac{35-50}{4} \leq z \leq \frac{45-50}{4}\right) = \Phi(-1.25) - \Phi(-3.75) = 0.10556.$

This means there is low chance of getting between 35 and 45 companies to register within a month period.

## 6.3  APPROXIMATE NORMAL DISTRIBUTION TO THE BINOMIAL DISTRIBUTION

In this section, we learn how to approximate normal distribution to the binomial distribution. The central limit theorem is the tool that allows us to do so. Suppose that we have about 500 public servants that are ready to take a promotion test in order to move to the next level of cadre. The chairman of the civil service commission claimed that 75% of the staff sitting for the test will pass at first sitting. If we want to find the probability that more than 300 public servants will pass the promotion test at the first sitting. Then, this is a binomial event with $n = 500$, $p = 0.75$, and $P(x > 350) =.$

It will be tedious calculating the required

$$P(x = 350) + P(x = 351) + P(x = 352) + \ldots + P(x = 500)$$

$$\binom{500}{350}(0.75)^{350}(0.75)^{150} + \binom{500}{351}(0.75)^{351}(0.75)^{149} + \ldots + \binom{500}{500}(0.75)^{500}(0.75)^{0}.$$

Due to computational effort, we can instead use a normal approximation to this problem. The general rule of thumb for the approximation is that the sample size ($n$) is sufficiently large, i.e., $np \geq 5$ and $n(1-p) \geq 5$.

Since $np = 500 \times 0.75 = 375 \geq 5$, then we can apply normal approximation.

Let $z = \frac{X-\mu}{\sigma}$.

Recall that the mean of a binomal distribution is $pq$ and the variace is $npq$.

We can re-define the $z$-score

$$z = \frac{X - np}{\sqrt{npq}}.$$

Thus, $\sigma^2 = npq = 500 \times 0.75 \times 0.25 = 93.75$ and $\sigma = 9.68$.

Since $x > 350$ implies that 350 not inclusive, it is possible to write it an approximation value as $x \geq 350.5$:

$$P(x > 350) \approx P(x \geq 350.5) = P\left(\frac{x - 375}{9.68} \geq \frac{350.5 - 375}{9.68}\right)$$

$$P(z \geq -2.53) = 1 - \Phi(-2.53) = 1 - 0.00570 = 0.9943.$$

This is interpreted that more than 350 staff sitting for the test will pass at first sitting.

## 6.4   USE OF THE NORMAL DISTRIBUTION IN BUSINESS PROBLEM SOLVING USING R

To generate normal distribution function, we use the function pnorm. The dnorm, qnorm, and rnorm are used fordensity, quantile function, and random generation for the normal distribution, respectively:

```
pnorm(q, mean =0, sd = 1, lower.tail = TRUE, log.p = FALSE)
dnorm(x, mean = 0, sd = 1, log = FALSE)
qnorm(p, mean = 0, sd = 1, lower.tail = TRUE, log.p = FALSE)
rnorm(n, mean = 0, sd = 1)
```

where

| | |
|---|---|
| q | vector of quantiles |
| mean | vector of means |
| sd | vector of standard deviations |
| log.p | logical; if TRUE, probabilities $p$ are given as $\log(p)$ |
| lower.tail | logical; if TRUE (default), probabilities are $P(X \leq x)$, otherwise, $P(X > x)$. |

Note that the lower tail of the normal curve is the direction of the tail to the left of a given point (value) while the upper tail is direction to the right side of the curve at a given point. Thus, the left-tailed test is when the critical region is on the left side of the distribution of the test value. The right-tailed test is when the critical region is on the right side of the distribution of the test value.

The following scripts are the solutions to the Examples 6.2, 6.3, and 6.4 above, with the use of R codes. It can be seen that we got the same results in R with less stress.

**# Example 6.2**

```
#  To calculate the probability of students scoring above 70
prob70<-pnorm (70, mean=65, sd=12.5, lower.tail=FALSE)
prob70
[1] 0.3445783
percent70<- prob70*100
percent70
[1] 34.45783
```

**# Example 6.3**

```
# (a) To calculate the probability that the machine will produce
#      between 78 and 85?
btw78_85 <- pnorm(85, 80, 5) - pnorm(78, 80, 5)
btw78_85
[1] 0.4967665

# (b) To calculate the probability that the machine will produce
#      less than 90?
less90 <- pnorm(90, 80, 5)
less90
[1] 0.9772499
```

# Example 6.4

```
# (a) To calculate the probability of new registration
#     will be less than 35
prob35<-pnorm (35, mean=50, sd=4, lower.tail=FALSE)
prob35
[1] 0.9999116


# (b) To calculate the probability of new registration will be 45
prob45<- pnorm (45, mean=50, sd=4, lower.tail=TRUE)
prob45
[1] 0.1056498


# (c) To calculate the probability of new registration will fall
#     between 35 and 45 new companies
btw35_45 <- pnorm(45, 50, 4) - pnorm(35, 50, 4)
[1] 0.1055614
```

## 6.5  EXERCISES

**6.1.** Suppose $X \sim Bin(100, 0.8)$. Calculate. (i) $P(x \leq 70)$, (ii) $P(x > 75)$, and (iii) $P(70 \leq x \leq 90)$.

**6.2.** A machine packs rice nominally in a 50-kg bag. It is observed that there is a variation in the actual weight that is normally distributed. Records show that the standard deviation of the distribution is 0.10 kg and the probability that the bag is underweight is 0.05. Find:

   (a) the mean value of the distribution; and

   (b) what value standard deviation is needed to ensure that the probability that a bag is underweight is 0.005. Assuming the mean is constant, and improvement in the machine relies on reduction in the value of standard deviation.

**6.3.** The Ozone cinemas revealed that movie customers spent an average of $2,000 on concessions with a standard deviation of $200. If the spending on concessions follows a normal distribution:

   (a) find the percentage of customers that will spend less than $1,800 on concenssions;

   (b) find the percentage of customers that will spend more than $1,800 on concenssions; and

   (c) find the percentage of customer that will more than $2,000 on concenssions.

**6.4.** Suppose we know that the survival rate of a new business is normally distributed with mean 60% and standard deviation 8%. (a) What is the probability that more than 25 out of 30 new businesses registered in the week will survive? (b) What is the probability that between 20 and 25 new businesses will survive?

**6.5.** The average lifetime of a light bulb is 4500 h with a standard deviation of 500 h. Assume that the average lifetime of light bulbs is normal. (a) Find the probability that the average life time of a bulb is between 4200 and 4700. (b) Find the probability that the average life time of a bulb exceed 4500.

**6.6.** Suppose the time spent (in min) in opening a new bank account is X with a probability density function of:

$$f(x) = \begin{cases} kx^2 & \text{for } x > 0 \\ 0 & \text{otherwise.} \end{cases}$$

(a) Find the value of $k$.

(b) Find the probabilities that time to spend to open a new account will less than 10 min.

CHAPTER 7

# Other Continuous Probability Distributions

This chapter will explain some commonly used distributions in the testing of as hypothesis. We will focus on the formulas and their uses in statistics. These distributions are Student's $t$-distribution, chi-square distribution, and F-distribution. We will see the conditions for using each of the distributions mentioned.

## 7.1   STUDENT-T DISTRIBUTION

The $t$-distribution was first discovered by W. S. Gosset and he published it under the pseudonym Student, therefore it is often called Student's $t$-distribution. The $t$-distribution is the ratio of standard normal distribution and square root of chi-square divided by its df. The degrees of freedom are the number of free choices left after removing a sample statistic.

Suppose $Z$ is normally distributed with mean 0 and standard deviation 1, $Z \sim N(0, 1)$, and $U$ is distributed chi-square with df $(v)$, $U \sim \chi^2(v)$. If $Z$ and $U$ are independent, then the random variable $t = \frac{Z}{\sqrt{\frac{U}{v}}}$ follows a $t$-distribution with $v$ degrees of freedom.

The pdf of $t$ with degrees of freedom $v$ is given by:

$$f(t) = \frac{\Gamma((v+1)/2)}{\sqrt{\pi v}\,\Gamma(v/2)\,(1 + t^2/v)^{(v+1)/2}}, \quad \text{for} \quad -\infty < t < \infty.$$

In general, when the sample size is less than 30 and population standard deviation is unknown, then the random variable $x$ is approximately normally distributed, thus it follows a Student $t$-distribution. Furthermore, the difference between $t$-distribution and normal distribution is negligible when the sample size is sufficiently large. When population standard deviation is unknown, estimating it from the sample results to a greater uncertainty and a more spread out distribution (see Fig. 7.1).

From Fig. 7.1, it can be seen that the graphs of $t$-distribution is similar to standard normal distribution in exception that $t$-distribution is a lower and wider; this attribute is prominent in the $t$-distribution with df (1). Also, the graphs show the absolute and relative error for normal approximation. The graph of $t$-distribution with df (30) is approximately standard normal distribution. Therefore, as the df increases, the $t$-distribution approaches the standard normal distribution.

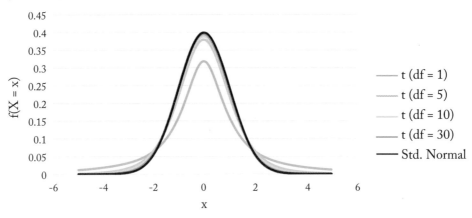

Figure 7.1: $t$-distribution with different degrees of freedom and standard normal distribution.

When the population standard deviation is unknown, the sample size is less than 30, and the random variable $x$ is approximately normally distributed, it follows a $t$-distribution. The test statistics is:

$$t = \frac{(\bar{x} - \mu)}{s/\sqrt{n}} \sim t_{(n-1),(\alpha/2)}.$$

When you use a $t$-distribution to estimate a population mean, the df are equal to one less than the sample size, $df = n - 1$.

**Properties of the $t$-Distribution**
The $t$-distribution has the following properties.

- The $t$-distribution is bell shaped and symmetric about the mean.

- The $t$-distribution is a family of curves, each determined by the degrees of freedom.

- The total area under a $t$-curve is 1 or 100%.

- The mean, median, and mode of the $t$-distribution are equal to zero.

- The variance of the $t$-distribution is $v/(v - 2)$, where $v$ is the degree of freedom and $v > 2$.

- When the degrees of freedom of $t$-distribution is sufficiently large, the $t$-distribution approaches the normal distribution.

**Example 7.1**

What is the value of $t$ in the following: (i) $t_{0.05}(20)$, (ii) $t_{0.01}(20)$, (iii) $t_{0.975}(25)$, and (iv) $t_{0.95}(25)$?

**Solution:**

Let's make use of the $t$-distribution table (see Appendix A).

(i) $t_{0.05}(20) = 1.725$.

We look at $t$-distribution table when significance level ($\alpha$) is 0.05 and df ($v$) is 20, then we get 1.725.

(ii) $t_{0.01}(20) = 2.528$.

We look at $t$-distribution table when significance level ($\alpha$) is 0.01 and df ($v$) is 20, then we get 2.528.

(iii) $t_{0.975} = 2.060$.

Because of the symmetry nature of $t$-distribution, we look $t$-distribution table when significance level ($\alpha$) is 0.025 and df ($v$) is 25, then we get 2.060.

(iv) $t_{0.95}(25) = 1.708$.

We use significance level ($\alpha$) of 0.05 and df ($v$) is 25, since $t$-distribution is symmetric, then we get 1.708.

**R Codes to Obtain $t$-Values Using Example 7.1**

The computation of the $t$-values in R is of the form:

```
qt(p, df, ncp, lower.tail = TRUE, log.p = FALSE)
```

where

| | |
|---|---|
| qt | is the quantile function for the $t$-distribution |
| p | is the vector of probabilities |
| ncp | is the non-centrality parameter delta; if omitted, use the central $t$-distribution |
| lower.tail | is logical; if TRUE (default), probabilities are $P[X \leq x]$, otherwise, $P[X > x]$ |
| log.p | is logical; if TRUE, probabilities $p$ are given as $\log(p)$. |

For the Example 7.1(i)–(iv), we can simply use the following R codes.

*# Example 7.1(i)*

```
alpha <- 0.05
df<-20
```

```
t.alpha <- qt(alpha, df )
t.alpha
[1] -1.724718
t.abs<-abs(t.alpha)   # t distribution is symmetric.
t.abs
[1] 1.724718
```

# *Example 7.1(ii)*

```
alpha<- 0.01
df<-20
t.alpha <- qt(alpha, df, lower.tail =TRUE )
t.alpha
[1] -2.527977
t.abs<-abs(t.alpha)   # t distribution is symmetric.
t.abs
[1] 2.527977
```

# *Example 7.1(iii)*

```
alpha<- 0.975
df<-25
t.alpha <- qt(alpha, df, lower.tail =TRUE )
t.alpha
[1] 2.059539
```

(iv) $t_{0.95}(25) = 2.485$.

# *Example 7.1(iv)*

```
alpha<- 0.95
df<-25
t.alpha <- qt(alpha, df, lower.tail =TRUE )
t.alpha
[1] 1.708141
```

## Example 7.2
Suppose a random number $X$ follows a $t$-distribution with $v = 10$ df. Calculate the probability that the absolute value of $X$ is less than 2.228.

**Solution:**

$$P\left(|X| < 2.228\right) = P(-2.228 < X < 2.228).$$

We write the probability in the RHS in terms of cumulative probabilities:

$$P\left(|X| < 2.228\right) = P\left(X < 2.228\right) - P\left(X < -2.228\right).$$

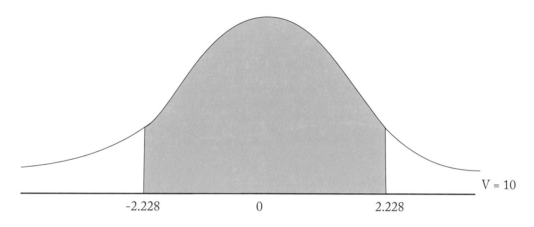

Figure 7.2: $t$-distribution.

Since $t$-distribution is symmetric and $t$-table does not contain have a negative $t$-values, we can write the probabilities as:

$$P\left(|X| < 2.228\right) = P\left(X < 2.228\right) - P\left(X > 2.228\right).$$

From the $t$-table, the $P\left(X < 2.228\right) = 0.975$ and $P\left(X > 2.228\right) = 0.025$. The required probability is

$$P\left(|X| < 2.228\right) = 0.975 - 0.025 = 0.95.$$

## 7.2   CHI-SQUARE DISTRIBUTION

In this section, we shall look at the definition, properties, and uses of chi-square. The chi-square is denoted by $\chi^2(v)$ with the degree of freedom $(v)$.

Let $Y_1, Y_2, \ldots, Y_n$ be mutually independent standard normal random variables, and let $X = Y_1^2 + Y_1^2 + \ldots + Y_n^2$ has a chi-square distribution. The pdf of the chi-square distribution is:

$$f\left(x\right) = \frac{e^{-x/2}x^{v/2}}{2^{v/2}\Gamma\left(\frac{v}{2}\right)}, \quad \text{for} \quad x \geq 0,$$

where $v$ is the shape parameter (df) and $\Gamma$ is the gamma function. For instance, $\Gamma(x) = (x - 1)$.

Chi-square distribution being a squared of standard normal random variable takes only non-negative values and it tends to be right skewed. Its skewness depends on the df or number of observations. As the number of observations increases, the more symmetrical the chi-square distribution becomes, and then tends to normal distribution. The higher the degrees of freedom, the less the skewness of the chi-square (see Fig. 7.3).

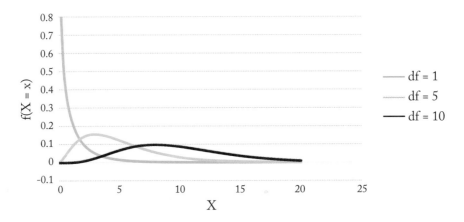

Figure 7.3: Chi-square distribution with different df.

The chi-square test statistics is given by:

$$X^2 = \sum \frac{(O_i - E_i)^2}{E_i} \sim \chi_v^2.$$

where $O_i$ is the observed value, $E_i$ is the expected value and $v$ is the df.

**Properties of the Chi-Square Distribution**
The chi-square distribution has the following properties.

- The chi-square distribution is a continuous probability distribution with the values ranging from 0 to $\infty$ (nonnegative).

- The mean of a chi-square distribution is the number of df, $v$.

- The mean of a chi-square distribution is the doubled the number of df, $2v$.

- Chi-square has an additive property. The sum of independent $\chi^2$ is itself a $\chi^2$ variate. Suppose two independent $\chi_1^2$ and $\chi_2^2$ with the df of $v_1$ and $v_2$, respectively, then $\chi_1^2 + \chi_2^2$ is the same as $\chi^2$ variate with degree of freedom $v_1 + v_2$.

## Uses of the Chi-Square Distribution

Chi-square can be use in the following ways.

- Independence of two criteria of the classification of qualitative variables.

- Relationships between categorical variables (contingency tables).

- Sample variance study when the underlying distribution is normal.

- Tests of deviations of differences between expected and observed frequencies (one-way tables).

- The chi-square test (a goodness-of-fit test). This is to test how well a sample data fits a certain distribution.

- Confidence interval estimation for a population standard deviation of a normal distribution from a sample standard deviation.

### Example 7.3

What is the value of chi-square in the following: (i) $\chi^2_{0.05}(15)$, (ii) $\chi^2_{0.995}(30)$, and (iii) $\chi^2_{0.900}(85)$.

### Solution:

We look at a chi-square table for the significance level $(\alpha)$ and the degree of freedom $(v)$.

(i) $\chi^2_{0.05}(15) = 7.261$.

(ii) $\chi^2_{0.995}(30) = 53.67$.

(iii) $\chi^2_{0.900}(85) = 102.07$.

We obtained the answer for $\chi^2_{0.900}(85) = 68.7845$ from finding the average of $\chi^2_{0.900}(80) = 96.5782$ and $\chi^2_{0.900}(90) = 107.565$, since we cannot see $\chi^2_{0.900}(85)$ directly from the chi-square table. We use the average method to estimate the value.

Note that we use the chi-square table that has the probabilities of $P[X \leq x]$.

### R Codes to Obtain Chi-Square Values from the Table Using Example 7.3

The chi-square can be obtain in R using the function:

```
qchisq(p, df, ncp, lower.tail = TRUE, log.p = FALSE)
```

where

|  |  |
|---|---|
| qchisq | is the quantile function for the Chi-square distribution |
| p | is the vector of probabilities |
| ncp | is the non-centrality parameter delta; if omitted, use the central $\chi^2$ distribution |
| lower.tail | is logical; if TRUE (default), probabilities are $P[X \leq x]$, otherwise, $P[X > x]$ |
| log.p | is logical; if TRUE, probabilities $p$ are given as $\log(p)$. |

The following are the codes to solve the Example 7.3(i)–(iii):

```
qchisq(0.05, df=15, lower.tail = TRUE)
[1] 7.260944
```

```
qchisq(0.995, df=30, lower.tail = TRUE)
[1] 53.67196
```

```
qchisq(0.900, df=85, lower.tail = TRUE)
[1] 102.0789
```

We easily got the inverse of the $p$-value for a chi-square distribution in Example 7.3.

## 7.3    F-DISTRIBUTION

The F-distribution is the ratio of two independent chi-square distributions divided by their degrees of freedom $v_1$ and $v_2$. The probability density function of the F-distribution is

$$f(x) = \frac{\Gamma\left(\frac{v_1+v_2}{2}\right)\left(\frac{v_1}{v_2}\right)^{\frac{v_1}{2}} x^{\frac{v}{2}-1}}{\Gamma\left(\frac{v_1}{2}\right)\Gamma\left(\frac{v_2}{2}\right)\left(1 + \frac{v_1 x}{v_2}\right)^{\left(\frac{v_1+v_2}{2}\right)}}, \quad x \geq 0,$$

where $v_1$ and $v_2$ are the shape parameter and $\Gamma$ is the gamma function.

The F-distribution is mainly spread out when the df are small. Thus, as the df decreases, the F-distribution is more dispersed. The distribution of F-distribution is asymmetric that has a minimum value of 0 and maximum of infinity. The curve reaches a peak not far to the right of 0, and then gradually approaches the highest value of F in the horizontal axis. The F-distribution approaches the horizontal axis but never touches the horizontal axis (see Fig. 7.4).

**Properties of the F-Distribution**
The F-distribution has the following properties.

- The F-distribution is asymmetric about the mean but skewed to the right.

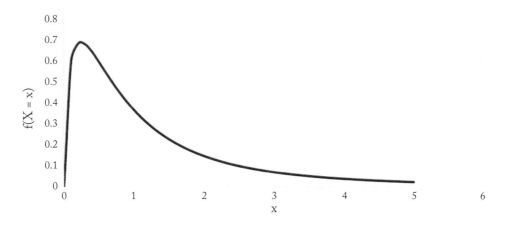

Figure 7.4: F-distribution with df $(v_1 = 3$ and $v_2 = 5)$.

- The F-distribution is a family of curves that determined by two df.

- The F-distribution is a continuous probability distribution with the values ranging from 0 to $\infty$ (nonnegative).

- The curve approaches normal as the df for the numerator and denumerator become larger.

- The mean of the F-distribution is $\frac{v_2}{v_2-2}$.

- The variance of the F-distribution is $\frac{2v_2^2(v_1+v_2-2)}{v_1(v_2-2)^2(v_2-4)}$.

- Any changes in the first parameter $(v_1)$ does not change the mean of the distribution, but the density of the distribution is shifted from the tail of the distribution toward the center.

**Uses of the F-Distribution**
The F-distribution is useful in the following.

- The F-distribution is used to test the validity of a multiple regression model.

- The F-distribution is used to test hypotheses about the equality of two independent population variance.

- It is used to draw an inference about the data that is drawn from a population.

## Example 7.4

What is the value of F in the following: (i) $F_{(0.05)}(8, 12)$, (ii) $F_{(0.95)}(10, 15)$, and (iii) $F_{(0.995)}(20, 50)$.

### Solution:

Let's look at F table for the significance level ($\alpha$) and the degrees of freedom ($v_1$ and $v_2$) for the numerator and denominator, respectively.

(i) $F_{(0.05)}(8, 12) = 0.3045$.

(ii) $F_{(0.95)}(10, 15) = 2.544$.

(iii) $F_{(0.995)}(20, 50) = 2.470$.

Note that we use the F table that has the probabilities of $P[X \leq x]$, the left side of the curve.

### R Codea to Obtain F Values from the F-Distribution Table Using Example 7.4

The F value can be obtained in R using the function:

```
qf(p, df1,df2, ncp, lower.tail = TRUE, log.p = FALSE)
```

where

|          |                                                          |
|----------|----------------------------------------------------------|
| qf       | is the quantile function for the F-distribution          |
| p        | is the vector of probabilities                           |
| df1      | is the degree of freedom for numerator                   |
| df2      | is the degree of freedom for denominator                 |
| ncp      | is the non-centrality parameter delta;                   |
|          | if omitted, use the central F-distribution               |
| lower.tail | is logical; if TRUE (default), probabilities are $P[X \leq x]$, |
|          | otherwise, $P[X > x]$                                     |
| log.p    | is logical; if TRUE, probabilities $p$ are given as $\log(p)$. |

With these short R statements we are able to obtain the F values for Example 7.4(i)–(iii).

```
qf (0.05, 8, 12, lower.tail = TRUE, log.p = FALSE)
[1] 0.3045124
```

```
qf (0.95, 10, 15, lower.tail = TRUE, log.p = FALSE)
[1] 2.543719
```

```
qf (0.995, 20, 50, lower.tail = TRUE, log.p = FALSE)
[1] 2.470161
```

## 7.4   EXERCISES

**7.1.**   (a) Mention the continuous probability distributions that you know.

(b) Define student $t$-distribution and state its properties.

(c) With the aid of charts, explain how $t$-distribution can be used as an approximation to the normal distribution.

(d) What is the value of $t$ in the following: (i) $t_{0.95}(18)$, (ii) $t_{0.1}(25)$, (iii) $t_{0.995}(30)$, and (iv) $t_{0.99}(10)$.

**7.2.**   (a) Define student chi-square distribution and state its properties.

(b) What are the uses of chi-square distribution?

(c) What is the value of chi-square in the following: (i) $\chi^2_{0.95}(20)$, (ii) $\chi^2_{0.995}(40)$, (iii) $\chi^2_{0.975}(25)$, and (iv) $\chi^2_{0.99}(50)$.

**7.3.**   (a) Define student F-distribution and state its properties.

(b) What are the uses of F-distribution?

(c) What is the value of $F$ in the following: (i) $F_{(0.95)}(10, 12)$, (ii) $F_{(0.99)}(5, 25)$, (iii) $F_{(0.05)}(10, 30)$, and (iv) $F_{(0.01)}(18, 10)$.

CHAPTER 8

# Sampling and Sampling Distribution

Sampling distributions emanated from a group of selected data being calculated using statistics such as mean, median, mode, range, standard deviation, and variance. The distribution is useful in testing a hypothesis and making inferences about the population.

The sampling distribution relies on the following:

- an underlying distribution of the population;

- the statistic under investigation;

- sampling techniques; and

- sample size.

In this chapter, we shall consider the probability and non-probability sampling, sampling techniques, sampling distribution of mean and proportion, and central limit theorem.

## 8.1  PROBABILITY AND NON-PROBABILITY SAMPLING

A method that uses random sampling techniques to generate a sample, where every sampling unit in the population has an equal chance of being selected, is called a **probability sampling**. Randomization is the key in probability sampling techniques. Suppose a population contains 100 sampling units, and each sampling unit has a chance of 1/100 being selected by probability sampling techniques. Under probability sampling, the sample selected gives a true representation of the population that it comes from. The most common probability samplings are simple random, systematic, stratified, and cluster samples.

**Advantages of Probability Sampling**
- The outcomes are reliable.

- It increases accuracy of error estimation.

- No sampling bias and systematic error.

- It is good in making inferences about the population.

**Disadvantage of Probability Sampling**
- It consumes time.

- More expensive than non-probability sampling.

- More complex than non-probability sampling.

**Non-Probability Sampling**

It involves a non-random sampling of the sampling units, thus only specific members of the population have a chance of being selected. The most widely used non-probability methods are judgment sampling, quota sampling, convenience sampling, and extensive sampling. A non-probability sampling technique is based on subjective judgment and it is used for exploratory studies, e.g., pilot survey.

**Advantages of Non-Probability Sampling**
- It easily gives the description about the sample.

- It saves time.

- Less expensive compared to probability sampling.

- It is effective when unfeasible to conduct probability sampling.

**Disadvantages of Non-Probability Sampling**
- Lack of representation of the population.

- Difficult to estimate sampling variability.

- Difficult to identify possible bias.

- Lower level of generalization of research findings.

# 8.2   PROBABILITY SAMPLING TECHNIQUES—SIMPLE RANDOM, SYSTEMATIC, STRATIFIED, AND CLUSTER SAMPLES

## 8.2.1   SIMPLE RANDOM SAMPLING (SRS)

In a **simple random sampling** (SRS) technique, each unit included in the sample has an equal chance of inclusion in the sample. In a homogenous population, SRS provides an unbiased and better estimate of the population parameters. In the process of selection, the probability of selecting the first sampling unit will not necessarily be the same probability of selecting second sampling unit.

In the event that every selection of the sampling unit remains constant for every selection with a chance of $1/N$, where $N$ is the total number of the elements in the population, then the procedure is called **simple random sampling with replacement** (SRSWR). In a SRSWR, there are $N^n$ possible samples with each sample having a $\frac{1}{N^n}$ chance of selection, where $n$ is the sample size.

However, if in the first selection, each member of the population has an equal chance of selection, with probability of $1/N$. In the selection of second unit, all the remaining sampling units have probability of $\frac{1}{N-1}$ of selection. Any successive selection in a SRS is referred as to a **simple random sample without replacement** (SRSWOR). If sampling is done without replacement, there are $\binom{N}{n}$ possible samples and each sample has a chance of $\frac{1}{\binom{N}{n}}$ selection. More often, the SRSWOR is regarded as a **simple random sample.**

The following methods are used to select units of a simple random sample.

1. **Random Number Table**

   In using a random number table, all units of the population are numbered either from 1 to $N$ or 0 to $N-1$. Suppose we have a population size of 50 and we want to select a sample of size 10. We can number sampling units in two digits like 01, 02,…, 49, 50. We shall read a two-digit random number from the random number table, any two-digit numbers that are greater than 50 are ignored, and any repetition of a number is also ignored if the sampling is without replacement (see Table 8.1).

   We can read the random number from any columns or row of the random number table. From Table 8.1, let's start from first column downward to form our two-digit numbers. Thus, we have: 11, 21, 10, 36, 49, 17, 24, 16, 29, and 12. Some numbers such as 73, 64, 51, 99, 71, 65, 95, 61, 78, 62, 59, and 96 are discarded in the list because they are not part of the population. Furthermore, let's consider a population of 100, and we are asked to take a random sample of 10 from the population. We shall read the random number table in 3-digits, that is we will assign a number from 001–100. From Table 8.1, we have: 047, 046, 098, 070, 024, 088, 004, 084, 094, and 097 in that order.

2. **Lottery Method**

   The lottery method is very close to modern methods of sample selection. This process involves labeling all sampling units from $1-N$ in the sampling frame. The same numbers $(1-N)$ from the sampling frame are written on slips of paper. Next, the slips are mixed thoroughly, and then selections are made randomly. This method is advisable when the size of the population is small. It may be difficult if the sample size is large since it is not easy to mix properly the heap of paper slips.

Table 8.1: Random digits

| | | | | | | | | | |
|---|---|---|---|---|---|---|---|---|---|
| 11164 | 36318 | 75061 | 37674 | 26320 | 75100 | 10431 | 20418 | 19228 | 91792 |
| 21215 | 91791 | 76831 | 58678 | 87054 | 31687 | 93205 | 43685 | 19732 | 08468 |
| 10438 | 44482 | 66558 | 37649 | 08882 | 90870 | 12462 | 41810 | 01806 | 02977 |
| 36792 | 26236 | 33266 | 66583 | 60881 | 97395 | 20461 | 36742 | 02852 | 50564 |
| 73944 | 04773 | 12032 | 51414 | 82384 | 38370 | 00249 | 80709 | 72605 | 67497 |
| | | | | | | | | | |
| 49563 | 12872 | 14063 | 93104 | 78483 | 72717 | 68714 | 18048 | 25005 | 04151 |
| 64208 | 48237 | 41701 | 73117 | 33242 | 42314 | 83049 | 21933 | 92813 | 04763 |
| 51486 | 72875 | 38605 | 29341 | 80749 | 80151 | 33835 | 52602 | 79147 | 08868 |
| 99756 | 26360 | 64516 | 17971 | 48478 | 09610 | 04638 | 17141 | 09227 | 10606 |
| 71325 | 55217 | 13015 | 72907 | 00431 | 45117 | 33827 | 92873 | 02953 | 85474 |
| | | | | | | | | | |
| 65285 | 97198 | 12138 | 53010 | 94601 | 15838 | 16805 | 61004 | 43516 | 17020 |
| 17264 | 57327 | 38224 | 29301 | 31381 | 38109 | 34976 | 65692 | 98566 | 29550 |
| 95639 | 99754 | 31199 | 92558 | 68368 | 04985 | 51092 | 37780 | 40261 | 14479 |
| 61555 | 76404 | 86210 | 11808 | 12841 | 45147 | 97438 | 60022 | 12645 | 62000 |
| 78137 | 98768 | 04689 | 87130 | 79225 | 08153 | 84967 | 64539 | 79493 | 74917 |
| | | | | | | | | | |
| 62490 | 99215 | 84987 | 28759 | 19177 | 14733 | 24550 | 28067 | 68894 | 38490 |
| 24216 | 63444 | 21283 | 07044 | 92729 | 37284 | 13211 | 37485 | 10415 | 36457 |
| 16975 | 95428 | 33226 | 55903 | 31605 | 43817 | 22250 | 03918 | 46999 | 98501 |
| 59138 | 39542 | 71168 | 57609 | 91510 | 77904 | 74244 | 50940 | 31553 | 62562 |
| 29478 | 59652 | 50414 | 31966 | 87912 | 87154 | 12944 | 49862 | 96566 | 48825 |
| | | | | | | | | | |
| 96155 | 95009 | 27429 | 72918 | 08457 | 78134 | 48407 | 26061 | 58754 | 05326 |
| 29621 | 66583 | 62966 | 12468 | 20245 | 14015 | 04014 | 35713 | 03980 | 03024 |
| 12639 | 75291 | 71020 | 17265 | 41598 | 64074 | 64629 | 63293 | 53307 | 48766 |
| 14544 | 37134 | 54714 | 02401 | 63228 | 26831 | 19386 | 15457 | 17999 | 18306 |
| 83403 | 88827 | 09834 | 11333 | 68431 | 31706 | 26652 | 04711 | 34593 | 22561 |
| | | | | | | | | | |
| 67642 | 05204 | 30697 | 44806 | 96989 | 68403 | 85621 | 45556 | 35434 | 09532 |
| 64041 | 99011 | 14610 | 40273 | 09482 | 62864 | 01573 | 82274 | 81446 | 32477 |
| 17048 | 94523 | 97444 | 59904 | 16936 | 39384 | 97551 | 09620 | 63932 | 03091 |
| 93039 | 89416 | 52795 | 10631 | 09728 | 68202 | 20963 | 02477 | 55494 | 39563 |
| 82244 | 34392 | 96607 | 17220 | 51984 | 10753 | 76272 | 50985 | 97593 | 34320 |

3. **Computer Generation**

Computers have some in-built programs that help to generate random samples at ease. These are mostly used in selection of winners of applicants for plots of lands, visa lottery, etc.

**Example 8.1**

Suppose a population contains the following: 4, 6, 10, 11, 15, 17, and 20 units. Select a sample size of 2. What are the possible samples with replacement and without replacement?

**Solution:**

Table 8.2: SRSWR and SRSWOR samples

| Samples | 4 | 6 | 10 | 11 | 15 | 17 | 20 |
|---|---|---|---|---|---|---|---|
| 4 | (4, 4) | (4, 6) | (4, 10) | (4, 11) | (4, 15) | (4, 17) | (4, 20) |
| 6 | (6, 4) | (6, 6) | (6, 10) | (6, 11) | (6, 15) | (6, 17) | (6, 20) |
| 10 | (10, 4) | (10, 6) | (10, 10) | (10, 11) | (10, 15) | (10, 17) | (10, 20) |
| 11 | (11, 4) | (11, 6) | (11, 10) | (11, 11) | (11, 15) | (11, 17) | (11, 20) |
| 15 | (15, 4) | (15, 6) | (15, 10) | (15, 11) | (15, 15) | (15, 17) | (15, 20) |
| 17 | (17, 4) | (17, 6) | (17, 10) | (17, 11) | (17, 15) | (17, 17) | (17, 20) |
| 20 | (20, 4) | (20, 6) | (20, 10) | (20, 11) | (20, 15) | (20, 17) | (20, 20) |

(a) SRSWR: Possible sample = $7^2$ = 49

| Samples | 4 | 6 | 10 | 11 | 15 | 17 | 20 |
|---|---|---|---|---|---|---|---|
| 4 | | | | | | | |
| 6 | (6, 4) | | | | | | |
| 10 | (10, 4) | (10, 6) | | | | | |
| 11 | (11, 4) | (11, 6) | (11, 10) | | | | |
| 15 | (15, 4) | (15, 6) | (15, 10) | (15, 11) | | | |
| 17 | (17, 4) | (17, 6) | (17, 10) | (17, 11) | (17, 15) | | |
| 20 | (20, 4) | (20, 6) | (20, 10) | (20, 11) | (20, 15) | (20, 17) | |

(b) SRSWOR: Possible sample = $\binom{7}{2}$ = 2

## 8.2.2   SYSTEMATIC SAMPLING

This sampling procedure is easier done than the simple random sampling, although it uses technique of SRS in selection of the first sample from the population. Thus, each sampling unit has an equal chance of selection in the first sample to be taken from the population. The subsequent selection follows a predefined pattern. Consider a population of $N$ from which a sample size of $n$ is drawn. Assume that $k = N/n$. Initially, a random sample shall be taken from 1–$k$ that will be the first sample, then for every $k$th unit in the population from a sample systematically. For example, a recruiting agency received 1,000 qualified applicants, out of which only 50 applicants are to be considered for jobs. If he decided to interview only 50 applicants by systematic sampling, then $k = \frac{1000}{50} = 20$. Therefore, a random sampling shall be done between 1–20, say 13th item is selected, so every 20th applicant in the population of 1,000 will form a sample (i.e., 13th, 33th, 53th, ..., 953th, 973th, and 993th).

### 8.2.2.1 Advantages of Systematic Sampling

- It is simple and convenient to actualize.

- It more easily represents a population without numbering each member of a sample.

- The samples from system sampling are based on precision in the member selection.

- The risk involved in the process of selection is minimal.

- It can be used in a heterogeneous population.

### 8.2.2.2 Disadvantages of Systematic Sampling

- It cannot be used where the size of the population is not available or being approximated.

- It requires a population to characterize with a natural degree of randomness in order to mitigate the risk of selecting samples.

- It has a higher risk of manipulation of data thereby increasing the likelihood of achieving a targeted outcome rather than randomness of a dataset.

## 8.2.3   CLUSTER SAMPLING

Cluster sampling is a technique of selecting all individuals or group of individuals through a random selection. Its procedure involves a selection of groups or clusters; then from each group the individual subjects are selected either by SRS or systematic random sampling. It is desirable for clusters to be made up of heterogeneous units or elements. The samples can be either entire cluster or group rather than a subset of the cluster or group. For example, if a survey is to take a sample of agro-allied companies in the western region of Nigeria. The western region of Nigeria is made up of six States, and it is fair to have samples representation from each of the state rather than concentrating on three or four States of the region. The commonly used cluster is geographical location.

Cluster sampling can be a single-stage or multi-stage cluster sampling. In a single-stage cluster sampling, clusters are selected by a SRS and then data is collected from every unit of the sampled clusters. However, a two-stage process involves a simple random sampling of clusters and then a SRS of the units in each of sampled cluster.

### 8.2.3.1 Advantages of Systematic Sampling

- It is economical to generate sampling frame.

- It is less time consuming for listing and implementation.

- It works for larger sample with a similar fixed cost.

#### 8.2.3.2 Disadvantages of Systematic Sampling

- It gives less information about each observation than SRS.

- It may show variation within the group.

- Elements of the cluster may possess similar attributes.

- High estimates of standard errors when compared with other probability sampling techniques.

### 8.2.4  STRATIFIED RANDOM SAMPLING

Stratified random sampling is a probability sampling technique in which the population is partitioned into relatively homogeneous groups know as *strata*. In each stratum, a simple random sample is use for the selection of the sampling units. Thus, the statistic computed from the strata is aggregated to make inference about the population. Suppose a team of researchers wants to know the average performance of students in a private university that has five faculties (Engineering, Science, Law, Social Science, and Medicine). Five hundred students study Engineering, 1,200 students study Science, 800 students study Law, 1,550 students study Social Science, and 350 students study Medicine. The distribution of the students population is depicted in the pie chart in Fig. 8.1.

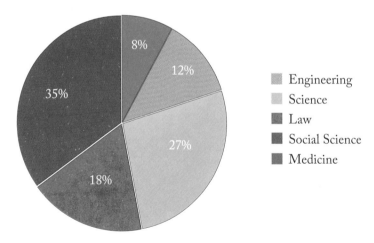

Figure 8.1: The distribution of students by faculty.

If a stratified random sample of 1,000 students are be selected in the above example, it is expected to select students according to the size of the faculties. That is, 120 students from Engineering, 270 students from Science, 180 students from Law, 350 students from Social Science, and 80 students from Medicine suppose to be among the selection to achieve a better precision.

#### 8.2.4.1 Advantages of Stratified Random Sampling

- It gives a high representation of the population.

- It allows a valid statistical inference from the data collected.

- It improves the potential for units to evenly distribute over the population, hence improve precision when compared with SRS.

#### 8.2.4.2 Disadvantages of Stratified Random Sampling

- It cannot be practically used if a complete list of the population is not available.

- The list of the population is needed to be clearly delineated into each stratum.

## 8.3   NON-PROBABILITY SAMPLING TECHNIQUES

### 8.3.1   JUDGMENT SAMPLING

Judgment sampling is a type of non-probability sampling technique where the researcher uses his own experience and prior knowledge about the situation before the commencement of selection; the sample is taken without use of any statistical tools. Suppose that a panel decides to understand the reasons why startup companies failed. The panel should understand that they should form the samples from the business owners to obtain useful information about the factors that responsible for failure in business. This process is called judgment sampling.

**Advantages of Judgment Sampling**

- The method is easily understood.

- It requires no specific knowledge of statistics.

- It consumes less time to actualize.

**Disadvantages of Judgment Sampling**

- The researcher may be biased in selecting the sample.

- There is no logic in the process of selection of the sample.

- It has no capacity to extrapolate the population as samples selection are not good representation of the population.

- In some cases, it gives rise to vague conclusions.

### 8.3.2    QUOTA SAMPLING

This is a non-probability sampling technique, therefore the samples selected have the same proportions of individuals as the entire population with as regard to known characteristics. Its procedures include the following.

- Dividing the population into exclusive sub-groups.

- Identification of proportions of the subgroups in the population and this proportion has to be maintained in the sampling process.

- Selection of subjects from subgroups using the same proportion in the previous step.

- Ensure the sample drawn is a representative of the population, thus, it is easy to understand the characteristics noticed in each subgroup. For example, if the population size is 2,000 consists of 1,200 men and 800 women and researcher is interested in the 30% of the population, it means that he will select a sample of 600 sampling units. The 600 sampling units is made up of 360 men and 240 women.

**Advantages of Quota Sampling**
- It allows sampling of a subgroup of interest and investigates the traits and characteristics.

- It helps to establish the relationship in terms of traits and characteristics between subgroups.

**Disadvantages of Quota Sampling**
- Selected characteristics of the population are accounted for while forming the subgroups.

- Its process may result to over-represent in the sample.

### 8.3.3    CONVENIENCE SAMPLING

This approach is an example of a non-probability sampling where a researcher draws a sample because of the "convenience" of the data sources. Here, convenience could be the nearest subjects or availability of resources to be needed in carry out the research project. It is also known as *accidental sampling*. It is commonly used in pilot studies before embarking on the main project. For example, to determine profitability of firms, a researcher may first look at some firms in his vicinity and sample opinions of the business owners in the area before extending the research work to a larger communities.

**Advantages of Convenient Sampling**
- It is time efficient.

- Its outcomes can be used to refine some questions in the questionnaire.

- It is less expensive since research is able to use available resources.

**Disadvantages of Convenient Sampling**
- It is not a good representative of the entire population.

- It may lead to a biased outcome and wrong conclusion because of uncontrollable sample representation.

## 8.4   SAMPLING DISTRIBUTION OF THE MEAN

1. The mean of the sampling distribution is equal to the mean of the population, that is, $\mu_{\overline{X}} = \mu$. To establish this fact, we can use the data in Example 8.1.

   Suppose a sample of size 2 is drawn from a population that contains the following: 4, 6, 10, 11, 15, 17, and 20 units.

   $$\text{The population mean} = \frac{4 + 6 + 10 + 11 + 15 + 17 + 20}{7} = 11.86.$$

   For SRSWR, the distribution of the sample means appears in Table 8.3.

Table 8.3: SRSWR distribution of samples

| Samples | 4 | 6 | 10 | 11 | 15 | 17 | 20 |
|---------|------|------|------|------|------|------|------|
| 4 | 4.0 | 5.0 | 7.0 | 7.5 | 9.5 | 10.5 | 12.0 |
| 6 | 5.0 | 6.0 | 8.0 | 8.5 | 10.5 | 11.5 | 13.0 |
| 10 | 7.0 | 8.0 | 10.0 | 10.5 | 12.5 | 13.5 | 15.0 |
| 11 | 7.5 | 8.5 | 10.5 | 11.0 | 13.0 | 14.0 | 15.5 |
| 15 | 9.5 | 10.5 | 12.5 | 13.0 | 15.0 | 16.0 | 17.5 |
| 17 | 10.5 | 11.5 | 13.5 | 14.0 | 16.0 | 17.0 | 18.5 |
| 20 | 12.0 | 13.0 | 15.0 | 15.5 | 17.5 | 18.5 | 20.0 |

$$\mu_{\overline{X}} = \frac{4.0 + 5.0 + 7.0 + \cdots + 17.5 + 18.5 + 20.0}{49} = 11.86.$$

Therefore, the mean of distribution of sample means is same as population mean.

For SRSWOR, the distribution of the sample means appear in Table 8.4.

$$\mu_{\overline{X}} = \frac{5.0 + 7.0 + 7.5 + \cdots + 16.0 + 17.5 + 18.5}{21} = 11.86.$$

Hence, the mean of distribution of sample means is same as population mean.

Table 8.4: SRSWOR distribution of samples

| Samples | 4 | 6 | 10 | 11 | 15 | 17 | 20 |
|---|---|---|---|---|---|---|---|
| 4 | | | | | | | |
| 6 | 5.0 | | | | | | |
| 10 | 7.0 | 8.0 | | | | | |
| 11 | 7.5 | 8.5 | 10.5 | | | | |
| 15 | 9.5 | 10.5 | 12.5 | 13.0 | | | |
| 17 | 10.5 | 11.5 | 13.5 | 14.0 | 16.0 | | |
| 20 | 12.0 | 13.0 | 15.0 | 15.5 | 17.5 | 18.5 | |

In summary, irrespective of the sampling processes, the mean of distribution of means still remain the mean of the population.

2. The standard error of the mean is equal to the ratio of the standard error of the population to the square root of the sample size. This can also be demonstrated as follows using (SRSWR) Table 8.3. The standard deviation of the population 4, 6, 10, 11, 15, 17, and 20 units is:

$$\sigma = \frac{(4 - 11.86)^2 + (6 - 11.86)^2 + \cdots + (20 - 11.86)^2}{7} = 5.38.$$

Similarly, the standard deviation of the distribution of sample means is calculated as:

$$\sigma_{\overline{X}} = \frac{(4 - 11.86)^2 + (5 - 11.86)^2 + \cdots + (18.5 - 11.86)^2 + (20 - 11.86)^2}{49} = 3.8065$$

$$\sigma_{\overline{X}} = \frac{\sigma}{\sqrt{n}} = \frac{5.38}{\sqrt{2}} = 3.8065.$$

This result shows the relationship between the standard deviation of distribution of means and the population standard deviation. That is, the standard deviation of distribution of means ($\sigma_{\overline{X}}$) is the population standard deviation ($\sigma$) divided by the square root of sample size ($n$).

**Sampling Distribution of the Mean Using R**

```
# To compute the mean of the population
pop=c(4,6,10, 11, 15, 17, 20)
pop_mean<-sum(pop)/7
pop_mean
[1] 11.85714
```

```
# To compute the mean of the distribution of means
# for SRS with replacement
sWR<-49
sampWR<- c(4, 5, 7, 7.5, 9.5, 10.5, 12, 5, 6, 8,
 8.5, 10.5, 11.5, 13, 7, 8, 10, 10.5, 12.5, 13.5,
 15, 7.5, 8.5, 10.5, 11, 13, 14, 15.5, 9.5, 10.5,
 12.5, 13, 15, 16, 17.5, 10.5, 11.5, 13.5, 14, 16,
 17, 18.5, 12, 13, 15, 15.5, 17.5, 18.5, 20)
sampWR_mean=sum(sampWR)/sWR
sampWR_mean
[1] 11.85714

# To compute the standard deviation of the distribution
# of means for SRS with replacement
sampWR_std<-sd(sampWR)
sampWR_std
[1] 3.845994

# To compute the mean of the distribution
# of means for SRS without replacement
sWOR<-21
sampWOR<-c(5,7,7.5,9.5,10.5,12,8,8.5,10.5,11.5,13,
           10.5,12.5,13.5,15,13,14,15.5,16,17.5,18.5)
sampWOR_mean<-sum(sampWOR)/sWOR
sampWOR_mean
[1] 11.85714

# Population standard deviation
p<-7
pop_std<-sd(pop)*sqrt((p-1)/p)
pop_std
[1] 5.38327

# Sample standard deviation
n<-2    # sample selection of 2
samp_std<- pop_std/sqrt(n)
samp_std
[1] 3.806546
```

## 8.5    CENTRAL LIMIT THEOREM AND ITS SIGNIFICANCE

The central limit theorem states that let $X_1, X_2, \ldots, X_n$ be a random sample from a distribution with finite mean ($\mu$) and finite variance ($\sigma^2$). For a sufficiently large sample size $n$, i.e., ($n \geq 30$), the following hold.

1. Sample mean ($\overline{X}$) is approximately normal.

2. The mean of the sample means is equal to the population mean $E\left(\overline{X}\right) = \mu$.

3. Variance $var(\overline{X}) = \sigma_{\overline{X}}^2 = \frac{\sigma^2}{n}$.

   This theorem can be written mathematically as:

$$\overline{X} \to N\left(\mu, \frac{\sigma^2}{n}\right) \quad \text{as} \quad n \to \infty.$$

Alternatively,

$$z = \frac{\overline{X} - \mu}{\sigma} \sim N(0, 1) \quad \text{as} \quad n \to \infty.$$

The main significance of the central limit theorem is that it enables us to make probability statements about the sample mean when compared with the population mean. Let's distinguish two separate variables with their corresponding distributions:

1. Let $X$ be a random variable that measures a single element from the population, then the distribution of $X$ is the same as distribution of the population with mean ($\mu$) and standard deviation ($\sigma$).

2. Let $\overline{X}$ be a sample mean from a population; then the distribution of $\overline{X}$ is its sampling mean with mean ($\mu_{\overline{X}}$) and standard deviation ($\sigma_{\overline{X}} = \sigma/\sqrt{n}$), where $n$ is the sample size.

**Example 8.2**
Let $\overline{X}$ be the mean of a random sample of 100 selected from a population of mean 30 and standard deviation of 5. (a) What is the mean and standard deviation of $\overline{X}$? (b) What is the probability that the value of $\overline{X}$ falls between 29 and 31? (c) What is the probability that value of $\overline{X}$ is more than 31?

**Solution:**

(a) $\mu_{\overline{X}} = \mu = 30$; $\sigma_{\overline{X}} = \frac{\sigma}{\sqrt{n}} = \frac{5}{\sqrt{100}} = 0.5$.

(b)

$$P(29 < \overline{X} < 31) = P\left(\frac{29 - \mu_{\overline{X}}}{0.5} \le z \le \frac{31 - \mu_{\overline{X}}}{0.5}\right)$$

$$= P\left(\frac{29 - 30}{0.5} \le z \le \frac{31 - 30}{0.5}\right)$$

$$= \Phi(2) - \Phi(-2) = 0.9772 - 0.0228 = 0.9544.$$

(c)

$$P\left(\overline{X} > 31\right) = 1 - P\left(\overline{X} \le 31\right) = 1 - P\left(\frac{31 - 30}{0.5}\right)$$

$$= 1 - \Phi(-2) = 1 - 0.9772 = 0.0228.$$

**R Codes**

*# Example 8.2a solution*

```
sampl.mean<-30
mu<- sampl.mean
sample.size<-100
sigma<-5
std.dev_mean<-sigma/sqrt(sample.size)
std.dev_mean
[1] 0.5
```

*# Example 8.2b solution*

```
sampl.mean<-mu
lower.mean<-29
z29<-(lower.mean- mu)/ std.dev_mean
p_29<-pnorm(z29, mean =0, sd = 1, lower.tail = TRUE,
   log.p = FALSE)
p_29
[1] 0.02275013
upper.mean<-31
z31<-(upper.mean- mu)/ std.dev_mean
p_31<-pnorm(z31, mean =0, sd = 1, lower.tail = TRUE,
   log.p = FALSE)
p_31
[1] 0.9772499
```

```
btw_p29_p31<- p_31- p_29
btw_p29_p31
[1] 0.9544997
```

# Example 8.2c solution

```
p.greater31<-1-p_31
p.greater31
[1] 0.02275013
```

## Example 8.3

A branch manager of a microfinance bank claims that the average number of customers that deposit cash on monthly basis is 1,250 customers with a standard deviation of 130 customers. Assume the distribution of cash lodgement is normal. Find:

(a) the probability that less than or equal to 1,220 customers will deposit cash in a month and

(b) the probability that the mean of a random sample of 15 months, less than 1,200 customers deposit cash.

## Solution:

(a)

$$P\left(X < 1220\right) = P\left(z \leq \frac{1220 - 1250}{130}\right) = P\left(z \leq -0.231\right) = 0.4090.$$

(b)

$$P\left(\overline{X} < 1200\right) = P\left(z \leq \frac{1200 - 1250}{\frac{130}{\sqrt{15}}}\right) = P\left(z \leq -1.49\right) = 0.0681.$$

## R Codes

# Example 8.3a solution

```
mean<-1250
std<-130
x<-1220
z<-(x- mean)/ std
p_1220<-pnorm(z, mean =0, sd = 1, lower.tail = TRUE, log.p = FALSE)
p_1220
[1] 0.408747
```

# Example 8.3b solution

```
mean<-1250
std<-130
n<-15
std.err<-std/sqrt(n)
x.bar<-1200
z.xbar<-(x.bar- mean)/ std.err
p.xbar_1200<-pnorm(z.xbar, mean =0, sd = 1,
  lower.tail = TRUE, log.p = FALSE)
p.xbar_1200
[1] 0.06816354
```

## 8.6   EXERCISES

**8.1.**   (a) Explain what you understand by the sampling distribution.

(b) Differentiate between probability sampling and non-probability sampling.

(c) What are the merits and demerits of probability sampling and non-probability sampling?

**8.2.**   (a) Mention and describe types of probability sampling techniques you know.

(b) State the advantages and disadvantages of the sampling techniques mentioned in (a).

**8.3.**   List non-probability sampling techniques and state the advantages and disadvantages of the techniques.

**8.4.**   With the aid of a demonstrative example, explain the concept of sampling distribution of means.

**8.5.**   (a) State the central limit theory and its importance.

(b) Assume that the length of time of calls is normal, with average of 60 s and standard deviation of 10 s. Find the probability that the average time obtained from a sample of 35 calls is 55 s of the entire population average.

**8.6.**   Suppose a normally distributed population has mean and standard deviation of 75 and 12, respectively.

(a) What is the probability that a random element $X$ selected from the population falls between 72 and 75?

(b) Calculate the mean and standard deviation of $\overline{X}$ for a random sample of size 30.

(c) Calculate the probability that the mean of selected sample size of 30 from the population is between 72 and 75.

CHAPTER 9

# Confidence Intervals for Single Population Mean and Proportion

When a statistic is computed from a sample of data to estimate the population parameter, due to the variability in the sample collected, we have to reduce our risk of estimation by constructing a range in which the exact value of the population parameter lies. This process gives us the self-assurance at a certain percentage that the estimate is capable of predicting the real value of the population of interest. This concept describes the *confidence interval* or *confidence limit*. In this chapter, we are focusing on the constructing of confidence interval (CI) for both mean and proportion.

## 9.1 POINT ESTIMATES AND INTERVAL ESTIMATES

When a sample is drawn from a population, the fact obtained or quality computed from the sample is called a *statistic*. This statistic is closely described the characteristics obtained from the population, and then the estimate or a single value from the sampled data is referred to as a **point estimate**. For example, a human resource person may want to know the productivity of workers in a firm. He can use the number of cases closed per month as a metric to measure productivity. He discovered that the average cases closed per month was 22; thus the value (22) is the point estimate.

On the other hand, in order to know how well the sample statistic accurately describes the population, we compute a range of values that we are confident enough to say the true value of population parameter lies. The interval estimate offers a measure of exactness of the point estimate by giving an interval that contains the plausible values. In most cases, we use a 95% confident limit for the estimation; this implies that we can boldly say that our estimation about the population plausible values fall within the specified range of values in 95 out of 100 cases. This phenomenon is referred to as **interval estimation**. For instance, a researcher may like to know the number of cars plying a road on a daily basis. He may conduct the traffic census for some days and conclude that the average number of car plying a road daily is between 180–200 cars. This scenario can be represented in normal curve, as shown in Fig. 9.1.

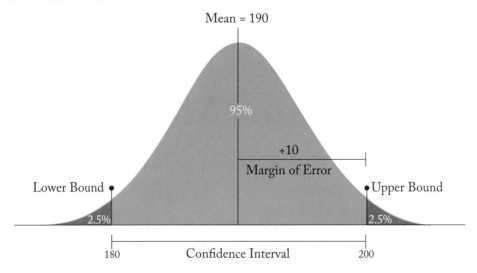

Figure 9.1: Confidence interval.

## 9.2   CONFIDENCE INTERVALS FOR MEAN

If a sample is drawn many times, there is a certain percentage of boldness that a range of values computed from the sample will probably contain an unknown population parameter, and this percentage is the CI. CI is the probability that a value will fall between an upper and a lower bound of a probability distribution. Suppose an analyst forecasted that the return on DJIA in the first quarter of the year will fall within −0.5% and +2.5% at 95% CI. This means that the analyst is 95% sure that the returns on DJIA in the first quarter of the year will lie between −0.5% and +2.5%. CIs can be used to bound numerous statistics such as the mean, proportion, and regression coefficients (covered in Chapter 11). CI is constructed as follows:

$$CI = sample\ statistic \pm critical\ value \times standard\ error\ of\ estimate.$$

For example, if the sample size $n < 30$, $\sigma$ is unknown, and the population is normally distributed, then we should use the Student $t$-distribution.

However, if $n < 30$, $\sigma$ is unknown, and the population is not normally distributed, then we should use nonparametric statistics (not covered in this book). Specifically, the CI for population mean is constructed as:

$$CI = \bar{x} \pm t_{n-1,q} \times \frac{s}{\sqrt{n}}. \tag{9.1}$$

A $100\,(1-\alpha)\%$ confidence region for $\mu$ contains:

$$\bar{x} - t_{n-1,q} \times \frac{s}{\sqrt{n}} \leq \mu \leq \bar{x} + t_{n-1,q} \times \frac{s}{\sqrt{n}}, \tag{9.2}$$

where $\alpha$ represents level of significance, $n$ represents sample size, $s$ is the standard deviation, $\bar{x}$ is the mean, $t$ is the critical region from the $t$-distribution table, and $q$ is the quantile (usually $q = 1 - \frac{\alpha}{2}$ for two-tailed test and $q = 1 - \alpha$ for one-tailed test).

Suppose we want to construct a 95% CI for an unknown population mean, then a 95% probability that CI will contain the true population mean could be calculated as follows:

$$P\left[\bar{x} - t_{n-1,\alpha/2} \times \frac{s}{\sqrt{n}} \leq \mu \leq \bar{x} + t_{n-1,\alpha/2} \times \frac{s}{\sqrt{n}}\right] = 0.95. \tag{9.3}$$

## Example 9.1

A random sample of 25 customers at a supermarket spent an average of $2,000 with a standard deviation of $200. Construct a 95% CI estimating the population mean of purchase made at the supermarket.

## Solution:

$$100(1 - \alpha)\% = 95\% \Rightarrow 100 - 100\alpha = 95 \Rightarrow \alpha = 0.05$$

$$\bar{x} = 2000, \quad s = 200, \quad n = 25, \quad t_{n-1,1-\alpha/2} = t_{24,0.975} = 2.064 (\text{from } t\text{-table})$$

$$CI = 2000 - \left(2.064 \times \frac{200}{\sqrt{25}}\right) \leq \mu \leq 2000 + \left(2.064 \times \frac{200}{\sqrt{25}}\right)$$

$$CI = 1,917.44 \leq \mu \leq 2,082.56.$$

This implies that the average purchase by the customers in the supermarket falls between $1,917.44 and $2,082.56.

## R Codes for the Example 9.1

The R code below shows how to use R to get CIs.

```
sample.mean <- 2000
sample.std <- 200
n <- 25
std.error <- qt(0.975,df=n-1)*sample.std/sqrt(n)
lower.limit <- sample.mean-std.error
upper.limit <- sample.mean+std.error
conf.interval<-c(lower.limit, upper.limit)
conf.interval
[1] 1917.444    2082.556
```

The average purchase by the customers in the supermarket lies between $1,917.44 and $2,082.56.

In addition, if $n \geq 30$ and $\sigma$ is known or $n < 30$, $\sigma$ is known, and the population is normally distributed, then we use:

$$\left[ \bar{x} - z_{1-\alpha/2} \times \frac{\sigma}{\sqrt{n}} \leq \mu \leq \bar{x} + z_{1-\alpha/2} \times \frac{\sigma}{\sqrt{n}} \right]. \tag{9.4}$$

If $n \geq 30$ and $\sigma$ is unknown, the standard deviation s of the sample is used to approximate the population standard deviation $\sigma$, then we have:

$$\left[ \bar{x} - z_{1-\alpha/2} \times \frac{s}{\sqrt{n}} \leq \mu \leq \bar{x} + z_{1-\alpha/2} \times \frac{s}{\sqrt{n}} \right]. \tag{9.5}$$

**Example 9.2**
A sales manager of a company envisage that there dramatic drop in the sale of a particular product. He took a simple random sample of 50 sales records from the previous days. The sales (in dollars) was recorded and some summary measures are provided: $n = 22$, $\bar{x} = 5200$ and $s = 400$. Assuming that the sales is approximately normal. (a) Construct a 95% CI for the mean sales of the product. (b) Interpret your result in (a).

**Solution:**

(a) $n = 50$, $\bar{x} = 5200$ and $s = 400$ and $z_{0.025} = 1.96$.

$$CI = 5,200 - \left( 1.96 \times \frac{400}{\sqrt{50}} \right) \leq \mu \leq 5,200 + \left( 1.96 \times \frac{400}{\sqrt{50}} \right)$$
$$CI = \$5,089.13 \leq \mu \leq \$5,310.87 \quad \text{or} \quad \mu = [\$5,089.13, \$5,310.87].$$

(b) The true sales of the product lies between \$5,089.13 and \$5,310.87.

**R Codes to Calculate the Confidence Interval for the Example 9.2**
```
sample.mean <- 5200
sample.std <- 400
n <- 50
std.error <- qnorm(0.975)*sample.std/sqrt(n)
lower.limit <- sample.mean-std.error
upper.limit <- sample.mean+std.error
conf.interval<-c(lower.limit, upper.limit)
conf.interval
[1] 5089.128    5310.872
```
This confirms results in the Example 9.2.

## 9.3    CONFIDENCE INTERVALS FOR PROPORTION

Suppose we are interested in estimating the proportion of people with a certain ailment in a population. Let's consider a diagnosis of such ailment as a "success" and lack of diagnosis of the ailment as a "failure." Let $X$ be the number of people with a diagnosis of the ailment, then the sample proportion is computed by $\hat{p} = \frac{x}{n}$ , where $n$ is the sample size.

The sampling distribution of $\hat{p}$ is approximately normal with $\mu_{\hat{p}} = p$ and $\sigma_{\hat{p}} = \frac{p(1-p)}{n}$.
Therefore, the CI for population proportion is calculated as:

$$CI = \hat{p} \pm z_{1-\frac{\alpha}{2}} \times \sqrt{\frac{\hat{p}(1-\hat{p})}{n}}. \tag{9.6}$$

The sampling distribution of $\hat{p}$ can be approximated by a normal distribution when $n\hat{p} \geq 5$.

**Example 9.3**
In an opinion poll to know whether to establish a National Grazing Reserve bill in Nigeria or not, a random sample of 8,500 participants were selected, only 6,250 respondents were in support of the bill while others moved against the bill. Construct 95% CI for the population proportion.

**Solution:**
Sample proportion $(\hat{p}) = \frac{6250}{8500} = 0.74$.
Since $n\hat{p} = 8500 \times 0.74 > 5$ and $n\hat{p} = 8500 \times 0.36 > 5$, then we can use normal distribution table.
From the normal table, $z_{(1-\frac{0.05}{2})} = 1.96$.

$$CI = 0.74 \pm 1.96 \times \sqrt{\frac{0.74(0.26)}{8500}}$$

$$CI = 0.74 - 1.96 \times \sqrt{\frac{0.74\,(0.26)}{8500}} \leq p \leq 0.74 + 1.96 \times \sqrt{\frac{0.74(0.26)}{8500}}$$

$$CI = 0.7307 \leq p \leq 0.7493.$$

Hence, the proportion of respondents that supported the National Grazing Reserve bill in Nigeria lies within 0.7307 and 0.7493.

**R Codes for the Computation of Confidence Interval for Proportion in Example 9.3**

```
sample.prop <- 0.74
n <- 8500
std.error <- qnorm(0.975)*sqrt(sample.prop*(1-sample.prop)/n)
lower.limit <- sample.prop-std.error
upper.limit <- sample.prop+std.error
```

```
conf.interval<-c(lower.limit, upper.limit)
conf.interval
[1] 0.7306752   0.7493248
```

The result shows that between 73% and 75% of the respondents supported the National Grazing Reserve bill in Nigeria.

**Example 9.4**
The manager of a commercial bank took a random sample of 120 customers' account numbers and found that 15 customers have not had bank verification number (BVN). Compute 90% CI for the proportion of all the bank customers that are yet to complete the BVN process.

**Solution:**

$$\hat{p} = \frac{15}{120} = 0.125$$

$$CI = 0.125 \pm 1.645 \times \sqrt{\frac{0.125(0.875)}{120}}$$

$$CI = 0.125 - 1.645 \times \sqrt{\frac{0.125\,(0.875)}{120}} \le p \le 0.125 + 1.645 \times \sqrt{\frac{0.125(0.875)}{120}}$$

$$CI = 0.075 \le p \le 0.1747.$$

The percentage of all the bank customers that are yet to complete the BVN process is between 7.5% and 17.5% of the bank customers.

**R Codes for the Computation of Confidence Interval for Proportion in Example 9.4**

```
sample.prop <- 0.125
sample.size <- 120
std.error <- qnorm(0.95)
          *sqrt(sample.prop*(1-sample.prop)/sample.size)
lower.limit <- sample.prop-std.error
upper.limit <- sample.prop+std.error
conf.interval<-c(lower.limit, upper.limit)
conf.interval
[1] 0.07534126 0.17465874
```

## 9.4   CALCULATING THE SAMPLE SIZE

Suppose we have given confidence level $(1 - \alpha)$ as well as the margin of error $(e)$, and we are asked to calculate the minimum number of sample size. This sample size is computed using the general formula:

$$n \geq \left(\frac{z_{1-\frac{\alpha}{2}}}{e}\right)^2 s^2, \tag{9.7}$$

where $s$ is the standard deviation of the sample.

**Example 9.5**

A researcher claimed that the standard deviation for the monthly utility bill for an individual household is \$50. He wants to estimate the mean of the utility bill in the present month using 95% of confidence level with the margin of error of 12 . How large a sample is required?

**Solution:**

$$n \geq \left(\frac{z_{0.975}}{12}\right)^2 (50)^2 = \left(\frac{1.96}{12}\right)^2 (50)^2 = 66.69 \approx 67 \text{ households.}$$

Therefore, the minimum sample size required is 67 households.

**R Codes to Calculate Sample Size Given a Standard Deviation and Margin of Error**

```
pop.std<-50
margin.err<-12
z.normal<-qnorm(0.975)
sample.size<- (pop.std * z.normal/margin.err)**2
sample.size
[1] 66.69199
round(sample.size, digits = 0)
[1] 67
```

However, we can calculate the sample size for proportion under two conditions.

(i) When $\hat{p}$ is known, the sample size is:

$$n \geq \left(\frac{z_{1-\frac{\alpha}{2}}}{e}\right)^2 \hat{p}(1-\hat{p}). \tag{9.8}$$

Note that $\sqrt{\hat{p}(1-\hat{p})}$ is the same as the standard deviation of a proportion $(s)$.

(ii) When $\hat{p}$ is unknown, the sample size is computed as:

$$n \geq \left(\frac{z_{1-\frac{\alpha}{2}}}{e}\right)^2 0.25. \tag{9.9}$$

This assumes that $\hat{p} = 0.5$.

## Example 9.6

In a survey, 60% of the respondents supported a paternal leave for male workers. Construct a 95% CI for the population proportion of workers who supported a paternal leave for male workers. The accuracy of your estimate must fall within 2.5% of the true population proportion. Find the minimum sample size to achieve this result.

## Solution:

$\hat{p} = \frac{60}{100} = 0.6$ and $\hat{q} = 0.4$.

To verify the sampling distribution of $\hat{p}$ to be approximated by the normal distribution, we have $n\hat{p} = 100 \times 0.6 > 5$ and $n\hat{q} = 100 \times 0.4 > 5$:

$$n \geq \left( \frac{z_{1-\frac{\alpha}{2}}}{e} \right)^2 \hat{p}(1 - \hat{p}).$$

$$n \geq \left( \frac{1.96}{0.025} \right)^2 (0.6)(0.4)$$

$$n \geq \left( \frac{1.96}{0.025} \right)^2 (0.6)(0.4) = 1475.17.$$

The minimum sample size should be at least 1,475 respondents.

**R Codes to Calculate Sample Size Given a Proportion and Margin of Error**

```
p.estimate<-0.6
q.estimate<-0.4
margin.err<-0.025
alpha<-0.05
qtile<-1-(alpha/2)
z.normal<-qnorm(0.975)
sample.size<- ((z.normal/margin.err)**2)* p.estimate* q.estimate
sample.size
[1] 1475.12
```

The survey will required a minimum of 1,475 respondents to achieve a margin of error of 2.5% at 95% CI.

## 9.5   FACTORS THAT DETERMINE MARGIN OF ERROR

The margin of error is defined as the product of critical value and standard error of estimate. For instance, a large sample size with unknown population standard deviation has a margin of error to be $z_{1-\alpha/2} \times \frac{s}{\sqrt{n}}$ where $z_{1-\alpha/2}$ is the critical region from a normal table, $s$ is the sample standard deviation, and $n$ is the sample size. This margin of error is determined by the sample size, the standard deviation, and the confidence level $(1-\alpha)$.

(a) When sample size increases, margin of error decreases and vice versa.

(b) The higher the standard deviation, the greater the uncertainty, thus, margin of error increases.

(c) The higher the confidence level, the greater the margin of error. For instance, at 95% confidence level, $z_{1-\alpha/2} = 1.96$ while at 99% confidence level $z_{1-\alpha/2} = 2.576$. Hence, the margin of error increases as the confidence level increases.

## 9.6    EXERCISES

**9.1.**  The scores of students Business Statistics course are normally distributed. If a random sample of 40 students are selected at random with mean 72 and standard deviation of 14, compute the 95% CI for the population mean.

**9.2.**  Research department of a telecommunication company wants to know the customers' usage (in hours) of a new service rendered. Assuming that the usage of the service is normally distributed, a random sample 3,000 customers under the new service is taken. They found that the mean usage is 7 h and standard deviation of 1 h 30 min. Construct a 99% CI for the mean usage of the service.

**9.3.**  During the recession period, the price of a bottle of 60 cl Coke rose. Due to variability in the price of Coke, retailers sold at diffferent prices. A random sample of 100 retailers were sampled with mean 150.20 naira and standard deviation of 23.5. Calculate the 95% CI.

**9.4.**  In the process of manufacturing bulbs, the probability that a bulb will be defective is 0.09. A random sample of 200 bulbs is selected, compute 95% confidence limit for the defective bulbs?

**9.5.**  In order to know the winner of the next presidential election in a country, a survey poll was conducted to allow the citizens to express their opinions about the contestants. If the 95% CI is not greater than 0.09, what number of random sample size of the respondents should be taken with the margin of error within 0.15 if the standard deviation is 20?

**9.6.**  A steel rolling company manufanuctures cyclindrical steel with the same length but different diameter (in mm). A random sample of 24 steels is checked and a mean diameter of 12.5 mm and standard deviation of 3 mm were observed. Compute the 95% CI for the mean diameter of the steels.

CHAPTER 10

# Hypothesis Testing for Single Population Mean and Proportion

Hypothesis testing is used to know whether there is enough statistical evidence in favor or against a belief about a population parameter. In this chapter, we will demonstrate how to use the concept of hypothesis to make a smart decision. We will also dwell on its applications in business.

## 10.1 NULL AND ALTERNATIVE HYPOTHESES

A hypothesis is a statement speculating upon the result of a research study which can be used to describe the population parameter. The hypothesis that in favor of the assumption is called the *null hypothesis*; this is the hypothesis under investigation we are trying to disprove. It is denoted by $H_0$. However, the hypothesis that we are left with should in case the null hypothesis fails is called *alternative hypothesis*. An alternative hypothesis is denoted by $H_1$. For example, if government wants to know if unemployment rate in the country is different from 5% aclaimed by the National Bureau of Statistics. The null hypothesis for this scenario is $H_0 : \mu = 5\%$ against the alternative hypothesis $H_1 : \mu \neq 5\%$.

## 10.2 TYPE I AND TYPE II ERRORS

A type I error occurs when rejecting the null hypothesis when null hypothesis is true. This error is also known as a *false positive*. The probability of rejecting a null hypothesis when it is true is denoted by $\alpha$, i.e., $P$ (rejecting $H_0|H_0$ is true) $= \alpha$. Type 1 error is sometimes called a *producer's risk* or a *false alarm*. This error is usually set by the researcher, the lower the $\alpha$ value, the lower of chance of committing type I error. The probability value ($p$-value) is often set to be 0.05, except in biomedical research where the $p$-value is set to be 0.01 because they deal with human life. The probability of committing a type I error is known as the test's *level of significance*.

A type II error occurs when accepting the alternative hypothesis (fails to reject the null hypothesis) when the alternative hypothesis is false. The probability of accepting an alternative hypothesis when it is actually false is denoted by $\beta$, i.e., $P$ (accepting $H_1|H_1$ is false) $= \beta$. The type II error is also known as *consumer's risk* or *misdetection*. The error is not predetermined by a researcher; rather, it is derived from the estimation of the distribution based on an alternative hypothesis and is usually unknown. The value of $1 - \beta$ is known as *power of a test*. The power of a test gives the probability of rejecting the null hypothesis when the null hypothesis is false. On the contrary, the level of significance is gives probability of rejecting the null hypothesis when the null hypothesis is true. The values of both $\alpha$ and $\beta$ are dependent, as one increases the other decreases. However, the increase in the sample size, $n$, causes both to decrease due to reduction in sampling error. Table 10.1 shows the types of errors and theirs respective probabilities.

Table 10.1: Statistical errors

|  |  | $H_0$ Rejected | Fail to Reject $H_0$ |
|---|---|---|---|
| $H_0$ | false | Correct decision $P = 1-\beta$ (power of a test) | Type II error $P = \beta$ |
| $H_0$ | true | Type I error $P = \alpha$ (level of significance) | Correct decision $P = 1-\alpha$ |

## 10.3   ACCEPTANCE AND REJECTION REGIONS

In the hypothesis testing procedure, the sampling region is divided into two—acceptance and rejection (critical) regions. The acceptance region contains a set of values for which a test statistic falls within the specified range. If the test statistic falls within the acceptance region, then the null hypothesis is accepted. On the other hand, the rejection region is the area of the curve where the test statistic falls outside the specified range. Thus, if the sample statistic falls within the rejection region, then the alternative hypothesis is accepted. Figure 10.1 shows the acceptance and critical regions for a two-tail normal test.

## 10.4   HYPOTHESIS TESTING PROCEDURES

In carrying out the testing of a hypothesis, the following are various steps to take.

(a) **State the Hypotheses:**

A hypothesis is stated based on the argument of interest. The hypothesis can be either a one-tail test or a two-tail test. A one-tail test is a test of a hypothesis where the region of rejection is on one side of the sampling distribution. Suppose that the null hypothesis stated that the population mean is greater than zero and the alternative hypothesis stated that the population mean is less than or equal to zero (i.e., $H_0 : \mu < 0$ against $H_1 : \mu \geq 0$). This implies that the rejection region would consist of a range of values located on the left side of sampling distribution; a set of values less than or equal to zero.

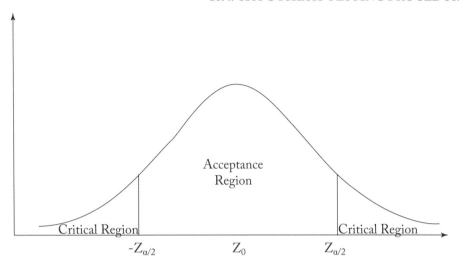

Figure 10.1: Two-tail normal test.

Alternatively, a two-tail test is a test hypothesis where the rejection region is on both sides of the sampling distribution. Assume that the null hypothesis stated that $H_0 : \mu = 0$ against the alternative hypothesis $H_1 : \mu \neq 0$. The non-directional sign would take the values from both sides of the sampling distribution; thus, the set of values on the right side of zero and on the left size of zero are the rejection regions. Hypotheses testing can be of the form:

$H_0 : \mu = 0$ vs. $H_1 : \mu \neq 0$ (two-tail test)

$H_0 : \mu = 0$ vs. $H_1 : \mu < 0$ (one-tail test)

$H_0 : \mu = 0$ vs. $H_1 : \mu > 0$ (one-tail test)

$H_0 : \mu > 0$ vs. $H_1 : \mu \leq 0$ (one-tail test)

$H_0 : \mu \geq 0$ vs. $H_1 : \mu < 0$ (one-tail test)

$H_0 : \mu < 0$ vs. $H_1 : \mu \geq 0$ (one-tail test)

$H_0 : \mu < 0$ vs. $H_1 : \mu \geq 0$ (one-tail test)

(b) **Specify the Level of Significance:**

Prior to the experiment, the researcher would have chosen the level of significance. In most cases, the level of significance is set to 10%, 5%, and 1% depending on the stringency of the research investigation. Suppose the level of significance is 5%; this indicates that there is likelihood that out of 100 cases, only 5 cases might result to rejecting the null hypothesis.

(c) **Compute the Value of the Test Statistic:**

The appropriate test statistic is compared with the critical value. The most commonly used test statistics are Student $t$-test, normal ($z$-test), chi-square, and F-test. The type of statistic to be used depends on the properties of the data. The typical example for a test statistic is:

$$t = \frac{\sqrt{n}\,(\bar{x} - \mu)}{s} \sim t_{n-1,\alpha/2}$$

or

$$z = \frac{\sqrt{n}\,(\bar{x} - \mu)}{s} \sim z_{,\alpha/2}.$$

(d) **Determine the Critical Value and Decision Rule:**

The critical region is the cut off point area of the rejection region. As long as the absolute value of the test statistic is greater than the critical value, the null hypothesis is rejected. The decision rule states that we should reject the null hypothesis if the absolute value of test statistic is higher than the critical value.

(e) **Draw a Conclusion:**

After a decision has been made whether to accept or reject the null hypothesis, the next process is to draw a conclusion about the parameter under investigation.

**Example 10.1**

In a pharmaceutical company, the operations manager claimed that the mean of the drugs produced by the company is 100 mg. If a random sample of 60 drugs is chosen with mean of 98 mg and standard deviation of 14 mg, test the hypothesis to justify the operations manager's claim, use $\alpha = 0.05$.

**Solution:**

(a) $H_0 : \mu = 100$ vs. $H_1 : \mu \neq 100$.

(b) $\alpha = 0.05$.

(c) Test statistic: $z = \frac{\sqrt{60}(98-100)}{14} = -1.1066$ (we use test statistic $z$ since the sample size is greater than 30).

(d) $z_{(0.975)} = 1.96$ (from the normal distribution table).

The stated hypothesis is a two-tailed test, therefore we use $z_{\left(1-\frac{\alpha}{2}\right)}$. However, if the stated hypothesis is a one-tailed test and sample size is is equal to or greater than 30, then we will use $z_{(1-\alpha)}$.

Decision rule: reject null hypothesis if $|-1.1066| > 1.96$, since test statistics is not greater than critical value, therefore we do not reject $H_0$.

(e) Conclusion: the data support the claim of the operations manager than the mean of the drugs produced is 100 mg.

The scripts below show how the question in Example 10.1 can be solved in R. The $z$-statistic and critical value are computed in R. This serves as a basis of comparison.

R Codes

```
# state the given parameters
xbar = 98            # sample mean
mu0 = 100            # hypothesized value
sigma = 14           # sample standard deviation
n = 60               # sample size
# use z-test since sample size is greater than 30
z = (xbar-mu0)/(sigma/sqrt(n))
z                    # test statistic
[1] -1.106567
```

This $z$-statistic is -1.1066.

```
# compute the critical value at 0.05 significance level

alpha = 0.05
z_alpha = qnorm(1-alpha/2)
z_alpha              # critical value
[1] 1.959964
```

The absolute value of computed $z$-statistic is 1.1066, which is less than the critical value of 1.96. Therefore, we do not reject null hypothesis and we conclude that the operations manager is right in his claim with the given data.

### Example 10.2
A stockbroker claimed that weekly average return on a stock is normal with an average of return of 0.5%. He took the 20 previous weeks return and found that the weekly average returns was 0.48 with standard deviation 0.08. At 5% level of significance, does his claim about the relevant? If the level of significance is reduce to 1%, compare the result.

### Solution:

(a) Hypothesis: $H_0 : \mu = 0.5\%$ vs. $H_1 : \mu \neq 0.5\%$.

(b) $\alpha = 0.05$.

(c) Test statistic: $t = \frac{\sqrt{20}(0.48-0.50)}{0.08} = -1.118$ (we use $t$-test because the sample size is less than 30). In this case, our sample size is 20.

(d) $t_{n-1,(1-\frac{\alpha}{2})} = t_{19,(0.975)} = 2.093$ (critical value for two-tailed test is obtained from student-$t$ table).

Decision rule: reject null hypothesis if $|-1.118| > 2.093$, since test statistics is not greater than critical value, therefore we do not reject $H_0$.

(e) Conclusion: the stockbroker is correct on his claim based on the data. Therefore, the average weekly returns of the stock is 0.5%.

At $\alpha = 0.01$, $t = -1.118$, $t_{n-1,(1-\frac{\alpha}{2})} = t_{19,(0.995)} = 2.861$ (obtained from the Student-$t$ table).

**Decision rule:** Reject null hypothesis if $|-1.118| > 2.861$. Since the absolute of test statistics is less than critical value, therefore we do not reject $H_0$.

**Conclusion:** We accept the null hypothesis based on the data, and conclude that the average weekly returns is 0.5%.

**Comparison:** The stockbroker is claim that the average weekly return is 0.5% is right at both 1% and 5% level of significance.

Let's demonstrate this Example 10.2 with R codes.

**R Codes**

```
# Given parameters
x.bar = 0.48
mu0 = 0.50
sigma = 0.08
sample.size = 20

# compute the t-statistics
t = (x.bar-mu0)/(sigma/sqrt(sample.size ))
t
[1] -1.118034

# compute the critical value at 0.05 significance level

alpha1 = 0.05
t.alpha1 = qt(1-alpha1/2, sample.size-1 )
```

```
t.alpha1
[1] 2.093024

# At 1% level of significance
alpha2 = 0.01
t.alpha2 = qt(1-alpha2/2, sample.size-1 )
t.alpha2
[1] 2.860935
```

These results are the same as the outcomes we obtained in Example 10.2.

**Example 10.3**

The National Bureau of Statistics (NBS) claimed that less than 10% of the graduate youths are unemployed while the opposition party argued that the percentage of graduate youths is more than NBS claims. To ascertain the validity of the claim, a random sample of 10,000 graduate youths are selected in which 1,250 graduate youths are unemployed. Test the hypothesis that less than 10% of the graduate youths are unemployed. (Hint: use $\alpha = 0.05$.)

**Solution:**

(a) Hypothesis: $H_0 : P < 10\%$ vs. $H_1 : P \geq 10\%$.

(b) $\alpha = 0.05$.

(c) $\hat{p} = 0.125$.

Test statistic: $z = \frac{\hat{p} - p_0}{\sqrt{\frac{p_0(1-p_0)}{n}}}$.

Here, we used $z$-statistics because the sample size is 10,000 which is large enough, that is, it is greater than 30.

$$z = \frac{0.125 - 0.1}{\sqrt{\frac{0.1(1-0.1)}{10000}}} = 8.3.$$

(d) **Critical value:** $z_{(1-\alpha)} = z_{(0.95)} = 1.64$ (Our hypothesis is one-tailed, thus $z_{(1-\alpha)}$ is to be used).

Decision rule: Reject null hypothesis if $z > z_{(0.95)}$, since $8.3 > 1.64$, then we reject null hypothesis.

(e) **Conclusion**: There is no evidence to support the claim of NBS that the percentage of unemployed graduate youths is less than 10% based on the data.

**Note:** There is a possibility that another set of dataset might justified the claim of the NBS. However, based on the information given in this particular question, no justification for the claim that the percentage of unemployed graduate youths is less than 10%.

The R codes below describe how the $z$-statistics for the proportion ($p$) and critical value can be obtained for proper comparison.

**R Codes**

```
# compute the z-statistic
p.hat = 0.125
p0 = 0.10
n = 10000
z = (p.hat-p0)/ sqrt (p0*(1-p0)/n)
z
[1] 8.333333

# compute the critical value at 0.05 significance level

alpha = 0.05
z.alpha = qnorm(1-alpha)
z.alpha
[1] 1.644854
```

The $z$-statistic and critical value under $z$ are 8.333333 and 1.644854, respectively.

**Example 10.4**

There is a popular saying that girls perform better than the boys. To justify that, a random sample of 1,500 students which consists of 950 boys was selected to participate in an entrance examination into the secondary schools. Out of the boys that participated, only 480 passed and only 455 girls passed. Test the hypothesis that girls perform better than boys at a 5% level of significance.

**Solution:**

(a) Let $\hat{p}$ be the proportion of girls that passed the examination and $p_0$ be the proportion of girls that participated in the examination.

Hypothesis: $H_0 : p > 0.5\%$ vs. $H_1 : p \leq 0.5$.

(b) $\alpha = 0.05$.

(c) $\hat{p} = 0.83$ and $p_0 = 0.5$.

Test statistic: $z = \dfrac{\hat{p}-p_0}{\sqrt{\frac{p_0(1-p_0)}{n}}}$

The $z$-statistic is used because the sample size is greater than 30:

$$z = \frac{0.83 - 0.50}{\sqrt{\frac{0.5(1-0.5)}{1500}}} = 25.56.$$

(d) **Critical value**: $z_{(1-\alpha)} = z_{(0.95)} = 1.64$ (from $z$-table with one tailed test).

Decision rule: Reject null hypothesis if $z > z_{(0.95)}$, since $25.56 > 1.64$, then we reject null hypothesis.

(e) **Conclusion**: The data supported the general claim that girls perform better than the boys.

**R Codes for Computing $z$-test for a Proportion and its Critical Value**

```
# compute the z-test for the proportion
p.cap = 0.83
p0 = 0.5
n = 1500
z = (p.cap-p0)/ sqrt (p0*(1-p0)/n)
z
[1] 25.56169

# compute the critical value at 0.05 significance level

alpha = 0.05
z.alpha = qnorm(1-alpha)
z.alpha
[1] 1.644854
```

Since both $z$-test for the proportion and critical value are the same as in Example 10.4. Therefore, we are arriving at the same conclusion.

## 10.5  EXERCISES

**10.1.**  (a) Define the following:

(i) null hypothesis and alternative hypothesis; and

(ii) type 1 and type 2 error.

(b) The resident doctor of a hospital stated that the weight of a newborn baby is 3.5 kg and above because of the kind of foods pregnant women ate during pregnancy. A random sample of the 20 newborn babies are selected from the records and find that the mean is 2.95 kg and the standard deviation is 0.85 kg. Test the hypothesis that the weight of newborn babies is greater than or equal to 3.5 kg, assuming the weight is normal (use $\alpha = 0.01$).

**10.2.**  The managing director claims that brewery company notices that the sales of the products decline less than 20% during Ramadan periods and summon the sales manager to investigate his claim. The sales manager collated the sales of the products during the month of Ramadan in the past 30 years. Table 10.2 shows the distribution of percentage decrease in the sales during Ramadan periods. What would you say about the managing director's claim?

Table 10.2: Sales of a brewery company during Ramadan

| Year | 1988 | 1989 | 1990 | 1991 | 1992 | 1993 | 1994 | 1995 | 1996 | 1997 |
|---|---|---|---|---|---|---|---|---|---|---|
| Decrease in sales (%) | 27.41 | 9.31 | 20.36 | 26.43 | 22.75 | 14.48 | 10.21 | 12.42 | 20.83 | 18.53 |

| Year | 1998 | 1999 | 2000 | 2001 | 2002 | 2003 | 2004 | 2005 | 2006 | 2007 |
|---|---|---|---|---|---|---|---|---|---|---|
| Decrease in sales (%) | 19.98 | 25.22 | 12.08 | 26.75 | 35.43 | 19.44 | 19.62 | 24.06 | 25.04 | 10.61 |

| Year | 2008 | 2009 | 2010 | 2011 | 2012 | 2013 | 2014 | 2015 | 2016 | 2017 |
|---|---|---|---|---|---|---|---|---|---|---|
| Decrease in sales (%) | 31.32 | 24.13 | 16.38 | 20.08 | 21.59 | 13.98 | 19.80 | 23.97 | 29.64 | 21.29 |

**10.3.** A quality assurance manager argued that the average lifetime of light bulbs is 520 h. To ascertain his claim, he took a random sample of 50 bulbs and the lifetime readings (in hours) are as follows:

427.82, 425.76, 395.28, 444.67, 437.26, 442.67, 424.36, 416.63, 431.49,
401.58, 407.57, 461.93, 436.58, 423.20, 429.79, 447.74, 430.27, 434.41,
414.26, 435.79, 427.24, 401.04, 433.63, 404.31, 400.14, 437.70, 437.36,
424.59, 410.77, 448.75, 421.52, 416.88, 427.79, 425.87, 412.31, 423.88,
397.12, 430.68, 418.87, 411.51, 418.85, 405.59, 416.06, 388.01, 439.83,
419.70, 443.24, 422.75, 419.85, 420.28

Test whether the population mean is 520 h at a significance level of 5%.

**10.4.** Due to the economic recession in Nigeria, the chairman of National Union Transport and Road Workers (N.U.T.R.W) wanted to increase their fares and he told to the management of the University of Lagos that the daily income of the taxi operators within the campus is less than N2,500 per daily. The institution set of a committee to confirm his affirmation, then the committee took a random sample of 15 taxi operators with average income of N2,580 and standard deviation of N200. Assume that the income is normal distributed, justify the claim of the chairman at level of significance of 5%.

**10.5.** (a) With the aid of illustration, explain what you understand about the acceptance and rejection region.

(b) Discuss the procedure involved in the testing of hypotheses.

(c) The manager of a grocery store insisted that a customer spent an average of NGN 5,000 or more for food on a daily basis. A random sample of 18 customers are selected from the sales records and found that the average sales is NGN 4,975 with variance of NGN 22,500. Test whether the manager's claim agrees with the sample collected. Assume that the sales of groceries is normal and use 5% significance level.

**10.6.** A Coca-Cola production plant produces bottles containing 35 cl of soda, the new manager suspected that the volume of the drink do not follow the specification ascribed on the bottle. He decided to take a sample of the products and the following measurements are obtained:

34.73,  36.02,  35.54,  34.72,  35.49,  35.15,  35.99,  35.35,
35.81,  34.98,  34.23,  35.45,  34.99,  34.75,  35.57,  34.40,
35.09,  34.20,  34.42,  36.09,  34.34,  35.81,  34.89

Test the $H_0 : \mu = 35$ cl against $H_1 : \mu \neq 35$ cl (use $\alpha = 0.05$).

**10.7.** A rector of a polytechnic institution said that not fewer than 52% of the students that graduated in the institution fully gained employment immediately after leaving the school. A random sample of 1,000 graduates of the institution are taken across different years to examine if they actually gained employment immediately after leaving the school. The table below shows the number of the graduates from the institution and employment status immediately after graduation.

| Employment status | Employed | Not employed |
|---|---|---|
| Number of graduated students | 542 | 458 |

Test whether the rector is right in his statement and test that $H_0 : p \geq 0.5$ against $H_1 : p < 0.5$, use $\alpha = 0.05$.

CHAPTER 11

# Regression Analysis and Correlation

This chapter will focus on how two or more variables are interrelated. We shall understand the two concepts in statistics—regression analysis and correlational analysis—and the relationship between the concepts. We shall discuss what to look for in the output of regression analysis and how the output can be interpreted. We shall elucidate on how to use regression analysis for forecasting.

## 11.1 CONSTRUCTION OF LINE FIT PLOTS

In showing the relationship between two variables, we can draw a line across the variables after plotting the scatter plot and ensuring the line passes through as many points as possible. The straight line that gives the best approximation in a given set of data is referred to as the **line of best fit**. Least squares method is the most accurate method of finding the line of best fit of a given dataset.

For example, Fig. 11.1 shows sales revenue ($'million) and amount spent on advertisement ($'million) of a production company.

## 11.2 TYPES OF REGRESSION ANALYSIS

There are many regression analyses which are based on different assumptions. We mention a few, and we will dwell on the first and second mentioned below:

1. simple linear regression;

2. multiple regression;

3. ridge regression;

4. quantile regression; and

5. Bayesian regression.

### 11.2.1 USES OF REGRESSION ANALYSIS

Regression analysis can be used for the following.

| Sales revenue ($'million) | 115 | 118 | 120 | 125 | 126 | 128 | 131 | 132 |
|---|---|---|---|---|---|---|---|---|
| Advertisement expenses ($'million) | 4 | 7 | 9 | 14 | 15 | 17 | 20 | 21 |

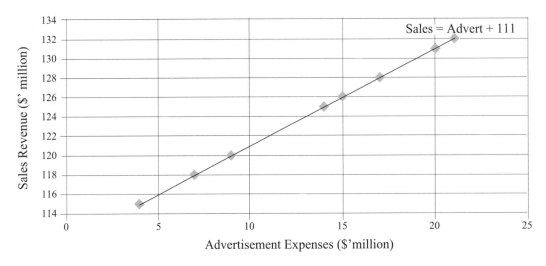

Figure 11.1: Chart of sales revenue on advertisement.

1. Causal analysis—to establish the relationship between two or more variables.

2. Forecasting an effect—it is used to predict a response variable fully knowing the independent variables.

3. Forecasting a trend—regression analysis can be used to predict trend in a dataset.

## 11.2.2  SIMPLE LINEAR REGRESSION

Simple linear regression is a statistical technique to show the relationship between one dependent variable and one independent variable. The dependent variable is denoted by $Y$ while the independent variable is denoted by $X$. The variables $X$ and $Y$ are linearly related. Simple linear regression can be used for the following: (a) description of the linear dependence of one variable on another variable; (b) prediction of one variable from the values of another variable; and (c) correction for the linear dependence of one variable on another variable.

The simple linear regression model is of the form:

$$Y_i = \beta_0 + \beta_1 X_i + \varepsilon_i, \tag{11.1}$$

where $\beta_0$ and $\beta_1$ are the intercept and regression coefficient of $X$ and $\varepsilon$ is the error term.

The solution to the regression coefficients in (11.1) can be derived using Least Square method:

$$e_i = Y_i - \beta_0 - \beta_1 X_i. \tag{11.2}$$

To find a minimum sum of squares of residuals you set the sum below equal to zero:

$$\sum_{i=1}^{n} (e_i)^2 = \sum_{i=1}^{n} (Y_i - \beta_0 - \beta_1 X_i)^2 = 0. \tag{11.3}$$

Taking partial derivative of (11.3) with respect to $\beta_1$:

$$\frac{\delta}{\delta \beta_0} \sum_{i=1}^{n} (Y_i - \beta_0 - \beta_1 X_i)^2 = -2 \left( n\beta_0 + \beta_1 \sum_{i=1}^{n} X_i - \sum_{i=1}^{n} Y_i \right) = 0. \tag{11.4}$$

Divide (11.4) by 2, and solve for $\beta_0$.
Then,

$$\beta_0 = \overline{Y} - \beta_1 \overline{X}. \tag{11.5}$$

Now,

$$\frac{\delta}{\delta \beta_1} \sum_{i=1}^{n} (Y_i - \beta_0 - \beta_1 X_i)^2 = -2 \sum_{i=1}^{n} \left( X_i Y_i - \beta_0 X_i - \beta_1 X_i^2 \right) = 0. \tag{11.6}$$

Substitute for the value of $\beta_0$ into (11.6):

$$\sum_{i=1}^{n} \left( X_i Y_i - (\overline{Y} - \beta_1 \overline{X}) X_i - \beta_1 X_i^2 \right) = 0$$

$$\sum_{i=1}^{n} \left( X_i Y_i - X_i \overline{Y} - \beta_1 X_i \overline{X} - \beta_1 X_i^2 \right) = 0$$

$$\sum_{i=1}^{n} \left( X_i Y_i - X_i \overline{Y} \right) - \beta_1 \sum_{i=1}^{n} \left( X_i^2 - X_i \overline{X} \right) = 0.$$

Therefore,

$$\beta_1 = \frac{\sum_{i=1}^{n} \left( X_i Y_i - X_i \overline{Y} \right)}{\sum_{i=1}^{n} \left( X_i^2 - X_i \overline{X} \right)} = \frac{\sum_{i=1}^{n} (X_i Y_i) - n\overline{X}\overline{Y}}{\sum_{i=1}^{n} (X_i^2) - n\overline{X}^2} = \frac{cov(X, Y)}{var(X)}. \tag{11.7}$$

## 11.2.3 ASSUMPTIONS OF SIMPLE LINEAR REGRESSION

1. There is a linear relationship between variable $Y$ and variable $X$.

2. The variable $X$ is deterministic or non-stochastic.

3. The error terms are statistically independent.

4. There is no correlation between $X$ and $\varepsilon_i$, that is, $Cov\,(X, \varepsilon_i) = 0$.

5. The error terms are distributed normally with mean zero and constant variance, i.e., $\varepsilon \sim N(0, \sigma^2)$.

6. There is no correlation between the error terms, i.e., no serial auto-correlation in the data.

7. The number of sample observations must greater than the number of parameters to be estimated.

8. For each of value of X, the distribution of residuals has equal variance, i.e., homoscedacity.

**Example 11.1**

In a business statistics class, the weight and height of 30 students were measured, as shown in Table 11.1.

(i) Find the regression of the weight on the height of the students.

(ii) Use your answer in (i) to estimate the value of student's weight when the height is 1.80?

Table 11.1: Weight and height of students

| Student | 1 | 2 | 3 | 4 | 5 | 6 | 7 | 8 | 9 |
|---|---|---|---|---|---|---|---|---|---|
| Height (m) | 1.43 | 1.10 | 2.24 | 1.36 | 2.26 | 1.25 | 1.74 | 1.55 | 1.51 |
| Weight (kg) | 92.18 | 77.76 | 65.44 | 114.19 | 82.81 | 106.66 | 94.44 | 75.32 | 67.35 |
| Student | 10 | 11 | 12 | 13 | 14 | 15 | 16 | 17 | 18 |
| Height (m) | 1.82 | 1.57 | 1.59 | 2.19 | 1.54 | 2.06 | 1.86 | 1.76 | 1.51 |
| Weight (kg) | 101.55 | 76.37 | 91.66 | 75.85 | 88.82 | 83.02 | 74.66 | 97.57 | 104.56 |
| Student | 19 | 20 | 21 | 22 | 23 | 24 | 25 | 26 | 27 |
| Height (m) | 2.39 | 1.83 | 2.02 | 1.99 | 1.40 | 1.54 | 1.60 | 1.88 | 1.52 |
| Weight (kg) | 113.36 | 64.71 | 103.79 | 70.02 | 78.35 | 80.70 | 90.54 | 91.55 | 82.57 |
| Student | 28 | 29 | 30 | | | | | | |
| Height (m) | 1.41 | 1.38 | 1.18 | | | | | | |
| Weight (kg) | 82.49 | 87.98 | 67.54 | | | | | | |

**Solution:**
From the data above, we obtained the following results:

$$\sum XY = 4347.56, \quad \sum Y = 2583.81, \quad \sum X = 50.48,$$

$$n = 30, \quad \overline{X} = 1.68, \quad \overline{Y} = 86.13,$$

$$\sum X^2 = 88.18.$$

Substitute for these values in Equation (11.7) above:

$$\beta_1 = \frac{\sum_{i=1}^{n}(X_i Y_i) - n\overline{X}\,\overline{Y}}{\sum_{i=1}^{n}(X_i{}^2) - n\overline{X}^2} = \frac{4347.56 - 30\,(1.68)\,(86.13)}{88.18 - 30(1.68)^2} = -0.042.$$

The slope of the regression is $-0.042$.
Then, substitute for $\overline{Y}$, $\overline{X}$, and $\beta_1$ in Equation (11.5), to get the constant term:

$$\beta_0 = \overline{Y} - \beta_1\overline{X} = 86.13 - (-0.042)\,(1.68) = 86.20.$$

(i) The regression model is Weight $= 86.20 - 0.042 * $ Height.

(ii) Weight $= 86.20 - 0.042 * 1.80 = 78.64$.

**To Estimate the Regression Estimates in R**
Assign values for height and weight in R as follows.

```
height<-c(1.43, 1.10, 2.24, 1.36, 2.26, 1.25, 1.74, 1.55, 1.51,
          1.82, 1.57, 1.59, 2.19, 1.54, 2.06, 1.86, 1.76, 1.51,
          2.39, 1.83, 2.02, 1.99, 1.40, 1.54, 1.60, 1.88, 1.52,
          1.41, 1.38, 1.18)
weight<-c(92.18, 77.76, 65.44, 114.19, 82.81, 106.66, 94.44, 75.32,
          67.35, 101.55, 76.37, 91.66, 75.85, 88.82, 83.02, 74.66,
          97.57, 104.56, 113.36, 64.71, 103.79, 70.02, 78.35, 80.70,
          90.54, 91.55, 82.57, 82.49, 87.98, 67.54)
```

Fit the model by regressing weight on height of the students and the results follow.

```
model.fit<-lm (weight~height)
summary(model.fit)


Call:
lm(formula = weight ~ height)

Residuals:
```

```
Min          1Q     Median     3Q       Max
-21.411   -10.132   -3.192    7.747   28.049


Coefficients:
             Estimate    Std. Error  t value    Pr(>|t|)
(Intercept)  86.19791    13.55401     6.360     6.99e-07 ***
height       -0.04214     7.90579    -0.005     0.996
---
Signif. codes:  0 `***' 0.001 `**' 0.01 `*' 0.05 `.' 0.1 ` ' 1


Residual standard error: 14.23 on 28 degrees of freedom
Multiple R-squared:  1.015e-06, Adjusted R-squared:  -0.03571
F-statistic: 2.841e-05 on 1 and 28 DF,  p-value: 0.9958
```

In the results above, the statistics for residuals, the coefficient estimates (with standard errors and the associated p-values), and all other statistics (Multiple R-squared, Adjusted R-squared, F-statistics, etc.) are shown in the output.

**Example 11.2**

Table 11.2 shows the log of gross domestic products (GDP) and the log of government spending in Nigeria between 1981–2015. Regress the log of GDP on the log of government spending and interpret your result.

**Solution:**

From the table above, we obtained the following:

$$\sum XY = 20140.45, \quad \sum Y = 907.92, \quad \sum X = 775.62,$$

$$n = 35, \quad \overline{X} = 22.16, \quad \overline{Y} = 25.94,$$

$$\sum X^2 = 17243.21.$$

Substitute for these values to compute regression coefficients ($\beta_0$ and $\beta_1$)

$$\beta_1 = \frac{\sum_{i=1}^{n}(X_i Y_i) - n\overline{XY}}{\sum_{i=1}^{n}(X_i^2) - n\overline{X}^2} = \frac{20140.45 - 35\,(22.16)\,(25.94)}{17243.21 - 35(22.16)^2} = 0.382$$

$$\beta_0 = \overline{Y} - \beta_1\overline{X} = 25.94 - (0.382)\,(22.16) = 17.475.$$

Thus, the regression model is LNGDP $= 17.475 + 0.382 * $ LNGEXP.

   **Interpretation:** This implies that 1% increase in the government spending would lead to 0.4% increase in gross domestic products.

Table 11.2: Gross domestic product

| Year | 1981 | 1982 | 1983 | 1984 | 1985 | 1986 | 1987 | 1988 | 1989 | 1990 |
|------|------|------|------|------|------|------|------|------|------|------|
| LNGDP (Y) | 25.545 | 25.535 | 25.483 | 25.463 | 25.543 | 25.451 | 25.337 | 25.410 | 25.473 | 25.593 |
| LNGEXP (X) | 21.082 | 21.105 | 21.128 | 21.150 | 21.171 | 21.192 | 21.213 | 21.233 | 21.253 | 21.273 |

| Year | 1991 | 1992 | 1993 | 1994 | 1995 | 1996 | 1997 | 1998 | 1999 | 2000 |
|------|------|------|------|------|------|------|------|------|------|------|
| LNGDP (Y) | 25.587 | 25.591 | 25.612 | 25.621 | 25.618 | 25.666 | 25.694 | 25.721 | 25.725 | 25.777 |
| LNGEXP (X) | 21.283 | 21.312 | 21.340 | 21.354 | 21.354 | 21.382 | 21.399 | 21.416 | 21.433 | 21.449 |

| Year | 2001 | 2002 | 2003 | 2004 | 2005 | 2006 | 2007 | 2008 | 2009 | 2010 |
|------|------|------|------|------|------|------|------|------|------|------|
| LNGDP (Y) | 25.820 | 25.858 | 25.956 | 26.247 | 26.281 | 26.360 | 26.426 | 26.486 | 26.554 | 26.629 |
| LNGEXP (X) | 21.320 | 21.377 | 21.103 | 22.998 | 23.098 | 23.404 | 23.854 | 24.069 | 24.076 | 24.188 |

| Year | 2011 | 2012 | 2013 | 2014 | 2015 |
|------|------|------|------|------|------|
| LNGDP (Y) | 26.677 | 26.719 | 26.771 | 26.832 | 26.859 |
| LNGEXP (X) | 24.233 | 24.213 | 24.105 | 24.032 | 24.028 |

**R Codes for Regressing the Log of Gross Domestic Products on the Log of Government Spending**

Assign the values for the log of GDP and the log of government spending (LNGEXP).

```
LNGDP<-c(25.545, 25.535, 25.483, 25.463, 25.543, 25.451, 25.337, 25.410,
         25.473, 25.593, 25.587, 25.591, 25.612, 25.621, 25.618, 25.666,
         25.694, 25.721, 25.725, 25.777, 25.820, 25.858, 25.956, 26.247,
         26.281, 26.360, 26.426, 26.486, 26.554, 26.629, 26.677, 26.719,
         26.771, 26.832, 26.859)
LNGEXP<-c(21.082, 21.105, 21.128, 21.150, 21.171, 21.192, 21.213, 21.233,
          21.253, 21.273, 21.283, 21.312, 21.340, 21.354, 21.354, 21.382,
          21.399, 21.416, 21.433, 21.449, 21.320, 21.377, 21.103, 22.998,
          23.098, 23.404, 23.854, 24.069, 24.076, 24.188, 24.233, 24.213,
          24.105, 24.032, 24.028)
data<-data.frame (LNGDP, LNGEXP)
model<-lm(LNGDP~LNGEXP, data)
summary(model)

Call:
lm(formula = LNGDP~LNGEXP)
```

```
Residuals:
  Min        1Q      Median       3Q        Max
-0.25038 -0.06998 -0.01893   0.04646   0.40962


Coefficients:
              Estimate    Std. Error  t value  Pr(>|t|)
(Intercept)   17.68058     0.39751    44.48    <2e-16 ***
LNGEXP         0.37273      0.01791    20.81    <2e-16 ***
---
Signif. codes:  0 `***' 0.001 `**' 0.01 `*' 0.05 `.' 0.1 ` ' 1


Residual standard error: 0.1328 on 33 degrees of freedom
Multiple R-squared:  0.9292,    Adjusted R-squared:  0.9271
F-statistic: 433.2 on 1 and 33 DF,  p-value: < 2.2e-16
```

From the output above, the regression coefficients are 17.68 and 0.37 for the intercept and slope, respectively.

## 11.3   MULTIPLE LINEAR REGRESSION

In simple linear regression, we considered two variables where one is the response and the other one is explanatory variable. In the case of multiple linear regression, it is an extension of simple linear regression whereby we have two or more explanatory variables that account for the variation in a dependent variable. Each of the explanatory variables $X_i$ is associated with a value of the response variable $Y$. The multiple linear regression model is of the form:

$$Y_i = \beta_0 + \beta_1 X_{i1} + \beta_2 X_{i2} + \beta_3 X_{i3} + \cdots + \beta_k X_{ik} + \varepsilon_{ik}, \text{ for } i = 1, 2, \ldots, n, \qquad (11.8)$$

where $\beta_0$ is a constant term, $\beta_1, \beta_2, \ldots, \beta_k$ are regression coefficients, $\varepsilon_{ik}$ is error term, and $\varepsilon_{ik} \sim N(0, \sigma^2)$.

The estimates of the regression coefficients $(\beta_0, \beta_1, \beta_2, \ldots, \beta_k)$ are the values that minimize the sum of squared errors for the residuals.

For two independents variables,

$$Y_i = \beta_0 + \beta_1 X_{i1} + \beta_2 X_{i2} + \varepsilon_{ik}. \qquad (11.9)$$

The regression coefficients can be estimated as:

$$\beta_1 = \frac{\left(\sum x_2^2\right)\left(\sum x_1 y\right) - \left(\sum x_1 x_2\right)\left(\sum x_2 y\right)}{\left(\sum X_1^2\right)\left(\sum X_2^2\right) - \left(\sum X_1 X_2\right)^2} \qquad (11.10)$$

$$\beta_2 = \frac{\left(\sum x_1^2\right)\left(\sum x_2 y\right) - \left(\sum x_1 x_2\right)\left(\sum x_1 y\right)}{\left(\sum x_1^2\right)\left(\sum x_2^2\right) - \left(\sum x_1 x_2\right)^2} \qquad (11.11)$$

$$\beta_0 = \overline{Y} - \beta_1 \overline{X}_1 - \beta_2 \overline{X}_2, \qquad (11.12)$$

where

$$\sum x_1 y = \sum X_1 Y - \frac{\left(\sum X_1\right)\left(\sum Y\right)}{N} \qquad (11.13)$$

$$\sum x_2 y = \sum X_2 Y - \frac{\left(\sum X_2\right)\left(\sum Y\right)}{N} \qquad (11.14)$$

$$\sum x_1 x_2 = \sum X_1 X_2 - \frac{\left(\sum X_1\right)\left(\sum X_2\right)}{N}. \qquad (11.15)$$

**Interpretation:** $\beta_0$ is the constant term or intercept at $Y$. $\beta_1$ is the change in $Y$ for each 1 unit change in $X_1$ while $X_2$ is held constant, and $\beta_2$ is the change in $Y$ for each 1 unit change in $X_2$ holding $X_1$ constant.

### Example 11.3
Table 11.3 shows the level of education ($X_1$), year of experience ($X_2$), and the log of monthly compesation of a company ($Y$). The level of education $X_1 = 1$ for primary education, $X_1 = 2$ for secondary education, $X_1 = 3$ for polytechnic graduate, $X_1 = 4$ for university Bachelor's degree, and $X_1 = 5$ for university Master's degree holder. Regress log of monthly compensation ($Y$) on level of education ($X_1$) and the year of experience in the company ($X_2$).

### Solution:
We obtained the following values from the data above:

$$\sum X_2^2 = 921, \quad \sum X_1^2 = 387, \quad \sum X_1 Y = 759.61, \quad \sum X_2 Y = 1165.55,$$

$$\sum X_1 X_2 = 499, \quad n = 35, \quad \sum X_1 = 107, \quad \sum X_2 = 167, \quad \sum Y = 242.76.$$

Table 11.3: Data for Example 11.3

| Level of education $(X_1)$ | Experience $(X_2)$ | Log of Compensation (Y) |
|:---:|:---:|:---:|
| 1 | 8 | 6.43 |
| 2 | 4 | 6.73 |
| 2 | 6 | 6.76 |
| 4 | 2 | 7.00 |
| 3 | 7 | 7.10 |
| 4 | 5 | 7.34 |
| 5 | 5 | 7.53 |
| 3 | 3 | 6.75 |
| 4 | 2 | 6.83 |
| 2 | 6 | 7.00 |
| 2 | 3 | 6.51 |
| 3 | 5 | 6.82 |
| 3 | 8 | 6.94 |
| 1 | 5 | 6.23 |
| 3 | 5 | 6.82 |
| 5 | 5 | 7.53 |
| 5 | 3 | 7.31 |
| 5 | 4 | 7.43 |
| 4 | 5 | 7.34 |
| 4 | 5 | 7.34 |
| 2 | 3 | 6.51 |
| 4 | 9 | 7.61 |
| 3 | 2 | 6.71 |
| 5 | 4 | 7.43 |
| 3 | 4 | 6.79 |
| 1 | 7 | 6.40 |
| 4 | 5 | 7.34 |
| 2 | 3 | 6.51 |
| 2 | 9 | 7.17 |
| 2 | 5 | 6.75 |
| 5 | 6 | 7.55 |
| 1 | 2 | 5.92 |
| 1 | 5 | 6.23 |
| 3 | 3 | 6.75 |
| 4 | 4 | 7.31 |

Compute the following and substitute the values for obtained the regression coefficients:

$$\sum x_1 y = 759.61 - \frac{(107)(242.76)}{35} = 17.458$$

$$\sum x_2 y = 1165.55 - \frac{(167)(242.76)}{35} = 7.238$$

$$\sum x_1 x_2 = 499 - \frac{(107)(167)}{35} = -11.543$$

$$\sum x_2^2 = 921 - \frac{(167)(167)}{35} = 124.171$$

$$\sum x_1^2 = 387 - \frac{(107)(107)}{35} = 59.886$$

$$\begin{aligned}
\beta_1 &= \frac{\left(\sum x_2^2\right)\left(\sum x_1 y\right) - \left(\sum x_1 x_2\right)\left(\sum x_2 y\right)}{\left(\sum x_1^2\right)\left(\sum x_2^2\right) - \left(\sum x_1 x_2\right)^2} \\
&= \frac{(124.171)(17.458) - (-11.543)(7.238)}{(59.886)(124.171) - (-11.543)^2} = 0.308 \\
\beta_2 &= \frac{(59.886)(7.238) - (-11.543)(17.458)}{(59.886)(124.171) - (-11.543)^2} = 0.084 \\
\beta_0 &= 6.94 - 0.308(3.06) - 0.084(4.77) = 5.597.
\end{aligned}$$

The regression coefficients are 5.597, 0.308, and 0.084 for $\beta_0$, $\beta_1$, and $\beta_2$, respectively. The model is $Y_i = 5.577 + 0.31 X_{i1} + 0.087 X_{i2}$.

**Interpretation:** This implies that 1 unit increase in the level of education would lead to a 31% increase in compensation holding years of experience constant. Also, for every unit increase in years of experience would lead to a 9% increase in compensation holding level of education constant.

R Codes for the Solution of Example 11.3
Input the values of level of education (edu), year of employment (empl), and log of compensation (comp).

```
edu<-c(1, 2, 2, 4, 3, 4, 5, 3, 4, 2, 2, 3, 3, 1, 3, 5, 5, 5, 4, 4,
    2, 4, 3, 5, 3, 1, 4, 2, 2, 2, 5, 1, 1, 3, 4)

empl<-c(8, 4, 6, 2, 7, 5, 5, 3, 2, 6, 3, 5, 8, 5, 5, 5, 3, 4, 5, 5,
    3, 9, 2, 4, 4, 7, 5, 3, 9, 5, 6, 2, 5, 3, 4)

comp<-c(6.43, 6.73, 6.76, 7, 7.10, 7.34, 7.53, 6.75, 6.83, 7, 6.51,
    6.82, 6.94, 6.23, 6.82, 7.53, 7.31, 7.43, 7.34, 7.34, 6.51,
```

7.61, 6.71, 7.43, 6.79, 6.40, 7.34, 6.51, 7.17, 6.75, 7.55,
5.92, 6.23, 6.75, 7.31)

Combine the variables (edu, empl, and comp) as a dataframe and then regress comp on edu, and empl.

```
mydata<-data.frame (edu, empl, comp)
multiple.reg<-lm(comp~edu+empl, mydata)
```

Obtain the regression coefficient and other statistics as follows:

```
summary(multiple.reg)


Call:
lm(formula = comp~edu + empl, data = mydata)


Residuals:
 Min       1Q      Median    3Q       Max                    .
-0.25870 -0.09077 -0.01283  0.07499  0.28368


Coefficients:
             Estimate   Std. Error   t value    Pr(>|t|)
(Intercept)  5.57723    0.07656      72.844     < 2e-16 ***
edu          0.30803    0.01540      20.002     < 2e-16 ***
empl         0.08717    0.01069       8.151     2.61e-09 ***
---
Signif. codes:  0 `***' 0.001 `**' 0.01 `*' 0.05 `.' 0.1 ` ' 1


Residual standard error: 0.1181 on 32 degrees of freedom
Multiple R-squared:  0.9308,    Adjusted R-squared:  0.9265
F-statistic: 215.3 on 2 and 32 DF,  p-value: < 2.2e-16
```

The regression coefficients are the same with Example 11.3 above and it is interpreted the same manner.

## 11.3.1 SIGNIFICANCE TESTING OF EACH VARIABLE

In this section, we are testing if the independent variables in the model is useful in the model, i.e., if the independent variable can usually help us predict the dependent variable ($y$). Therefore, to determine whether variable $X_1$ is making a useful contribution in the model, we have to test its significance by setting hypotheses as shown below.

Hypothesis: $H_0 : \beta_1 = 0$ vs. $H_1 : \beta_1 \neq 0$.
Test statistic: $t = \frac{\beta_1}{se(\beta_1)} \sim t_{1-\frac{\alpha}{2},n-2}$.
Decision rule: Reject $H_0$ if $|t| \geq t_{1-\frac{\alpha}{2},n-2}$.

**Example 11.4**
In Example 11.3, test whether the null hypothesis that $\beta_1$ is significantly different from zero i.e., $H_0 : \beta_1 = 0$ vs. $H_1 : \beta_1 \neq 0$.

**Solution:**
Hypothesis: $H_0 : \beta_1 = 0$ vs. $H_1 : \beta_1 \neq 0$.
Test statistic: $t = \frac{0.30803}{0.01540} = 20.002$.
Critical value: $t_{0.975,33} = 2.042$.
Decision rule: Reject $H_0$ if $|t| \geq t_{0.975,33}$, since $20.002 \geq 2.042$, then we reject $H_0$.
Conclusion: The coefficient of level of education $X_1$ is significantly different from zero.

**Note:** This result gives the same conclusion with the model in Example 11.3.

## 11.3.2 INTERPRETATION OF REGRESSION COEFFICIENTS AND OTHER OUTPUT

(a) **Regression coefficients**: The magnitude of the coefficient of each independent variable gives the size of the effect that the independent variable has on dependent variable and the sign $(-/+)$ on the regression coefficient tells the direction of the effect. In general, the coefficient gives how much the dependent variable would change when the independent variable change by 1 unit, keeping all other independent variables constant.

For example, if we fit a model, $Y = 2.5 + 0.5X_1 - 0.8X_2$, this can be interpreted as: the $Y$-intercept can be intepreted as the predicted value for $Y$ when both $X_1$ and $X_2$ are zero. Therefore, you would expect 2.5 unit when $X_1 = 0$ and $X_2 = 0$. For every unit increse in $Y$ would lead to 0.5 unit increase in $X_1$ while $X_2$ is held constant, also for every unit in $Y$ would lead to 0.8 unit decrease in $X_2$ holding $X_1$constant.

(b) $t$-**value:** This is the ratio of the coefficient and the standard error of the coefficient. The rule of thumb is that the absolute value of $t$ must be 2 or more to show the significance of the coefficient. $T$-value is used to determine the $p$-value corresponding to Student $t$-distribution.

(c) $P$-**value:** It indicates that theprobability that the estimated coefficient is not reliable. The less the $p$-value the more it is reliable under the significance level. For example, if the level of significance is 5% or (10%) it means than the value of $p$ is less than 5% or (10%)

indicates that the estimated coefficient is reliable, otherwise it is unreliable and it should be discarded from the model.

(d) **Multiple R-squared**: This shows the fraction (percentage) of the variation in a response variable that is accounted for by independent variables in the model. It indicates how well the terms fit the data. In addition, the adjusted R-squared is used to adjust for the number of terms in a model. As long as you add more independent variables to a model, the R-squared continue to increase in value, even when the variable is useless in the model. However, the adjusted R-squared will increase if you add useful independent variable in the model, otherwise the value of adjusted R-squared will decrease. The R-squared rages from 0 to 1 but the adjusted R-squared can dip down to the negative value.

(e) **F-statistics:** This test for the significance of the overall coefficients whether the regression model provides a better fit to the data than a model with no independent variables.

(f) **Durbin–Watson:** It is used to test for the autocorrelation assumption of the error terms. That is, to make sure that no correlation between the error terms $Cov(\varepsilon_i, \varepsilon_{i-1}) = 0$. Autocorrelation may be caused by omission of important explanatory variable, misspecification of the model, and systematic error in measurement. The consequences of autocorrelation include the least square estimators will be inefficient and the estimated variances of the regression coefficients will be biased and inconsistent, thus hypothesis testing is no longer valid. Furthermore, Durbin–Watson ranges from 0–4. The value of 2 indicates no autocorrelation between the error terms, between 0 to $< 2$ is a positive autocorrelation and between 2 and 4 is negative autocorrelation. A rule of thumb for Durbin–Watson is that for a relatively normal data, the test statistic should fall within 1.5–2.5.

**Regression Output in R**

After inputting the values for dependent and independent variables and combined the series into dataframe, then the R function `lm()` is used to regress the dependent variable on the set of independent variables. The function `summary()` gives the result below, as explained in Example 11.2. We shall discuss most important results in this output; the regression coefficients of the model are 17.68 and 0.37 with the corresponding $p$-values of 2e-16 each. This is very close to 0 and much less than 5%. This indicates that the coefficients are reliable. Adjusted R-squared (0.93) indicates that 93% variation in GDP is explained by variation government expenditure. This shows that the model fits well. Also, the $p$-value of F-statistics is 2.2e-16, indicating that all the regression coefficients (intercept and slope) are jointly significant.

```
Call:
lm(formula = LNGDP~LNGEXP)

Residuals:
```

```
 Min       1Q       Median     3Q       Max
-0.25038 -0.06998 -0.01893  0.04646   0.40962


Coefficients:
            Estimate   Std. Error  t value   Pr(>|t|)
(Intercept)  17.68058    0.39751    44.48    <2e-16 ***
LNGEXP        0.37273    0.01791    20.81    <2e-16 ***
---
Signif. codes:  0 `***' 0.001 `**' 0.01 `*' 0.05 `.' 0.1 ` ' 1


Residual standard error: 0.1328 on 33 degrees of freedom
Multiple R-squared:  0.9292,    Adjusted R-squared:  0.9271
F-statistic: 433.2 on 1 and 33 DF,  p-value: < 2.2e-16
```

## 11.4  PEARSON CORRELATION COEFFICIENT

The simple linear regression analysis shows the relationship between two variables that are linearly related. The correlation analysis is a measure of strength or level of association between variables. The correlation is measured by the Pearson correlation coefficient and it is denoted by "r". The statistic "r" ranges from −1 to +1. If the value of "r" is zero, it implies that there is no linear association between the variables. As the value of correlation coefficient "r" move close to zero (0), the linear association between the variables becomes weaker. Conversely, as the value of the correlation coefficient "r" far away from zero and approaches ±1, the linear association between the variables becomes stronger. When the correlation coefficient is exactly 1, it is called a *perfect positive correlation* and when the correlation coefficient is exactly −1, then it is known as a *perfect negative correlation* (see Fig. 11.2).

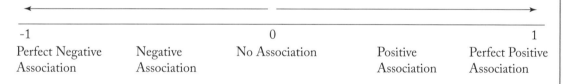

| -1 | | 0 | | 1 |
|---|---|---|---|---|
| Perfect Negative Association | Negative Association | No Association | Positive Association | Perfect Positive Association |

Figure 11.2: Pearson correlation coefficient "r".

The significance of a relationship is determined whether the Pearson's correlation coefficient "r" is a meaningful reflection of the linear relationship between the two variables or whether the relationship occurred by chance. For a given significant value ($\alpha = 0.05$), the probability that Pearson's correlation coefficient "r" value comes by chance is 5% or less.

Pearson's correlation coefficient "r" between variables $X$ and $Y$ can be defined as:

$$r_{XY} = \frac{\sum_{i=1}^{n} (X_i - \overline{X})(Y_i - \overline{Y})}{\sqrt{\sum_{i=1}^{n} (X_i - \overline{X})^2} \sqrt{\sum_{i=1}^{n} (Y_i - \overline{Y})^2}}. \tag{11.16}$$

Alternatively,

$$r_{XY} = \frac{n \sum_{i=1}^{n} X_i Y_i - \left(\sum_{i=1}^{n} Y_i\right)\left(\sum_{i=1}^{n} X_i\right)}{\sqrt{\left[n \sum_{i=1}^{n} X^2 - \left(\sum_{i=1}^{n} X_i\right)^2\right]\left[n \sum_{i=1}^{n} Y^2 - \left(\sum_{i=1}^{n} Y_i\right)^2\right]}} = \frac{Cov(X,Y)}{S_X . S_Y}, \tag{11.17}$$

where $\overline{X}$ and $\overline{Y}$ are the means of $X$ and $Y$, respectively.
$Cov(X, Y)$ is the covariance between $X$ and $Y$.
$S_X$ and $S_Y$ are standard deviations of $X$ and $Y$, respectively.

### 11.4.1 ASSUMPTIONS OF CORRELATION TEST

The followings are the assumptions under the use of Pearson correlation test.

1. There must be independent observations.

2. The population correlation assumed to be zero, i.e., $\rho = 0$.

3. The bivariates are normally distributed in the population.

### 11.4.2 TYPES OF CORRELATION

See Fig. 11.3.

### 11.4.3 COEFFICIENT OF DETERMINATION

The coefficient of determination is defined as the square of the correlation coefficient and it is denoted by $r^2$. It measures the strength of the relationship between two variables. The coefficient of determination is a measure of ratio of proportion variance explained by the model. That is, it measures the percentage of variation in dependent variable that is accounted for, by the variation in the independent variable. For instance, if $r = 0.9$, then coefficient of determination $r^2 = 0.81$. This indicates that 81% variation in the dependent variable is accounted for by the variation in indepedent variable. Thus, the remaining 19% variation in dependent variable cannot be explained by the variation in th independent variable.

### 11.4.4 TEST FOR THE SIGNIFICANCE OF CORRELATION COEFFICIENT (R)

This significance test is used to test the null hupothesis that $r_{XY} = 0$. We should bear in mind that the sampling distribution of $r$ is approximately normal when sample size is large ($n \geq 30$), and distributed $t$ when the sample size is small ($n < 30$).

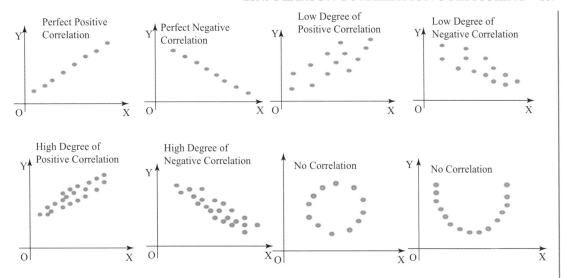

Figure 11.3: Types of correlation. Source: `https://www.slideshare.net/RamKumarshah/co` `rrelation-and-regression-56561989`.

The $t$-test statistics for the significance of the correlation coefficient $r$ is defined as:

$$t = r\sqrt{\frac{n-2}{1-r^2}} \sim t_{1-\frac{\alpha}{2}, n-2}. \tag{11.18}$$

However, when n is sufficiently large ($n \geq 30$), we use the standardized score for the $r$ using Fisher $z$-transformation ($z'$) to test for the significance of the correlation coefficient $r$:

$$z' = 0.5\left(\ln(1+r) - \ln(1-r)\right) \quad \sim z_{(1-\frac{\alpha}{2})}. \tag{11.19}$$

The result in (11.19) is compared with the appropriate normal table.

**Example 11.5**
Using the compensation data in Example 11.3,

(i) calculate the Pearson's correlation coefficient between $X_2$ and $Y$;

(ii) compute coefficient of determination in (i); and

(iii) test for the significant of the Pearson's correlation coefficient between $X_2$ and $Y$.

**Solution:**

(i) From the data in Example 11.3, we obtained the following values:

$$\sum X_2^2 = 921, \quad \sum X_1^2 = 387, \quad \sum X_1 Y = 759.61, \quad \sum X_2 Y = 1165.55,$$

$$\sum X_1 X_2 = 499, \quad n = 35, \quad \sum X_1 = 107, \quad \sum X_2 = 167,$$

$$\sum Y = 242.76, \quad \sum Y^2 = 1690.23.$$

The formula for the correlation coefficient is given by:

$$r_{X_2 Y} = \frac{n \sum_{i=1}^{n} X_{2i} Y_i - \left(\sum_{i=1}^{n} Y_i\right)\left(\sum_{i=1}^{n} X_{2i}\right)}{\sqrt{\left[n \sum_{i=1}^{n} X_{2i}^2 - \left(\sum_{i=1}^{n} X_{2i}\right)^2\right]\left[n \sum_{i=1}^{n} Y^2 - \left(\sum_{i=1}^{n} Y_i\right)^2\right]}}.$$

Substituting for the values in the formula, we have

$$r_{X_2 Y} = \frac{35(1165.55) - (242.76)(167)}{\sqrt{\left[35(921) - (167)^2\right]\left[35(1690.23) - (242.76)^2\right]}} = 0.26.$$

(ii) Coefficient of determination $r^2 = 0.07$.

(iii) Hypothesis: $H_0 : r_{X_2 Y} = 0$ vs. $H_1 : r_{X_2 Y} \neq 0$.

$$t = r\sqrt{\frac{n-2}{1-r^2}} = 0.26\sqrt{\frac{33}{0.93}} = 1.55.$$

Critical value: $t_{0.975, 33} = 2.042$.
Decision rule: Reject $H_0$ if t $\geq t_{0.975, 33}$, since $1.55 < 2.042$, then we do not reject null hypothesis.
Conclusion: The correlation coefficient between $X_2$ and $Y$ are not significantly different from zero.

**The R Script for Testing Correlation Coefficient for Small Sample**
In the code below, we will use R to obtain the correlation coefficient and CI for the correlation. We compute the correlation between years of experience (empl) and compensation on level of education (comp). We got our $t$-statistic to be 1.53 with corresponding $p$-value of 0.14. This indicates that the correlation between empl and comp is not statistically significant. In addition, at 95% confidence interval, the true correlation between the two variable should lie between $-0.08$ and $0.54$.

**# Pearson's product-moment correlation using Example 11.5 compesation data**

```
cor.test(mydata$empl, mydata$comp, method='pearson')

        Pearson's product-moment correlation

data:   mydata$empl and mydata$comp
t = 1.5264, df = 33, p-value = 0.1364
alternative hypothesis: true correlation is not equal to 0
95 percent confidence interval:
-0.08359426  0.54353702
sample estimates:
   cor
0.2568063
```

## Example 11.6

Use the following data to test for the significance of correlation coefficient:
$n = 50, r = 0.75$ and $\alpha = 1\%$.

## Solution:

Hypothesis: $H_0 : \rho = 0$ vs. $H_1 : \rho \neq 0$.
Test statistic:

$$z' = 0.5 \left( \ln \left( 1 + r \right) - \ln \left( 1 - r \right) \right).$$

Substitute for the value of r to get $z'$:

$$z' = 0.5 * \left( \ln \left( 1 + 0.75 \right) - \ln \left( 1 - 0.75 \right) \right) = 0.973.$$

Critical value: $z_{(1-\frac{\alpha}{2})} = z_{0.995} = 2.57$ (from the normal table).
Decision rule: Reject $H_0$ if $|z'| \geq z_{0.975}$, since $0.973 < 2.57$, then we do not reject null hypothesis.
Conclusion: The correlation coefficient is not significantly different from zero.

**The R Script for Testing Correlation Coefficient for Large Sample**
This is simplify version on how to compute Fisher $z$-transformation $(z')$ for the test of significance of the correlation coefficient, $r$.
The Fisher $z$-transformation $(z')$ for $r$

```
r<-0.75
z.prime<-0.5*(log(1+0.75)-log(1-0.75))
z.prime
[1] 0.9729551
```

Compute the critical value at 0.01 significance level

```
alpha = 0.01
z.prime = qnorm(1-alpha/2)
z.prime
[1] 2.575829
```

This result is similar to the result we obtained in Example 11.6.

## 11.5  EXERCISES

**11.1.**   **(a)** What do you understand about the concept of regression analysis?

   **(b)** With the aid of an example, differentiate between simple linear regression and multiple linear regression.

   **(c)** Table 11.4 shows data on the GDP and the government investment in Nigeria between 1981 and 2016. Regress GDP growth rate on the total investment (% GDP) and interpret your result.

**11.2.**   **(a)** List the types of regression analysis you know.

   **(b)** What are the assumptions of the simple linear regression?

   **(c)** Table 11.5 shows the log of space area (measured in sq. feet), log of number of bedrooms, and the log of house price (measured in $'million).

   (i) Perform a regression analysis to show the relationship between the three (3) variables. Take a log of house prices as the dependent variable ($Y$).

   (ii) Interpret your result.

   (iii) Comment on the output .

**11.3.**   **(a)** What do you understand about correlation coefficient?

   **(b)** What are the assumptions of the correlation test?

   **(c)** Explain the coefficient of determination.

   **(d)** The summary statistics for the two variables are given below:

$$\sum XY = 216.24, \quad \sum X = 21.20, \quad \sum Y = 204.21,$$

$$\sum X^2 = 22.90, \quad \sum Y^2 = 2187.59, \quad n = 20.$$

   (i) Calculate the Pearson's correlation coefficient (r).

   (ii) Test for the significance of r.

**11.4.**   **(a)** Show that the least square estimates for the simple linear regression are given as:

$$\beta_0 = \overline{Y} - \beta_1 \overline{X} \quad \text{and}$$

$$\beta_1 = \frac{Cov(X, Y)}{Var(X)}.$$

Table 11.4: GDP and government investment in Nigeria

| Year | GDP Growth Rate | Total Investment (% GDP) | Year | GDP Growth Rate | Total Investment (% GDP) |
|------|------|------|------|------|------|
| 1981 | -13.13 | 35.22 | 1999 | 0.47 | 6.99 |
| 1982 | -1.05 | 31.95 | 2000 | 5.32 | 7.02 |
| 1983 | -5.05 | 23.01 | 2001 | 4.41 | 7.58 |
| 1984 | -2.02 | 14.22 | 2002 | 3.78 | 7.01 |
| 1985 | 8.32 | 11.97 | 2003 | 10.35 | 9.90 |
| 1986 | -8.75 | 15.15 | 2004 | 33.74 | 7.39 |
| 1987 | -10.75 | 13.61 | 2005 | 3.44 | 5.46 |
| 1988 | 7.54 | 11.87 | 2006 | 8.21 | 8.27 |
| 1989 | 6.47 | 11.74 | 2007 | 6.83 | 9.25 |
| 1990 | 12.77 | 14.25 | 2008 | 6.27 | 8.32 |
| 1991 | -0.62 | 13.73 | 2009 | 6.93 | 12.09 |
| 1992 | 0.43 | 12.75 | 2010 | 7.84 | 16.56 |
| 1993 | 2.09 | 13.55 | 2011 | 4.89 | 15.53 |
| 1994 | 0.91 | 11.17 | 2012 | 4.28 | 14.16 |
| 1995 | -0.31 | 7.07 | 2013 | 5.39 | 14.17 |
| 1996 | 4.99 | 7.29 | 2014 | 6.31 | 15.08 |
| 1997 | 2.80 | 8.36 | 2015 | 2.65 | 14.83 |
| 1998 | 2.72 | 8.60 | 2016 | -1.62 | 12.60 |

**(b)** With the aid of diagram, explain the different types of correlation you know.

**11.5.** The strength (MPa) of a steel and the diameter (mm) are measured, as shown in the table below.

| Diameter (mm) | 75 | 80 | 85 | 90 | 95 | 100 | 105 | 110 | 115 | 120 |
|------|------|------|------|------|------|------|------|------|------|------|
| Strength (MPa) | 250 | 320 | 350 | 400 | 435 | 480 | 500 | 520 | 550 | 570 |

**(a)** Draw a scatter diagram to illustrate the information.

**(b)** Calculate the least square line of regression of Strength (MPa).

**(c)** Interpret the model.

**(d)** Estimate the strength (MPa) of the steel when the diameter (mm) is 150.

Table 11.5: Log table

| Log of space area (sq. feet) | 8.51 | 8.77 | 8.55 | 8.63 | 7.49 | 8.61 | 8.55 | 8.44 | 8.42 | 8.34 |
|---|---|---|---|---|---|---|---|---|---|---|
| Log of number of bedrooms | 1.61 | 1.39 | 1.39 | 0.69 | 1.10 | 1.61 | 1.39 | 1.39 | 1.39 | 1.61 |
| Log of house price ($' m) | 0.34 | 0.22 | 0.30 | 0.18 | 0.20 | 0.26 | 0.35 | 0.27 | 0.14 | 0.41 |

| Log of space area (sq. feet) | 8.39 | 8.52 | 8.69 | 8.60 | 8.40 | 8.39 | 8.25 | 8.71 | 8.55 | 8.55 |
|---|---|---|---|---|---|---|---|---|---|---|
| Log of number of bedrooms | 1.10 | 1.61 | 1.10 | 0.69 | 1.61 | 1.10 | 1.10 | 1.61 | 1.39 | 1.39 |
| Log of house price ($' m) | 0.17 | 0.24 | 0.22 | 0.22 | 0.35 | 0.19 | 0.10 | 0.48 | 0.43 | 0.35 |

| Log of space area (sq. feet) | 8.48 | 8.38 | 8.76 | 8.59 | 8.37 | 8.47 | 8.63 | 8.56 | 8.61 | 8.22 |
|---|---|---|---|---|---|---|---|---|---|---|
| Log of number of bedrooms | 1.61 | 1.10 | 1.10 | 0.69 | 1.10 | 1.10 | 1.10 | 1.10 | 1.61 | 1.39 |
| Log of house price ($' m) | 0.36 | 0.23 | 0.48 | 0.25 | 0.18 | 0.23 | 0.29 | 0.20 | 0.36 | 0.34 |

**11.6.** The following table shows the prices (N) of bread in a supermarket and the quantity sold in a week.

| Price ($X$) | 100 | 200 | 500 | 750 | 1000 | 1500 | 1800 | 2000 |
|---|---|---|---|---|---|---|---|---|
| Quantity sold ($Y$) | 55 | 49 | 40 | 37 | 35 | 27 | 15 | 8 |

(a) Plot the data on a scatter diagram.

(b) Draw the regression line on your scatter diagram.

(c) From the regression equation obtained in (b), estimate the quantity to be sold if the price (N) of the bread is N2,200.

(d) Calculate Pearson's correlation coefficient between price of bread and quantity sold.

**11.7.** The weekly number of sales in the two complementary commodities (DVD player and DVD disk) are given in the following table.

| Week ($X$) | 1 | 2 | 3 | 4 | 5 | 6 | 7 | 8 |
|---|---|---|---|---|---|---|---|---|
| DVD player | 20 | 23 | 18 | 25 | 15 | 17 | 16 | 20 |
| DVD disks | 38 | 39 | 25 | 28 | 23 | 26 | 25 | 30 |

(a) Calculate Pearson's correlation coefficient between the number of sales of a DVD player and DVD disk.

(b) Give interpretation of your result in (a).

(c) Test hypothesis about $r = 0$.

CHAPTER 12

# Poisson Distribution

The Poisson distribution was developed by the French mathematician Simeon Denis Poisson in 1837. The Poisson distribution is a discrete probability distribution. It is used to approximate the count of events that occur randomly and independently. The Poisson distribution may calculate number of instances that should occur in a certain amount of time, distance, area, or volume. For instance, the random variable could be used to estimate the number of radioactive decays in a given period of time for a certain amount of the radioactive material. If you know the rate of decay for that amount of the material you can use the Poisson distribution as a good estimate of the amount of decays. We shall elaborate on Poisson statistical properties, the derivation of the mean and the variance of a Poisson distribution, and an application of the Poisson distribution. Its practicality shall be demonstrated in the worked examples.

## 12.1 POISSON DISTRIBUTION AND ITS PROPERTIES

A discrete random variable $(X)$ is said to be a Poisson distribution function if it has a pdf of the form:

$$f(x) = \frac{\lambda^x e^{-\lambda}}{x!}, \quad x = 0, 1, 2, \ldots, \infty, \tag{12.1}$$

where $\lambda$ is the shape parameter that indicates the average occurrence per interval and $e$ is the Euler's constant, approximately 2.7183.

In Fig. 12.1, it is shown that the Poisson data skewed right and the skewness is less pronounced as the lambda, $\lambda$, which is the mean of the distribution increases. Poisson is closer to symmetric as the mean $(\lambda)$ of the distribution increases.

This distribution is most applicable where we have a rare event and the number of trials is large. It implies that the rate of occurrence is small, near to zero in a large number of trials. Some examples of a Poisson distribution are the occurrence of the dropping of a fish from the sky during rainfall, the occurrence of a fatal accident within a city, the number of automobiles arriving at a traffic light with a specified period of time, the number of typographical errors in a textbook, among others.

Poisson takes the values from zero to infinity, and the expected occurrences remain unchanged throughout the experiment. For a Poisson random variable, these two conditions should be met: the number of successes in two disjoint time intervals is independent and the probability of success in a short time interval is proportional to the entire length of the time interval. Alternatively, a Poisson random variable can also be applied to disjoint regions of space. Fig-

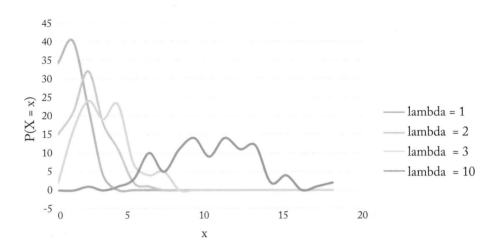

Figure 12.1: Poisson distributions.

| X | 0.1 | 0.2 | 0.3 | 0.4 | 0.5 | 0.6 | 0.7 | 0.8 | 0.9 | 1.0 |
|---|------|------|------|------|------|------|------|------|------|------|
| 0 | 0.9048 | 0.8187 | 0.7408 | 0.6703 | 0.6065 | 0.5488 | 0.4966 | 0.4493 | 0.4066 | 0.3679 |
| 1 | 0.0905 | 0.1637 | 0.2222 | 0.2681 | 0.3033 | 0.3293 | 0.3476 | 0.3595 | 0.3659 | 0.3679 |
| 2 | 0.0045 | 0.0164 | 0.0333 | 0.0536 | 0.0758 | 0.0988 | 0.1217 | 0.1438 | 0.1647 | 0.1839 |
| 3 | 0.0002 | 0.0011 | 0.0033 | 0.0072 | 0.0126 | 0.0198 | 0.0284 | 0.0383 | 0.0494 | 0.0613 |
| 4 | 0.0000 | 0.0001 | 0.0003 | 0.0007 | 0.0016 | 0.0030 | 0.0050 | 0.0077 | 0.0111 | 0.0153 |
| 5 | 0.0000 | 0.0000 | 0.0000 | 0.0001 | 0.0002 | 0.0004 | 0.0007 | 0.0012 | 0.0020 | 0.0031 |
| 6 | 0.0000 | 0.0000 | 0.0000 | 0.0000 | 0.0000 | 0.0000 | 0.0001 | 0.0002 | 0.0003 | 0.0005 |
| 7 | 0.0000 | 0.0000 | 0.0000 | 0.0000 | 0.0000 | 0.0000 | 0.0000 | 0.0000 | 0.0000 | 0.0001 |

| X | 1.1 | 1.2 | 1.3 | 1.4 | 1.5 | 1.6 | 1.7 | 1.8 | 1.9 | 2.0 |
|---|------|------|------|------|------|------|------|------|------|------|
| 0 | 0.3329 | 0.3012 | 0.2725 | 0.2466 | 0.2231 | 0.2019 | 0.1827 | 0.1653 | 0.1496 | 0.1353 |
| 1 | 0.3662 | 0.3614 | 0.3543 | 0.3452 | 0.3347 | 0.3230 | 0.3106 | 0.2975 | 0.2842 | 0.2707 |
| 2 | 0.2014 | 0.2169 | 0.2303 | 0.2417 | 0.2510 | 0.2584 | 0.2640 | 0.2678 | 0.2700 | 0.2707 |
| 3 | 0.0738 | 0.0867 | 0.0998 | 0.1128 | 0.1255 | 0.1378 | 0.1496 | 0.1607 | 0.1710 | 0.1804 |
| 4 | 0.0203 | 0.0260 | 0.0324 | 0.0395 | 0.0471 | 0.0551 | 0.0636 | 0.0723 | 0.0812 | 0.0902 |
| 5 | 0.0045 | 0.0062 | 0.0084 | 0.0111 | 0.0141 | 0.0176 | 0.0216 | 0.0260 | 0.0309 | 0.0361 |
| 6 | 0.0008 | 0.0012 | 0.0018 | 0.0026 | 0.0035 | 0.0047 | 0.0061 | 0.0078 | 0.0098 | 0.0120 |
| 7 | 0.0001 | 0.0002 | 0.0003 | 0.0005 | 0.0008 | 0.0011 | 0.0015 | 0.0020 | 0.0027 | 0.0034 |
| 8 | 0.0000 | 0.0000 | 0.0001 | 0.0001 | 0.0001 | 0.0002 | 0.0003 | 0.0005 | 0.0006 | 0.0009 |
| 9 | 0.0000 | 0.0000 | 0.0000 | 0.0000 | 0.0000 | 0.0000 | 0.0001 | 0.0001 | 0.0001 | 0.0002 |

| X | 2.1 | 2.2 | 2.3 | 2.4 | 2.5 | 2.6 | 2.7 | 2.8 | 2.9 | 3.0 |
|---|------|------|------|------|------|------|------|------|------|------|
| 0 | 0.1225 | 0.1108 | 0.1003 | 0.0907 | 0.0821 | 0.0743 | 0.0672 | 0.0608 | 0.0550 | 0.0498 |
| 1 | 0.2572 | 0.2438 | 0.2306 | 0.2177 | 0.2052 | 0.1931 | 0.1815 | 0.1703 | 0.1596 | 0.1494 |
| 2 | 0.2700 | 0.2681 | 0.2652 | 0.2613 | 0.2565 | 0.2510 | 0.2450 | 0.2384 | 0.2314 | 0.2240 |
| 3 | 0.1890 | 0.1966 | 0.2033 | 0.2090 | 0.2138 | 0.2176 | 0.2205 | 0.2225 | 0.2237 | 0.2240 |
| 4 | 0.0992 | 0.1082 | 0.1169 | 0.1254 | 0.1336 | 0.1414 | 0.1488 | 0.1557 | 0.1622 | 0.1680 |
| 5 | 0.0417 | 0.0476 | 0.0538 | 0.0602 | 0.0668 | 0.0735 | 0.0804 | 0.0872 | 0.0940 | 0.1008 |
| 6 | 0.0146 | 0.0174 | 0.0206 | 0.0241 | 0.0278 | 0.0319 | 0.0362 | 0.0407 | 0.0455 | 0.0504 |

Table of Poisson Probabilities

For a given value of $\lambda$, entry indicates the probability of a specifiec value of $X$.

Figure 12.2: Table of Poisson probabilities.

ure 12.2 shows the table of Poisson probabilities for a given value of $\lambda$ and the number of success recorded. The values in this table are computed using the formula in Equation (12.1) above. This Poisson table can be read directly without computational effort again. For example, suppose that a car dealer sells on the average two exotic cars per week and we want to calculate the probability that in a given week, he will sell one exotic car. We can check the table of Possion probabilities where mean ($\lambda = 2$) and the number of success ($x = 1$). From the table of Poisson probabilities, the required probability is 0.2707; this result is the same by substituting for $\lambda = 2$ and $x = 1$ in Equation (12.1) above. Using the formula, we have:

$$f(1) = \frac{2^1 e^{-2}}{1!} = 0.270671.$$

## 12.2 MEAN AND VARIANCE OF A POISSON DISTRIBUTION

In this section, we derive the mean and variance of a Poisson distribution mathematically. Here, you will see that the mean and variance of a Poisson distribution are equal.

**Mean**

The following is our standard form of the mean:

$$E(x) = \sum x f(x).$$

Substituting the Poisson function we get

$$E(x) = \sum_{x=0}^{\infty} x \frac{\lambda^x e^{-\lambda}}{x!}$$

or

$$E(x) = \sum_{x=0}^{\infty} x \frac{\lambda^{x-1} e^{-\lambda} \lambda}{x(x-1)!}$$

and

$$E(x) = \lambda \sum_{x=0}^{\infty} \frac{\lambda^{x-1} e^{-\lambda}}{(x-1)!}$$

since

$$\sum_{x=0}^{\infty} \frac{\lambda^{x-1} e^{-\lambda}}{(x-1)!} = 1.$$

Therefore,

$$E(x) = \lambda. \tag{12.2}$$

So the mean of the Poisson distribution is lambda.

**Variance**

Using our standard formula for variance we have

$$variance = E\left(x^2\right) - \left(E\left(x\right)\right)^2.$$

We will use the following clever fact to simplify the formula for variance of the Poisson distribution in the following few steps.

From $x^2 = x\left(x-1\right) + x$.

Then, $E\left(x^2\right) = E\left(x(x-1)\right) + E\left(x\right).$

$$E\left(x(x-1)\right) = \sum_{x=0}^{\infty} x\left(x-1\right) f(x)$$

$$E\left(x(x-1)\right) = \sum_{x=0}^{\infty} x\left(x-1\right) \frac{\lambda^x e^{-\lambda}}{x!}$$

$$E\left(x(x-1)\right) = \sum_{x=0}^{\infty} x\left(x-1\right) \frac{\lambda^{x-2} e^{-\lambda}\lambda^2}{x(x-1)(x-2)!}$$

$$E\left(x(x-1)\right) = \lambda^2 \sum_{x=0}^{\infty} \frac{\lambda^{x-2} e^{-\lambda}}{(x-2)!}$$

Since $\sum_{x=0}^{\infty} \frac{\lambda^{x-2} e^{-\lambda}}{(x-2)!} = 1.$

Then $E\left(x(x-1)\right) = \lambda^2.$

And, therefore,

$$var(x) = E\left(x(x-1)\right) + E\left(x\right) - \left(E\left(x\right)\right)^2.$$

And since $E(x) = \lambda$ from our derivation of the mean above,

$$var(x) = \lambda^2 + \lambda - \lambda^2.$$

Thus,

$$var(x) = \lambda. \tag{12.3}$$

Also, the variance of the Poisson distribution is lambda. This shows that the mean and variance of a Poisson distribution are the same.

**Example 12.1**

A paper mill produces writing pads and the probability of a writing pad being defective is 0.02. If a sample of 800 writing pads is selected, what is the probability that: (a) none are defective, (b) one defective, (c) two are defectives, and (d) three or more are defective writing pads.

**Solution:**
In Example 11.1, the probability of a writing pad being defective $(p) = 0.02$ and sample selected $n = 800$.
Calculate the lambda (mean),

$$\lambda = np = 800 * 0.02 = 16.$$

(a) The probability that none of the selected sample are defective:

$$f(0) = \frac{16^0 e^{-16}}{0!} = e^{-16}.$$

(b) The probability that one is defective:

$$f(1) = \frac{16^1 e^{-16}}{1!} = 16e^{-16}.$$

(c) The probability that two writing pads are defectives:

$$f(2) = \frac{16^2 e^{-16}}{2!} = 128e^{-16}.$$

(d) The probability that three or more writing pads are defectives:

$$f(x \geq 3) = 1 - (f(0) - f(1) - f(2)) = 1 - e^{-16} - 16e^{-16} - 128e^{-16}$$
$$f(x \geq 3) = 1 - f(x < 3) = 1 - e^{-16} - 16e^{-16} - 128e^{-16} = 0.999.$$

**R Codes**
The following are solutions to Example 12.1.
To calculate the probability of a Poisson distribution, the general format is:

```
ppois(q, lambda, lower.tail = TRUE, log.p = FALSE)
```

where

| | |
|---|---|
| q | vector of quantiles |
| lambda | vector of positive means |
| lower.tail | logical; if TRUE(default), probabilities are $P(X \leq x)$, otherwise $P(X > x)$ |
| log.p | logical; if TRUE, probabilities $P$ are given as $\log(p)$. |

1. The probability that none of the selected samples are defective:

```
n<-800
p<-0.02
lambda <-n*p
ppois(0, lambda=16, lower = TRUE)
[1] 1.125352e-07
```

This result is the same as $e^{-16}$ gotten in Example 12.1 above.

2. The probability that one is defective:

```
exact.1<-ppois(1, lambda=16)- ppois(0, lambda=16)
[1] 1.800563e-06
```

The evaluation of the quantity $16e^{-16}$ gives 1.800563e-06.

3. The probability that two writing pads are defectives:

```
exact.2<-ppois(2, lambda=16) - ppois(1, lambda=16)
[1] 1.44045e-05
```

The answer 1.44045e-05 is the same as $128e^{-16}$.

4. The probability that three or more writing pads are defectives:

```
ppois(3, lambda=16, lower = FALSE)    # upper tail
[1] 0.9999069
```

The upper tail is used here because we are considering the right side of the value 3 or value of 3 and above. Thus, we are able to use R code to solve the problem in Example 12.1 above.

## Example 12.2

The number of arrivals of customers into an eatery per minute has a Poisson with mean 3. Assuming that the number of arrivals in two different minutes are independent. Find the probability that:

1. no calls come in a period of a minute;

2. one call comes in a period of a minute; and

3. at least two customers will arrive in a given two-minute period.

**Solution:**

The mean of the Poisson distribution is 3.

1. $\lambda = 3$.

   Substitute for $\lambda = 3$ and $x = 0$

   $$f(0) = \frac{3^0 e^{-3}}{0!} = 0.0498.$$

2. The probability that one call comes in a period of a minute;

   $$f(1) = \frac{3^1 e^{-3}}{1!} = 0.1494.$$

3. The probability that at least two customers will arrive in a given two-minute period:

   $$f(x \geq 2) = 1 - f(0) - f(1)$$
   $$f(x \geq 2) = 1 - 0.0498 - 0.1494$$
   $$f(x \geq 2) = 0.8009.$$

**R Codes to Calculate the Probability of the Poisson Distribution in Example 12.2**

```
lambda =3
p0<-ppois(0, lambda=3, lower = TRUE)
[1] 0.04978707
```

The probability that no calls come in a period of a minute is 0.0498.

```
exact.p1<- ppois(1, lambda) - ppois(0, lambda)
[1] 0.1493612
```

Despite omitting the option "lower" in the statement above, R assumes `lower.tail = TRUE` by default.

```
p.greater2<- 1- p0 - exact.p1
[1] 0.8008517
```

The probability that at least two customers will arrive in a given two-minute period is 0.8009. We got similar results with Example 12.2 above.

**Example 12.3**

The operational manager has the option of using one of the two machines (A and B) to produce a particular product. He knew that the energy output of both machines is represented well by a Poisson distribution with machine A having a mean of 8.25 and machine B has a mean of 7.50. Assuming that the energy input remains the same, the efficiency of machine A is $f(x) = 2x^2 - 8x + 6$ and the efficiency of machine B is $f(y) = y^2 + 2y + 1$. Which of the machines has the maximum expected efficiency?

**Solution:**

Machine A expected efficiency is:

$$E(x) = E(2x^2 - 8x + 6)$$
$$E(x) = 2E(x^2) - 8E(x) + E(6).$$

From a general equation,

$$Var(x) = E(x^2) - (E(x))^2.$$

It implies that

$$E(x^2) = Var(x) + (E(x))^2.$$

Substitute for $E(x^2)$ to we get

$$E(x) = 2\left[Var(x) + (E(x))^2\right] - 8E(x) + 6.$$

Also, substitute for the mean and variance of the distribution to get

$$E(x) = 2\left[8.25 + 8.25^2\right] - (8 \times 8.25) + 6 = 92.63.$$

Machine B's expected efficiency is:

$$E(y) = E(y^2 + 2y + 1)$$
$$E(y) = E(y^2) + 2E(y) + E(1)$$
$$E(y) = \left[Var(y) + E(y)^2\right] + 2E(y) + 1,$$

since

$$E(y^2) = V(y) + E(y)^2.$$

Therefore,

$$E(y) = \left[7.50 + 7.50^2\right] + (2 \times 7.50) + 1 = 79.75.$$

Machine A is more efficient than machine B.

**R Codes for the Example 12.3**

We assigned for the values of mean and variance to be 8.25 each:

```
# compute efficiency for machine A
mean.x<-8.25
var.x<-8.25
```

Referring to $E(x) = 2\left[Var(x) + (E(x))^2\right] - 8E(x) + 6$, we obtained efficiency for the machine A as eff.x.

```
eff.x<-2*(var.x+mean.x**2)-8*mean.x+6
[1] 92.625
```

Also, we assigned for the values of mean and variance to be 7.50 each and then compute efficiency for machine B:

```
# compute efficiency for machine B
mean.y<-7.50        # expected efficiency
var.y<-7.50         # variance efficiency
eff.y<- var.y+mean.y**2+2*mean.y+1
[1] 79.75
```

The efficiency of machine A is 92.63 and machine B is 79.75, therefore machine A is more efficient.

## 12.3  APPLICATION OF POISSON DISTRIBUTION

Poisson distribution has its application in various aspects of life. A few areas shall be considered in this section. In healthcare, the Poisson distribution is helpful in birth detection and genetic mutations. It also helps to model the occurrence of rare disseases such as leukemia. In the area of transport, Poisson is good at accounting and predicting the occurrence of accidents in a high-way, monitoring the number of automobiles arriving at a traffic light within a one-hour period. Poisson can also be applied in the telecomunication and communication sectors by determining the number of calls received by the customer care center within a minute and the number of network failures per day. In the area of production, it can be used to capture the failure of a machine per month and the number of defective products in a production line.

## 12.4  POISSON TO APPROXIMATE THE BINOMIAL

The Poisson distribution is a special case of the binomial distribution and Poisson is useful in handling rare events. In the event that the binomial random variable has an extremely large number of trials ($n$) and the probability of success ($p$) is very small, then the Poisson distribution provides a good approximation of the binomial distribution when $n \geq 100$ and $np \leq 10$.

**Proof.** The Poisson ($\lambda$) is an approximation to the binomial ($n, p$) for a large $n$, small $p$, and $\lambda = np$.
Then $p = \frac{\lambda}{n}$.
Substitute for $p$ into the binomial distribution and then take the limit as $n$ tends to infinity:

$$\lim_{n\to\infty} P(X = k) = \lim_{n\to\infty} \frac{n!}{(n-k)!k!}\left(\frac{\lambda}{n}\right)^k\left(1 - \frac{\lambda}{n}\right)^{n-k}. \tag{12.4}$$

Take out the constant terms in (12.4):

$$\lim_{n\to\infty} P(X = k) = \frac{\lambda^k}{k!} \lim_{n\to\infty} \frac{n!}{(n-k)!} \left(\frac{1}{n}\right)^k \left(1 - \frac{\lambda}{n}\right)^n \left(1 - \frac{\lambda}{n}\right)^{-k}. \tag{12.5}$$

We can take the limit of the RHS one term after the other in (12.5):

$$\lim_{n\to\infty} \frac{n!}{(n-k)!} \left(\frac{1}{n}\right)^k$$

$$\lim_{n\to\infty} \frac{n\,(n-1)\,(n-2)\ldots(n-k)(n-k-1)}{(n-k)\,(n-k-1)\ldots(1)} \left(\frac{1}{n}\right)^k$$

$$\lim_{n\to\infty} \frac{n\,(n-1)\,(n-2)\ldots(n-k+1)}{n^k}. \tag{12.6}$$

As $n \to \infty$, then $k$ terms tend to 1.
Equation (12.6) can be written as:

$$\lim_{n\to\infty} \frac{n(n-1)(n-2)\ldots(n-k+1)}{n^k} \left(\frac{n}{n}\right)\left(\frac{n-1}{n}\right)\left(\frac{n-2}{n}\right)\ldots\left(\frac{n-k+1}{n}\right). \tag{12.7}$$

The second step is to take the limit of the middle term in (12.5):

$$\lim_{n\to\infty} \left(1 - \frac{\lambda}{n}\right)^n. \tag{12.8}$$

Since $e = 2.718$, then

$$e = \lim_{x\to\infty} \left(1 - \frac{1}{x}\right)^x. \tag{12.9}$$

Let $x = -\frac{n}{\lambda}$.
Substitute for $x$ into (12.8); then we have

$$\lim_{n\to\infty} \left(1 - \frac{\lambda}{n}\right)^n = \lim_{x\to\infty} \left(1 - \frac{1}{x}\right)^{x(-\lambda)} = e^{-\lambda}. \tag{12.10}$$

Take the limit of the last term of the RHS of (12.5):

$$\lim_{n\to\infty} \left(1 - \frac{\lambda}{n}\right)^{-k}. \tag{12.11}$$

As $n \to \infty$, then $(1)^{-k}$ tends to 1.

Putting all the results (12.7), (12.10) and (12.11) together into (12.5), we have

$$\lim_{n \to \infty} P(X = k) = \frac{\lambda^k}{k!} \lim_{n \to \infty} \frac{n!}{(n-k)!} \left(\frac{1}{n}\right)^k \left(1 - \frac{\lambda}{n}\right)^n \left(1 - \frac{\lambda}{n}\right)^{-k}$$

$$= \left(\frac{\lambda^k}{k!}\right) (1) \left(e^{-\lambda}\right) (1). \tag{12.12}$$

Therefore, $P(\lambda, k) = \left(\frac{\lambda^k e^{-\lambda}}{k!}\right)$.

This gives Poisson distribution with $k$ successes per period given parameter $\lambda$.    □

## Example 12.4

Suppose a random variable $X$ has a binomial distribution with $n = 120$ and $p = 0.01$, and use the Poisson distribution to calculate the following: (a) $P(X = 0)$, (b) $P(X = 1)$, (c) $P(X = 2)$, and (d) $P(X > 2)$.

## Solution:

(a) $\lambda = np = 1.2$.

$$P(X = 0) = \frac{1.2^0 e^{-1.2}}{0!} = 0.3012.$$

(b) $P(X = 1) = \frac{1.2^1 e^{-1.2}}{1!} = 0.3614.$

(c) $P(X = 2) = \frac{1.2^2 e^{-1.2}}{2!} = 0.2169.$

(d) $P(X > 2) = 1 - P(X \leq 2) = 1 - P(X = 0) - P(X = 1) - P(X = 2) = 0.1205.$

## R Codes for Example 12.4

Let's write some short codes in R to solve the Example 12.4 above:

```
# Question 12.4a
n<-120
p<-0.01
lambda = n*p
p0<-ppois(0, lambda, lower = TRUE)
[1] 0.3011942
```

The probability that $P(X = 0)$ is 0.3012:

```
# Question 12.4b
p1<-ppois(1, lambda, lower = TRUE) - p0
[1] 0.3614331
```

The probability that $P(X = 1)$ is 0.3614:

```
# Question 12.4c
p2<-ppois(2, lambda)-ppois(1, lambda)
p2
[1] 0.2168598
```

The probability that $P(X = 2)$ is 0.2169:

```
# Question 12.4d
p.greater2<-1-ppois(2, lambda, lower=TRUE)
p.greater2
[1] 0.1205129
```

The probability that $P(X > 2)$ is 0.1205.

## 12.5 EXERCISES

**12.1.** **(a)** Define the Poission distribution and the properties of the distribution.

**(b)** Show that the mean and the variance of a Poisson distribution are equal.

**(c)** A production manager took a sample of 25 textbooks and examined them for the number of defectives pages. The outcome of his findings is summarized in the table below.

Find the probability of finding a textbook chosen at random that contains two or more defective pages.

| Number of defectives | 0 | 1 | 2 | 3 | 4 | 5 |
|---|---|---|---|---|---|---|
| Frequency | 10 | 4 | 3 | 2 | 3 | 3 |

**12.2.** **(a)** Show that the Poisson $(\theta)$ is an approximation to the binomial $(n, p)$ as $n \to \infty$ and $p \to 0$.

**(b)** Consider a random variable $X$ that has a binomial distribution with $n = 100$ and $p = 0.005$. Use the Poisson distribution to calculate the following: (i) $P(X = 0)$, (ii) $P(X = 1)$, and (iii) $P(X > 1)$.

**12.3.** **(a)** Explain the area of life that Poisson process be applied.

**(b)** The ABC company supplies a supermarket with some groceries weekly. Experience has shown that 3% of the total supply in a given week of the groceries is defective. If the manager of the supermarket decides to check the number of defective items for a particular grocery and he took a sample of 105 items, what is the probability that: (i) none of the product is defective? (ii) one of the products is defective? (iii) 2 or more of the products are defective?

**12.4.** A specialist hospital recorded 200 deliveries in every 30 days and the management of the hospital observed that most of the deliveries took place in the early hours of the day, between 12:00 AM and 3:00 AM. Therefore, the management decided to make as many staff as possible available during these time periods to show their dedication to work. Using the Poisson distribution, find the probability of delivering: (a) no baby, (b) one baby, (c) two babies, and (d) three babies in the early hours of the day. Hence, how many days in a 30-day time period would 4 or more deliveries are expected?

**12.5.** An insurance company sells a special life insurance policy to people that are over the age of 50. The actuarial probability that somebody of age 50 and above will die within one year of the policy is 0.0008. If the special life insurance policy is sold to 7,500 people of the same age group, this is an indication that there is possibility that 6 people aged 50 years or older will die within the next year. What is the probability that the insurance company will pay exactly 6 claims on the 7,500 policies sold in the next year?

**12.6.** A car dealer claimed that he sold an average of three new brand cars per week. Assuming that the sales follow a Poisson distribution, what is the probability that: (a) he will sell exactly three new cars, (b) less than three new cars, or (c) more than three new cars in a given week?

CHAPTER 13

# Uniform Distributions

## 13.1  UNIFORM DISTRIBUTION AND ITS PROPERTIES

Let $X$ be a continuous random variable. Then $X$ is said to be a uniform distribution over the interval $[a, b]$ if its probability density function is defined as:

$$f(x) = \frac{1}{b-a}, \quad a \leq x \leq b.$$

The uniform distribution is denoted as $X \sim U(a, b)$. The uniform distribution is also known as **rectangular distribution**.

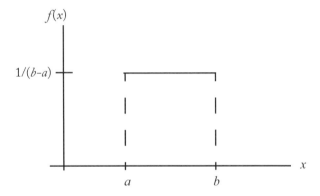

Figure 13.1: A uniform distribution.

Figure 13.1 shows a rectangle with the length of the base $(b - a)$ and a height of $\frac{1}{b-a}$. The total area under the curve of pdf is the product of the height of the rectangle and length of the base, thus the total area is 1. The area under $f(x)$ and between the points $a$ and $b$ is expected to be 1 and $f(x) > 0$, therefore, $f(x)$ is a probability density function. There is an infinite number of possible values of $a$ and $b$, thus there is an infinite number of possible uniform distributions. The commonly used continuous uniform distribution is $a = 0$ and $b = 1$. Uniform distribution is useful when every variable has an equal or exact chance of happening.

## 13.2  MEAN AND VARIANCE OF A UNIFORM DISTRIBUTION

We shall derive the mean and then the variance of a uniform distribution in this section.

**Mean**

The expected value of $X$

$$E(x) = \int_a^b x f(x)\, dx.$$

Substituting for $f(x)$ yields

$$E(x) = \int_a^b \frac{x}{b-a}\, dx.$$

Solving the integral yields

$$E(x) = \left[ \frac{x^2}{2(b-a)} \right]_a^b$$

$$E(x) = \left[ \frac{b^2}{2(b-a)} - \frac{a^2}{2(b-a)} \right] = \frac{b^2 - a^2}{2(b-a)}$$

$$E(x) = \frac{(b+a)(b-a)}{2(b-a)} = \frac{(b+a)}{2}.$$

So the mean is $\frac{(b+a)}{2}$ and it is an average of the two limits ($a$ and $b$).

**Variance**

The variance of a uniform distribution is derived as follows:

$$Var(x) = E(x^2) - (E(x))^2$$

$$E(x^2) = \int_a^b x^2 f(x)\, dx$$

$$E(x^2) = \int_a^b x^2 \frac{1}{b-a}\, dx$$

$$E(x^2) = \frac{1}{b-a} \int_a^b x^2 dx.$$

Solving the integral we get

$$E(x^2) = \frac{1}{b-a} \left[ \frac{x^3}{3} \right]_a^b$$

$$E(x^2) = \frac{1}{3(b-a)} [x^3]_a^b$$

$$E(x^2) = \frac{1}{3(b-a)} [b^3 - a^3],$$

since $[b^3 - a^3] = (b^2 + ab + a^2)(b - a)$.

Then, $E\left(x^2\right) = \frac{1}{3(b-a)}\left[(b^2 + ab + a^2)(b - a)\right]$

$$E\left(x^2\right) = \frac{1}{3}\left[(b^2 + ab + a^2)\right],$$

since

$$Var(x) = E\left(x^2\right) - (E\left(x\right))^2.$$

Then,

$$Var(x) = \frac{1}{3}\left[(b^2 + ab + a^2)\right] - \left(\frac{(b + a)}{2}\right)^2$$

$$Var(x) = \frac{(b^2 + ab + a^2)}{3} - \frac{(b + a)^2}{4}$$

$$Var(x) = \frac{4(b^2 + ab + a^2) - 3(b + a)^2}{12}$$

$$Var(x) = \frac{4b^2 + 4ab + 4a^2 - 3b^2 - 6ab - 3a^2}{12}$$

$$Var(x) = \frac{b^2 - 2ab + a^2}{12}$$

$$Var(x) = \frac{(b - a)^2}{12}.$$

Hence, the variance of a uniform distribution is $\frac{(b-a)^2}{12}$. That means, the square of the difference of point $a$ and $b$ divided by 12.

**Example 13.1**

Upon arriving at his office building, John wanted to take an elevator to the 10th floor where his office is located. Due to the congestion of the building, it takes between 0 and 60 s before the elevator arrives at the ground floor. Assuming that the arrival of the elevator to the ground floor is uniformly distributed. (a) What is the probability that the elevator takes less than 15 s to arrive at the ground floor? (b) Find the mean of the arrival of the elevator to the ground floor. (c) Find the standard deviation of the arrival of the elevator to the ground floor.

**Solution:**

(a) Let the intervals in seconds be $a = 0$, $b = 60$, and $c = 15$.

$$P\,(0 \le x \le 15) = \int_0^{15} \frac{1}{b-a}\,dx$$

$$P\,(0 \le x \le 15) = \int_0^{15} \frac{1}{60-0}\,dx$$

$$P\,(0 \le x \le 15) = \left[\frac{x}{60}\right]_0^{15}$$

$$P\,(0 \le x \le 15) = \left[\frac{15-0}{60}\right] = 0.25.$$

The possibility that the elevator will arrive in 15 s is one fourth of the time.
(b) $mean = E\,(x) = \frac{(b+a)}{2}$.

$$E\,(x) = \frac{(60+0)}{2} = 30 \text{ s}.$$

The mean arrival time is 30 s.
(c) $Var\,(x) = \frac{(b-a)^2}{12} = \frac{(60-0)^2}{12} = \frac{60^2}{12}.$

$$SD\,(x) = \sqrt{\frac{60^2}{12}} = \frac{60}{\sqrt{12}} = 17.32 \text{ s}.$$

The standard deviation is just over 17 s.

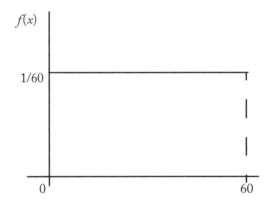

Figure 13.2: Interval in seconds.

### R Codes of a Uniform Distribution
The distribution function of a uniform distribution in R is generated by function *punif*. The format is:

```
punif(q, min = 0, max = 1, lower.tail = TRUE, log.p = FALSE)
```

where

|  |  |
|---|---|
| *q* | vector of quintiles |
| *min* | lower limit of the distribution |
| *max* | upper limit of the distribution |
| *lower.tail* | logical; if TRUE (default), probabilities are $P[X \leq x]$, otherwise, $P[X > x]$ |
| *log.p* | logical; if TRUE, probabilities $p$ are given as $\log(p)$. |

The R code that provides the solutions to Example 13.1 is as follows.

# *Solution to Example 13.1a*

```
punif(15,min=0,max=60)
[1] 0.25
```

The probability that the elevator will arrive in 15 s is 0.25.

# *Solution to Example 13.1b*

```
min<-0
max<-60
punif(15,min=0,max=60)
```

# *Solution to Example 13.1c*

```
mean.x<-(max+min)/2
mean.x
[1] 30
```

The mean arrival time is 30 s.

# *Solution to Example 13.1d*

```
var.x<-((max-min)**2)/12
sd.x<-sqrt(var.x)
sd.x
[1] 17.32051
```

The standard deviation is about 17 s.

## Example 13.2

In a debate competition that consists of 10 participants, the moderator gave each participant 5 min to talk on the debate topic. (a) Find the probability that the participants will finish their talk within 3 min and 30 s. (b) How many of these participants can finish up the talk within 3 min and 30 s?

**Solution:**

Let's convert all the time interval to seconds.

Interval (in second) of probability distribution $= [0, 300]$.

$$f(x) = \frac{1}{b-a} = \frac{1}{300}$$

$$P(0 \leq x \leq 210) = \int_0^{210} \frac{1}{300} dx$$

$$P(0 \leq x \leq 210) = \left[\frac{x}{300}\right]_0^{210}$$

$$P(0 \leq x \leq 210) = \left[\frac{210}{300}\right] = 0.7.$$

Therefore, the probability that the participants will finish their talk within 3 min and 30 s is 0.7. The number of participants that can finish up the talk within 3 min and 30 s is: $0.7 \times 10 = 7$ participants.

**R Codes**

*# Solution to Example 13.2a*

```
p.210<-punif(210,min=0,max=300)
p.210
[1] 0.7
```

The possibility that the participants will finish their talk within 3 min and 30 s is 0.7.

*# Solution to Example 13.2b*

```
n.participants<- p.210*10
n.participants
[1] 7
```

Thus, 7 participants can finish up the talk within 3 min and 30 s.

**Example 13.3**

Two friends, Peter and Paul, agreed to meet at the school library for a study session. Both of them randomly arrive between 5:45 PM and 6.00 PM. What is the probability that Peter arrives at the venue at least 5 min before Paul?

**Solution:**

Let $x$ be arrival time for Peter and $y$ be arrival time for Paul.

Time interval = 6:00 PM − 5:45 PM = 15 min.

Time interval of probability distribution = $[0, 15]$.

$$f(x) = \frac{1}{b-a} = \frac{1}{15}$$

$$P(x \geq 5) = \int_{5}^{15} \frac{1}{15} dx$$

$$P(x \geq 5) = \left[\frac{x}{15}\right]_{5}^{15}$$

$$P(x \geq 5) = \frac{15}{15} - \frac{5}{15} = \frac{10}{15} = 0.67.$$

The possibility that Peter arrives at the venue at least 5 min before Paul is 0.67.

R Codes

*# Solution to Example 13.3*

```
p.greater5<-1-punif(5,min=0,max=15)
p.greater5
[1] 0.6666667
```

This result (0.67) gives the possibility of Peter arriving the venue at least 5 min before Paul.

**Example 13.4**

A filling station manager claimed that the minimum volume of PMS sold per day is 5,000 L and the maximum of the product sold is 6,500 L per daily. Assume that the service at the filling station is uniform distribution. Find the probability that the volume of the product to be sold per day will fall between 5,500 and 6,200 L.

**Solution:**

Given $a = 5,000$ and $b = 6,500$,

$$f(x) = \frac{1}{b-a} = \frac{1}{1500}$$

$$P(5500 \leq x \leq 6200) = \int_{5500}^{6200} \frac{1}{1500} dx$$

$$P(5500 \leq x \leq 6500) = \left[\frac{x}{1500}\right]_{5500}^{6200}$$

$$P(5500 \leq x \leq 6500) = \frac{6200}{1500} - \frac{5500}{1500} = 0.47.$$

R Codes

*# Solution to Example 13.4*

```
p.6200<-punif(6200,min=5000,max=6500)
[1] 0.8
```

The probability that the volume of the product to be sold per day is 6,200 L is 0.8.

```
p.5500<-punif(5500,min=5000,max=6500)
[1] 0.3333333
```

The probability that the volume of the product to be sold per day is 5,500 L is 0.33.

```
btw5500_6200<-p.6200-p.5500
btw5500_6200
[1] 0.4666667
```

The probability that the volume of the product to be sold per day will fall between 5,500 and 6,200 L is 0.47; this is the difference in the probability of sale of 6,200 L and 5,500 L.

## 13.3  EXERCISES

**13.1.** **(a)** Define the continous uniform distribution

**(b)** Suppose $X$ has a uniform distribution on the interval $[10, 50]$. That is, $X \sim U(10, 50)$. Find the probability that: (i) $P(X \leq 25)$, (ii) $P(20 \leq X \leq 32)$, and (iii) $P(X \geq 32)$.

**13.2.** **(a)** Let $X \sim U(\alpha, \beta)$ and show that the mean of a uniform distribution is $\frac{(\beta+\alpha)}{2}$ and variance $\frac{(\beta-\alpha)^2}{12}$.

**(b)** If $f(x) = 3x^2, 0 \leq x \leq 2$. Find the expected of $X$.

**13.3.** The waiting time for a bus to arrive at a bus stop is 10 min. Find the probability that a bus will come within 7 min of waiting at the bus stop. Asume that the waiting time is uniformly distributed.

**13.4.** A recruitment agency conducted an interview for 20 job seekers and scheduled 5 min for each of the job seekers to express themselves on what changes and contributions they could bring into the company to which they were applying. Find the probability that: (a) the job seekers finish within 3 min, and (b) the job seekers finish after 3 min. (c) How many of these job seekers can express themselves for more than 3 min?

**13.5.** Suppose $X \sim U(2, 10)$. (a) What is the probability density function $f(x)$ of $X$? (b) Sketch the probability density function $f(x)$ of $X$. (c) What is $P(5 \leq X \leq 10)$? (d) What is $E\left(2X^2 - X\right)$?

# APPENDIX A

# Tables

We provide tables in the following pages.

Standard Normal Distribution Values ($z \leq 0$)

| $z$ | 0.00 | 0.01 | 0.02 | 0.03 | 0.04 | 0.05 | 0.06 | 0.07 | 0.08 | 0.09 |
|------|---------|---------|---------|---------|---------|---------|---------|---------|---------|---------|
| 0.0 | 0.50000 | 0.49601 | 0.49202 | 0.48803 | 0.48405 | 0.48006 | 0.47608 | 0.47210 | 0.46812 | 0.46414 |
| 0.1 | 0.46017 | 0.45621 | 0.45224 | 0.44828 | 0.44433 | 0.44038 | 0.43644 | 0.43251 | 0.42858 | 0.42466 |
| 0.2 | 0.42074 | 0.41683 | 0.41294 | 0.40905 | 0.40517 | 0.40129 | 0.39743 | 0.39358 | 0.38974 | 0.38591 |
| 0.3 | 0.38209 | 0.37828 | 0.37448 | 0.37070 | 0.36693 | 0.36317 | 0.35942 | 0.35569 | 0.35197 | 0.34827 |
| 0.4 | 0.34458 | 0.34090 | 0.33724 | 0.33360 | 0.32997 | 0.32636 | 0.32276 | 0.31918 | 0.31561 | 0.31207 |
| 0.5 | 0.30854 | 0.30503 | 0.30153 | 0.29806 | 0.29460 | 0.29116 | 0.28774 | 0.28434 | 0.28096 | 0.27760 |
| 0.6 | 0.27425 | 0.27093 | 0.26763 | 0.26435 | 0.26109 | 0.25785 | 0.25463 | 0.25143 | 0.24825 | 0.24510 |
| 0.7 | 0.24196 | 0.23885 | 0.23576 | 0.23270 | 0.22965 | 0.22663 | 0.22363 | 0.22065 | 0.21770 | 0.21476 |
| 0.8 | 0.21186 | 0.20897 | 0.20611 | 0.20327 | 0.20045 | 0.19766 | 0.19489 | 0.19215 | 0.18943 | 0.18673 |
| 0.9 | 0.18406 | 0.18141 | 0.17879 | 0.17619 | 0.17361 | 0.17106 | 0.16853 | 0.16602 | 0.16354 | 0.16109 |
| 1.0 | 0.15866 | 0.15625 | 0.15386 | 0.15151 | 0.14917 | 0.14686 | 0.14457 | 0.14231 | 0.14007 | 0.13786 |
| 1.1 | 0.13567 | 0.13350 | 0.13136 | 0.12924 | 0.12714 | 0.12507 | 0.12302 | 0.12100 | 0.11900 | 0.11702 |
| 1.2 | 0.11507 | 0.11314 | 0.11123 | 0.10935 | 0.10749 | 0.10565 | 0.10384 | 0.10204 | 0.10027 | 0.09853 |
| 1.3 | 0.09680 | 0.09510 | 0.09342 | 0.09176 | 0.09012 | 0.08851 | 0.08692 | 0.08534 | 0.08379 | 0.08226 |
| 1.4 | 0.08076 | 0.07927 | 0.07780 | 0.07636 | 0.07493 | 0.07353 | 0.07215 | 0.07078 | 0.06944 | 0.06811 |
| 1.5 | 0.06681 | 0.06552 | 0.06426 | 0.06301 | 0.06178 | 0.06057 | 0.05938 | 0.05821 | 0.05705 | 0.05592 |
| 1.6 | 0.05480 | 0.05370 | 0.05262 | 0.05155 | 0.05050 | 0.04947 | 0.04846 | 0.04746 | 0.04648 | 0.04551 |
| 1.7 | 0.04457 | 0.04363 | 0.04272 | 0.04182 | 0.04093 | 0.04006 | 0.03920 | 0.03836 | 0.03754 | 0.03673 |
| 1.8 | 0.03593 | 0.03515 | 0.03438 | 0.03363 | 0.03288 | 0.03216 | 0.03144 | 0.03074 | 0.03005 | 0.02938 |
| 1.9 | 0.02872 | 0.02807 | 0.02743 | 0.02680 | 0.02619 | 0.02559 | 0.02500 | 0.02442 | 0.02385 | 0.02330 |
| 2.0 | 0.02275 | 0.02222 | 0.02169 | 0.02118 | 0.02068 | 0.02018 | 0.01970 | 0.01923 | 0.01876 | 0.01831 |
| 2.1 | 0.01786 | 0.01743 | 0.01700 | 0.01659 | 0.01618 | 0.01578 | 0.01539 | 0.01500 | 0.01463 | 0.01426 |
| 2.2 | 0.01390 | 0.01355 | 0.01321 | 0.01287 | 0.01255 | 0.01222 | 0.01191 | 0.01160 | 0.01130 | 0.01101 |
| 2.3 | 0.01072 | 0.01044 | 0.01017 | 0.00990 | 0.00964 | 0.00939 | 0.00914 | 0.00889 | 0.00866 | 0.00842 |
| 2.4 | 0.00820 | 0.00798 | 0.00776 | 0.00755 | 0.00734 | 0.00714 | 0.00695 | 0.00676 | 0.00657 | 0.00639 |
| 2.5 | 0.00621 | 0.00604 | 0.00587 | 0.00570 | 0.00554 | 0.00539 | 0.00523 | 0.00509 | 0.00494 | 0.00480 |
| 2.6 | 0.00466 | 0.00453 | 0.00440 | 0.00427 | 0.00415 | 0.00403 | 0.00391 | 0.00379 | 0.00368 | 0.00357 |
| 2.7 | 0.00347 | 0.00336 | 0.00326 | 0.00317 | 0.00307 | 0.00298 | 0.00289 | 0.00280 | 0.00272 | 0.00264 |
| 2.8 | 0.00256 | 0.00248 | 0.00240 | 0.00233 | 0.00226 | 0.00219 | 0.00212 | 0.00205 | 0.00199 | 0.00193 |
| 2.9 | 0.00187 | 0.00181 | 0.00175 | 0.00170 | 0.00164 | 0.00159 | 0.00154 | 0.00149 | 0.00144 | 0.00140 |
| 3.0 | 0.00135 | 0.00131 | 0.00126 | 0.00122 | 0.00118 | 0.00114 | 0.00111 | 0.00107 | 0.00104 | 0.00100 |
| 3.1 | 0.00097 | 0.00094 | 0.00090 | 0.00087 | 0.00085 | 0.00082 | 0.00079 | 0.00076 | 0.00074 | 0.00071 |
| 3.2 | 0.00069 | 0.00066 | 0.00064 | 0.00062 | 0.00060 | 0.00058 | 0.00056 | 0.00054 | 0.00052 | 0.00050 |
| 3.3 | 0.00048 | 0.00047 | 0.00045 | 0.00043 | 0.00042 | 0.00040 | 0.00039 | 0.00038 | 0.00036 | 0.00035 |
| 3.4 | 0.00034 | 0.00033 | 0.00031 | 0.00030 | 0.00029 | 0.00028 | 0.00027 | 0.00026 | 0.00025 | 0.00024 |
| 3.5 | 0.00023 | 0.00022 | 0.00022 | 0.00021 | 0.00020 | 0.00019 | 0.00019 | 0.00018 | 0.00017 | 0.00017 |

Standard Normal Distribution Values ($z \geq 0$)

| $z$ | 0.00 | 0.01 | 0.02 | 0.03 | 0.04 | 0.05 | 0.06 | 0.07 | 0.08 | 0.09 |
|---|---|---|---|---|---|---|---|---|---|---|
| 0.0 | 0.50000 | 0.50399 | 0.50798 | 0.51197 | 0.51595 | 0.51994 | 0.52392 | 0.52790 | 0.53188 | 0.53586 |
| 0.1 | 0.53983 | 0.54380 | 0.54776 | 0.55172 | 0.55567 | 0.55962 | 0.56356 | 0.56749 | 0.57142 | 0.57535 |
| 0.2 | 0.57926 | 0.58317 | 0.58706 | 0.59095 | 0.59483 | 0.59871 | 0.60257 | 0.60642 | 0.61026 | 0.61409 |
| 0.3 | 0.61791 | 0.62172 | 0.62552 | 0.62930 | 0.63307 | 0.63683 | 0.64058 | 0.64431 | 0.64803 | 0.65173 |
| 0.4 | 0.65542 | 0.65910 | 0.66276 | 0.66640 | 0.67003 | 0.67364 | 0.67724 | 0.68082 | 0.68439 | 0.68793 |
| 0.5 | 0.69146 | 0.69497 | 0.69847 | 0.70194 | 0.70540 | 0.70884 | 0.71226 | 0.71566 | 0.71904 | 0.72240 |
| 0.6 | 0.72575 | 0.72907 | 0.73237 | 0.73565 | 0.73891 | 0.74215 | 0.74537 | 0.74857 | 0.75175 | 0.75490 |
| 0.7 | 0.75804 | 0.76115 | 0.76424 | 0.76730 | 0.77035 | 0.77337 | 0.77637 | 0.77935 | 0.78230 | 0.78524 |
| 0.8 | 0.78814 | 0.79103 | 0.79389 | 0.79673 | 0.79955 | 0.80234 | 0.80511 | 0.80785 | 0.81057 | 0.81327 |
| 0.9 | 0.81594 | 0.81859 | 0.82121 | 0.82381 | 0.82639 | 0.82894 | 0.83147 | 0.83398 | 0.83646 | 0.83891 |
| 1.0 | 0.84134 | 0.84375 | 0.84614 | 0.84849 | 0.85083 | 0.85314 | 0.85543 | 0.85769 | 0.85993 | 0.86214 |
| 1.1 | 0.86433 | 0.86650 | 0.86864 | 0.87076 | 0.87286 | 0.87493 | 0.87698 | 0.87900 | 0.88100 | 0.88298 |
| 1.2 | 0.88493 | 0.88686 | 0.88877 | 0.89065 | 0.89251 | 0.89435 | 0.89617 | 0.89796 | 0.89973 | 0.90147 |
| 1.3 | 0.90320 | 0.90490 | 0.90658 | 0.90824 | 0.90988 | 0.91149 | 0.91308 | 0.91466 | 0.91621 | 0.91774 |
| 1.4 | 0.91924 | 0.92073 | 0.92220 | 0.92364 | 0.92507 | 0.92647 | 0.92785 | 0.92922 | 0.93056 | 0.93189 |
| 1.5 | 0.93319 | 0.93448 | 0.93574 | 0.93699 | 0.93822 | 0.93943 | 0.94062 | 0.94179 | 0.94295 | 0.94408 |
| 1.6 | 0.94520 | 0.94630 | 0.94738 | 0.94845 | 0.94950 | 0.95053 | 0.95154 | 0.95254 | 0.95352 | 0.95449 |
| 1.7 | 0.95543 | 0.95637 | 0.95728 | 0.95818 | 0.95907 | 0.95994 | 0.96080 | 0.96164 | 0.96246 | 0.96327 |
| 1.8 | 0.96407 | 0.96485 | 0.96562 | 0.96638 | 0.96712 | 0.96784 | 0.96856 | 0.96926 | 0.96995 | 0.97062 |
| 1.9 | 0.97128 | 0.97193 | 0.97257 | 0.97320 | 0.97381 | 0.97441 | 0.97500 | 0.97558 | 0.97615 | 0.97670 |
| 2.0 | 0.97725 | 0.97778 | 0.97831 | 0.97882 | 0.97932 | 0.97982 | 0.98030 | 0.98077 | 0.98124 | 0.98169 |
| 2.1 | 0.98214 | 0.98257 | 0.98300 | 0.98341 | 0.98382 | 0.98422 | 0.98461 | 0.98500 | 0.98537 | 0.98574 |
| 2.2 | 0.98610 | 0.98645 | 0.98679 | 0.98713 | 0.98745 | 0.98778 | 0.98809 | 0.98840 | 0.98870 | 0.98899 |
| 2.3 | 0.98928 | 0.98956 | 0.98983 | 0.99010 | 0.99036 | 0.99061 | 0.99086 | 0.99111 | 0.99134 | 0.99158 |
| 2.4 | 0.99180 | 0.99202 | 0.99224 | 0.99245 | 0.99266 | 0.99286 | 0.99305 | 0.99324 | 0.99343 | 0.99361 |
| 2.5 | 0.99379 | 0.99396 | 0.99413 | 0.99430 | 0.99446 | 0.99461 | 0.99477 | 0.99492 | 0.99506 | 0.99520 |
| 2.6 | 0.99534 | 0.99547 | 0.99560 | 0.99573 | 0.99585 | 0.99598 | 0.99609 | 0.99621 | 0.99632 | 0.99643 |
| 2.7 | 0.99653 | 0.99664 | 0.99674 | 0.99683 | 0.99693 | 0.99702 | 0.99711 | 0.99720 | 0.99728 | 0.99736 |
| 2.8 | 0.99744 | 0.99752 | 0.99760 | 0.99767 | 0.99774 | 0.99781 | 0.99788 | 0.99795 | 0.99801 | 0.99807 |
| 2.9 | 0.99813 | 0.99819 | 0.99825 | 0.99831 | 0.99836 | 0.99841 | 0.99846 | 0.99851 | 0.99856 | 0.99861 |
| 3.0 | 0.99865 | 0.99869 | 0.99874 | 0.99878 | 0.99882 | 0.99886 | 0.99889 | 0.99893 | 0.99896 | 0.99900 |
| 3.1 | 0.99903 | 0.99906 | 0.99910 | 0.99913 | 0.99916 | 0.99918 | 0.99921 | 0.99924 | 0.99926 | 0.99929 |
| 3.2 | 0.99931 | 0.99934 | 0.99936 | 0.99938 | 0.99940 | 0.99942 | 0.99944 | 0.99946 | 0.99948 | 0.99950 |
| 3.3 | 0.99952 | 0.99953 | 0.99955 | 0.99957 | 0.99958 | 0.99960 | 0.99961 | 0.99962 | 0.99964 | 0.99965 |
| 3.4 | 0.99966 | 0.99968 | 0.99969 | 0.99970 | 0.99971 | 0.99972 | 0.99973 | 0.99974 | 0.99975 | 0.99976 |
| 3.5 | 0.99977 | 0.99978 | 0.99978 | 0.99979 | 0.99980 | 0.99981 | 0.99981 | 0.99982 | 0.99983 | 0.99983 |

Student's $t$-distribution

The table gives the values of $t_{\alpha;\,\nu}$ where
$\Pr(T_\nu > t_{\alpha;\,\nu}) = \alpha$, with $\nu$ degrees of freedom

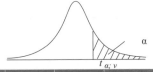

| α \ ν | 0.1 | 0.05 | 0.025 | 0.01 | 0.005 | 0.001 | 0.0005 |
|---|---|---|---|---|---|---|---|
| 1 | 3.078 | 6.314 | 12.076 | 31.821 | 63.657 | 318.310 | 636.620 |
| 2 | 1.886 | 2.920 | 4.303 | 6.965 | 9.925 | 22.326 | 31.598 |
| 3 | 1.638 | 2.353 | 3.182 | 4.541 | 5.841 | 10.213 | 12.924 |
| 4 | 1.533 | 2.132 | 2.776 | 3.747 | 4.604 | 7.173 | 8.610 |
| 5 | 1.476 | 2.015 | 2.571 | 3.365 | 4.032 | 5.893 | 6.869 |
| 6 | 1.440 | 1.943 | 2.447 | 3.143 | 3.707 | 5.208 | 5.959 |
| 7 | 1.415 | 1.895 | 2.365 | 2.998 | 3.499 | 4.785 | 5.408 |
| 8 | 1.397 | 1.860 | 2.306 | 2.896 | 3.355 | 4.501 | 5.041 |
| 9 | 1.383 | 1.833 | 2.262 | 2.821 | 3.250 | 4.297 | 4.781 |
| 10 | 1.372 | 1.812 | 2.228 | 2.764 | 3.169 | 4.144 | 4.587 |
| 11 | 1.363 | 1.796 | 2.201 | 2.718 | 3.106 | 4.025 | 4.437 |
| 12 | 1.356 | 1.782 | 2.179 | 2.681 | 3.055 | 3.930 | 4.318 |
| 13 | 1.350 | 1.771 | 2.160 | 2.650 | 3.012 | 3.852 | 4.221 |
| 14 | 1.345 | 1.761 | 2.145 | 2.624 | 2.977 | 3.787 | 4.140 |
| 15 | 1.341 | 1.753 | 2.131 | 2.602 | 2.947 | 3.733 | 4.073 |
| 16 | 1.337 | 1.746 | 2.120 | 2.583 | 2.921 | 3.686 | 4.015 |
| 17 | 1.333 | 1.740 | 2.110 | 2.567 | 2.898 | 3.646 | 3.965 |
| 18 | 1.330 | 1.734 | 2.101 | 2.552 | 2.878 | 3.610 | 3.922 |
| 19 | 1.328 | 1.729 | 2.093 | 2.539 | 2.861 | 3.579 | 3.883 |
| 20 | 1.325 | 1.725 | 2.086 | 2.528 | 2.845 | 3.552 | 3.850 |
| 21 | 1.323 | 1.721 | 2.080 | 2.518 | 2.831 | 3.527 | 3.819 |
| 22 | 1.321 | 1.717 | 2.074 | 2.508 | 2.819 | 3.505 | 3.792 |
| 23 | 1.319 | 1.714 | 2.069 | 2.500 | 2.807 | 3.485 | 3.767 |
| 24 | 1.318 | 1.711 | 2.064 | 2.492 | 2.797 | 3.467 | 3.745 |
| 25 | 1.316 | 1.708 | 2.060 | 2.485 | 2.787 | 3.450 | 3.725 |
| 26 | 1.315 | 1.706 | 2.056 | 2.479 | 2.779 | 3.435 | 3.707 |
| 27 | 1.314 | 1.703 | 2.052 | 2.473 | 2.771 | 3.421 | 3.690 |
| 28 | 1.313 | 1.701 | 2.048 | 2.467 | 2.763 | 3.408 | 3.674 |
| 29 | 1.311 | 1.699 | 2.045 | 2.462 | 2.756 | 3.396 | 3.659 |
| 30 | 1.310 | 1.697 | 2.042 | 2.457 | 2.750 | 3.385 | 3.646 |
| 40 | 1.303 | 1.684 | 2.021 | 2.423 | 2.704 | 3.307 | 3.551 |
| 60 | 1.296 | 1.671 | 2.000 | 2.390 | 2.660 | 3.232 | 3.460 |
| 120 | 1.289 | 1.658 | 1.980 | 2.358 | 2.617 | 3.160 | 3.373 |
| ∞ | 1.282 | 1.645 | 1.960 | 2.326 | 2.576 | 3.090 | 3.291 |

# F-distribution (Upper tail probability = 0.05) Numerator df = 1 to 10

| df2\df1 | 1 | 2 | 3 | 4 | 5 | 6 | 7 | 8 | 10 |
|---|---|---|---|---|---|---|---|---|---|
| 1 | 161.448 | 199.500 | 215.707 | 224.583 | 230.162 | 233.986 | 236.768 | 238.883 | 241.882 |
| 2 | 18.513 | 19.000 | 19.164 | 19.247 | 19.296 | 19.330 | 19.353 | 19.371 | 19.396 |
| 3 | 10.128 | 9.552 | 9.277 | 9.117 | 9.013 | 8.941 | 8.887 | 8.845 | 8.786 |
| 4 | 7.709 | 6.944 | 6.591 | 6.388 | 6.256 | 6.163 | 6.094 | 6.041 | 5.964 |
| 5 | 6.608 | 5.786 | 5.409 | 5.192 | 5.050 | 4.950 | 4.876 | 4.818 | 4.735 |
| 6 | 5.987 | 5.143 | 4.757 | 4.534 | 4.387 | 4.284 | 4.207 | 4.147 | 4.060 |
| 7 | 5.591 | 4.737 | 4.347 | 4.120 | 3.972 | 3.866 | 3.787 | 3.726 | 3.637 |
| 8 | 5.318 | 4.459 | 4.066 | 3.838 | 3.687 | 3.581 | 3.500 | 3.438 | 3.347 |
| 9 | 5.117 | 4.256 | 3.863 | 3.633 | 3.482 | 3.374 | 3.293 | 3.230 | 3.137 |
| 10 | 4.965 | 4.103 | 3.708 | 3.478 | 3.326 | 3.217 | 3.135 | 3.072 | 2.978 |
| 11 | 4.844 | 3.982 | 3.587 | 3.357 | 3.204 | 3.095 | 3.012 | 2.948 | 2.854 |
| 12 | 4.747 | 3.885 | 3.490 | 3.259 | 3.106 | 2.996 | 2.913 | 2.849 | 2.753 |
| 13 | 4.667 | 3.806 | 3.411 | 3.179 | 3.025 | 2.915 | 2.832 | 2.767 | 2.671 |
| 14 | 4.600 | 3.739 | 3.344 | 3.112 | 2.958 | 2.848 | 2.764 | 2.699 | 2.602 |
| 15 | 4.543 | 3.682 | 3.287 | 3.056 | 2.901 | 2.790 | 2.707 | 2.641 | 2.544 |
| 16 | 4.494 | 3.634 | 3.239 | 3.007 | 2.852 | 2.741 | 2.657 | 2.591 | 2.494 |
| 17 | 4.451 | 3.592 | 3.197 | 2.965 | 2.810 | 2.699 | 2.614 | 2.548 | 2.450 |
| 18 | 4.414 | 3.555 | 3.160 | 2.928 | 2.773 | 2.661 | 2.577 | 2.510 | 2.412 |
| 19 | 4.381 | 3.522 | 3.127 | 2.895 | 2.740 | 2.628 | 2.544 | 2.477 | 2.378 |
| 20 | 4.351 | 3.493 | 3.098 | 2.866 | 2.711 | 2.599 | 2.514 | 2.447 | 2.348 |
| 21 | 4.325 | 3.467 | 3.072 | 2.840 | 2.685 | 2.573 | 2.488 | 2.420 | 2.321 |
| 22 | 4.301 | 3.443 | 3.049 | 2.817 | 2.661 | 2.549 | 2.464 | 2.397 | 2.297 |
| 23 | 4.279 | 3.422 | 3.028 | 2.796 | 2.640 | 2.528 | 2.442 | 2.375 | 2.275 |
| 24 | 4.260 | 3.403 | 3.009 | 2.776 | 2.621 | 2.508 | 2.423 | 2.355 | 2.255 |
| 25 | 4.242 | 3.385 | 2.991 | 2.759 | 2.603 | 2.490 | 2.405 | 2.337 | 2.236 |
| 26 | 4.225 | 3.369 | 2.975 | 2.743 | 2.587 | 2.474 | 2.388 | 2.321 | 2.220 |
| 27 | 4.210 | 3.354 | 2.960 | 2.728 | 2.572 | 2.459 | 2.373 | 2.305 | 2.204 |
| 28 | 4.196 | 3.340 | 2.947 | 2.714 | 2.558 | 2.445 | 2.359 | 2.291 | 2.190 |
| 29 | 4.183 | 3.328 | 2.934 | 2.701 | 2.545 | 2.432 | 2.346 | 2.278 | 2.177 |
| 30 | 4.171 | 3.316 | 2.922 | 2.690 | 2.534 | 2.421 | 2.334 | 2.266 | 2.165 |
| 35 | 4.121 | 3.267 | 2.874 | 2.641 | 2.485 | 2.372 | 2.285 | 2.217 | 2.114 |
| 40 | 4.085 | 3.232 | 2.839 | 2.606 | 2.449 | 2.336 | 2.249 | 2.180 | 2.077 |
| 45 | 4.057 | 3.204 | 2.812 | 2.579 | 2.422 | 2.308 | 2.221 | 2.152 | 2.049 |
| 50 | 4.034 | 3.183 | 2.790 | 2.557 | 2.400 | 2.286 | 2.199 | 2.130 | 2.026 |
| 55 | 4.016 | 3.165 | 2.773 | 2.540 | 2.383 | 2.269 | 2.181 | 2.112 | 2.008 |
| 60 | 4.001 | 3.150 | 2.758 | 2.525 | 2.368 | 2.254 | 2.167 | 2.097 | 1.993 |
| 70 | 3.978 | 3.128 | 2.736 | 2.503 | 2.346 | 2.231 | 2.143 | 2.074 | 1.969 |
| 80 | 3.960 | 3.111 | 2.719 | 2.486 | 2.329 | 2.214 | 2.126 | 2.056 | 1.951 |
| 90 | 3.947 | 3.098 | 2.706 | 2.473 | 2.316 | 2.201 | 2.113 | 2.043 | 1.938 |
| 100 | 3.936 | 3.087 | 2.696 | 2.463 | 2.305 | 2.191 | 2.103 | 2.032 | 1.927 |
| 110 | 3.927 | 3.079 | 2.687 | 2.454 | 2.297 | 2.182 | 2.094 | 2.024 | 1.918 |
| 120 | 3.920 | 3.072 | 2.680 | 2.447 | 2.290 | 2.175 | 2.087 | 2.016 | 1.910 |
| 130 | 3.914 | 3.066 | 2.674 | 2.441 | 2.284 | 2.169 | 2.081 | 2.010 | 1.904 |
| 140 | 3.909 | 3.061 | 2.669 | 2.436 | 2.279 | 2.164 | 2.076 | 2.005 | 1.899 |
| 150 | 3.904 | 3.056 | 2.665 | 2.432 | 2.274 | 2.160 | 2.071 | 2.001 | 1.894 |
| 160 | 3.900 | 3.053 | 2.661 | 2.428 | 2.271 | 2.156 | 2.067 | 1.997 | 1.890 |
| 180 | 3.894 | 3.046 | 2.655 | 2.422 | 2.264 | 2.149 | 2.061 | 1.990 | 1.884 |
| 200 | 3.888 | 3.041 | 2.650 | 2.417 | 2.259 | 2.144 | 2.056 | 1.985 | 1.878 |
| 220 | 3.884 | 3.037 | 2.646 | 2.413 | 2.255 | 2.140 | 2.051 | 1.981 | 1.874 |
| 240 | 3.880 | 3.033 | 2.642 | 2.409 | 2.252 | 2.136 | 2.048 | 1.977 | 1.870 |
| 260 | 3.877 | 3.031 | 2.639 | 2.406 | 2.249 | 2.134 | 2.045 | 1.974 | 1.867 |
| 280 | 3.875 | 3.028 | 2.637 | 2.404 | 2.246 | 2.131 | 2.042 | 1.972 | 1.865 |
| 300 | 3.873 | 3.026 | 2.635 | 2.402 | 2.244 | 2.129 | 2.040 | 1.969 | 1.862 |
| 400 | 3.865 | 3.018 | 2.627 | 2.394 | 2.237 | 2.121 | 2.032 | 1.962 | 1.854 |
| 500 | 3.860 | 3.014 | 2.623 | 2.390 | 2.232 | 2.117 | 2.028 | 1.957 | 1.850 |
| 600 | 3.857 | 3.011 | 2.620 | 2.387 | 2.229 | 2.114 | 2.025 | 1.954 | 1.846 |
| 700 | 3.855 | 3.009 | 2.618 | 2.385 | 2.227 | 2.112 | 2.023 | 1.952 | 1.844 |
| 800 | 3.853 | 3.007 | 2.616 | 2.383 | 2.225 | 2.110 | 2.021 | 1.950 | 1.843 |
| 900 | 3.852 | 3.006 | 2.615 | 2.382 | 2.224 | 2.109 | 2.020 | 1.949 | 1.841 |
| 1000 | 3.851 | 3.005 | 2.614 | 2.381 | 2.223 | 2.108 | 2.019 | 1.948 | 1.840 |
| ∞ | 3.841 | 2.996 | 2.605 | 2.372 | 2.214 | 2.099 | 2.010 | 1.938 | 1.831 |

## F-distribution (Upper tail probability = 0.05) Numerator df = 12 to 40

| df2\df1 | 12 | 14 | 16 | 18 | 20 | 24 | 28 | 32 | 36 | 40 |
|---|---|---|---|---|---|---|---|---|---|---|
| 1 | 243.906 | 245.364 | 246.464 | 247.323 | 248.013 | 249.052 | 249.797 | 250.357 | 250.793 | 251.143 |
| 2 | 19.413 | 19.424 | 19.433 | 19.440 | 19.446 | 19.454 | 19.460 | 19.464 | 19.468 | 19.471 |
| 3 | 8.745 | 8.715 | 8.692 | 8.675 | 8.660 | 8.639 | 8.623 | 8.611 | 8.602 | 8.594 |
| 4 | 5.912 | 5.873 | 5.844 | 5.821 | 5.803 | 5.774 | 5.754 | 5.739 | 5.727 | 5.717 |
| 5 | 4.678 | 4.636 | 4.604 | 4.579 | 4.558 | 4.527 | 4.505 | 4.488 | 4.474 | 4.464 |
| 6 | 4.000 | 3.956 | 3.922 | 3.896 | 3.874 | 3.841 | 3.818 | 3.800 | 3.786 | 3.774 |
| 7 | 3.575 | 3.529 | 3.494 | 3.467 | 3.445 | 3.410 | 3.386 | 3.367 | 3.352 | 3.340 |
| 8 | 3.284 | 3.237 | 3.202 | 3.173 | 3.150 | 3.115 | 3.090 | 3.070 | 3.055 | 3.043 |
| 9 | 3.073 | 3.025 | 2.989 | 2.960 | 2.936 | 2.900 | 2.874 | 2.854 | 2.839 | 2.826 |
| 10 | 2.913 | 2.865 | 2.828 | 2.798 | 2.774 | 2.737 | 2.710 | 2.690 | 2.674 | 2.661 |
| 11 | 2.788 | 2.739 | 2.701 | 2.671 | 2.646 | 2.609 | 2.582 | 2.561 | 2.544 | 2.531 |
| 12 | 2.687 | 2.637 | 2.599 | 2.568 | 2.544 | 2.505 | 2.478 | 2.456 | 2.439 | 2.426 |
| 13 | 2.604 | 2.554 | 2.515 | 2.484 | 2.459 | 2.420 | 2.392 | 2.370 | 2.353 | 2.339 |
| 14 | 2.534 | 2.484 | 2.445 | 2.413 | 2.388 | 2.349 | 2.320 | 2.298 | 2.280 | 2.266 |
| 15 | 2.475 | 2.424 | 2.385 | 2.353 | 2.328 | 2.288 | 2.259 | 2.236 | 2.219 | 2.204 |
| 16 | 2.425 | 2.373 | 2.333 | 2.302 | 2.276 | 2.235 | 2.206 | 2.183 | 2.165 | 2.151 |
| 17 | 2.381 | 2.329 | 2.289 | 2.257 | 2.230 | 2.190 | 2.160 | 2.137 | 2.119 | 2.104 |
| 18 | 2.342 | 2.290 | 2.250 | 2.217 | 2.191 | 2.150 | 2.119 | 2.096 | 2.078 | 2.063 |
| 19 | 2.308 | 2.256 | 2.215 | 2.182 | 2.155 | 2.114 | 2.084 | 2.060 | 2.042 | 2.026 |
| 20 | 2.278 | 2.225 | 2.184 | 2.151 | 2.124 | 2.082 | 2.052 | 2.028 | 2.009 | 1.994 |
| 21 | 2.250 | 2.197 | 2.156 | 2.123 | 2.096 | 2.054 | 2.023 | 1.999 | 1.980 | 1.965 |
| 22 | 2.226 | 2.173 | 2.131 | 2.098 | 2.071 | 2.028 | 1.997 | 1.973 | 1.954 | 1.938 |
| 23 | 2.204 | 2.150 | 2.109 | 2.075 | 2.048 | 2.005 | 1.973 | 1.949 | 1.930 | 1.914 |
| 24 | 2.183 | 2.130 | 2.088 | 2.054 | 2.027 | 1.984 | 1.952 | 1.927 | 1.908 | 1.892 |
| 25 | 2.165 | 2.111 | 2.069 | 2.035 | 2.007 | 1.964 | 1.932 | 1.908 | 1.888 | 1.872 |
| 26 | 2.148 | 2.094 | 2.052 | 2.018 | 1.990 | 1.946 | 1.914 | 1.889 | 1.869 | 1.853 |
| 27 | 2.132 | 2.078 | 2.036 | 2.002 | 1.974 | 1.930 | 1.898 | 1.872 | 1.852 | 1.836 |
| 28 | 2.118 | 2.064 | 2.021 | 1.987 | 1.959 | 1.915 | 1.882 | 1.857 | 1.837 | 1.820 |
| 29 | 2.104 | 2.050 | 2.007 | 1.973 | 1.945 | 1.901 | 1.868 | 1.842 | 1.822 | 1.806 |
| 30 | 2.092 | 2.037 | 1.995 | 1.960 | 1.932 | 1.887 | 1.854 | 1.829 | 1.808 | 1.792 |
| 35 | 2.041 | 1.986 | 1.942 | 1.907 | 1.878 | 1.833 | 1.799 | 1.773 | 1.752 | 1.735 |
| 40 | 2.003 | 1.948 | 1.904 | 1.868 | 1.839 | 1.793 | 1.759 | 1.732 | 1.710 | 1.693 |
| 45 | 1.974 | 1.918 | 1.874 | 1.838 | 1.808 | 1.762 | 1.727 | 1.700 | 1.678 | 1.660 |
| 50 | 1.952 | 1.895 | 1.850 | 1.814 | 1.784 | 1.737 | 1.702 | 1.674 | 1.652 | 1.634 |
| 55 | 1.933 | 1.876 | 1.831 | 1.795 | 1.764 | 1.717 | 1.681 | 1.653 | 1.631 | 1.612 |
| 60 | 1.917 | 1.860 | 1.815 | 1.778 | 1.748 | 1.700 | 1.664 | 1.636 | 1.613 | 1.594 |
| 70 | 1.893 | 1.836 | 1.790 | 1.753 | 1.722 | 1.674 | 1.637 | 1.608 | 1.585 | 1.566 |
| 80 | 1.875 | 1.817 | 1.772 | 1.734 | 1.703 | 1.654 | 1.617 | 1.588 | 1.564 | 1.545 |
| 90 | 1.861 | 1.803 | 1.757 | 1.720 | 1.688 | 1.639 | 1.601 | 1.572 | 1.548 | 1.528 |
| 100 | 1.850 | 1.792 | 1.746 | 1.708 | 1.676 | 1.627 | 1.589 | 1.559 | 1.535 | 1.515 |
| 110 | 1.841 | 1.783 | 1.736 | 1.698 | 1.667 | 1.617 | 1.579 | 1.549 | 1.524 | 1.504 |
| 120 | 1.834 | 1.775 | 1.728 | 1.690 | 1.659 | 1.608 | 1.570 | 1.540 | 1.516 | 1.495 |
| 130 | 1.827 | 1.769 | 1.722 | 1.684 | 1.652 | 1.601 | 1.563 | 1.533 | 1.508 | 1.488 |
| 140 | 1.822 | 1.763 | 1.716 | 1.678 | 1.646 | 1.595 | 1.557 | 1.526 | 1.502 | 1.481 |
| 150 | 1.817 | 1.758 | 1.711 | 1.673 | 1.641 | 1.590 | 1.552 | 1.521 | 1.496 | 1.475 |
| 160 | 1.813 | 1.754 | 1.707 | 1.669 | 1.637 | 1.586 | 1.547 | 1.516 | 1.491 | 1.470 |
| 180 | 1.806 | 1.747 | 1.700 | 1.661 | 1.629 | 1.578 | 1.539 | 1.508 | 1.483 | 1.462 |
| 200 | 1.801 | 1.742 | 1.694 | 1.656 | 1.623 | 1.572 | 1.533 | 1.502 | 1.476 | 1.455 |
| 220 | 1.796 | 1.737 | 1.690 | 1.651 | 1.618 | 1.567 | 1.528 | 1.496 | 1.471 | 1.450 |
| 240 | 1.793 | 1.733 | 1.686 | 1.647 | 1.614 | 1.563 | 1.523 | 1.492 | 1.466 | 1.445 |
| 260 | 1.790 | 1.730 | 1.683 | 1.644 | 1.611 | 1.559 | 1.520 | 1.488 | 1.463 | 1.441 |
| 280 | 1.787 | 1.727 | 1.680 | 1.641 | 1.608 | 1.556 | 1.517 | 1.485 | 1.459 | 1.438 |
| 300 | 1.785 | 1.725 | 1.677 | 1.638 | 1.606 | 1.554 | 1.514 | 1.482 | 1.456 | 1.435 |
| 400 | 1.776 | 1.717 | 1.669 | 1.630 | 1.597 | 1.545 | 1.505 | 1.473 | 1.447 | 1.425 |
| 500 | 1.772 | 1.712 | 1.664 | 1.625 | 1.592 | 1.539 | 1.499 | 1.467 | 1.441 | 1.419 |
| 600 | 1.768 | 1.708 | 1.660 | 1.621 | 1.588 | 1.536 | 1.495 | 1.463 | 1.437 | 1.414 |
| 700 | 1.766 | 1.706 | 1.658 | 1.619 | 1.586 | 1.533 | 1.492 | 1.460 | 1.434 | 1.412 |
| 800 | 1.764 | 1.704 | 1.656 | 1.617 | 1.584 | 1.531 | 1.490 | 1.458 | 1.432 | 1.409 |
| 900 | 1.763 | 1.703 | 1.655 | 1.615 | 1.582 | 1.529 | 1.489 | 1.457 | 1.430 | 1.408 |
| 1000 | 1.762 | 1.702 | 1.654 | 1.614 | 1.581 | 1.528 | 1.488 | 1.455 | 1.429 | 1.406 |
| ∞ | 1.752 | 1.692 | 1.644 | 1.604 | 1.571 | 1.517 | 1.476 | 1.444 | 1.417 | 1.394 |

# Cumulative Binomial Distribution - 1

| n | x | .01 | .05 | .10 | .15 | .20 | p .25 | .30 | .35 | .40 | .45 | .50 |
|---|---|-----|-----|-----|-----|-----|-----|-----|-----|-----|-----|-----|
| 2 | 0 | 0.9801 | 0.9025 | 0.8100 | 0.7225 | 0.6400 | 0.5625 | 0.4900 | 0.4225 | 0.3600 | 0.3025 | 0.2500 |
|   | 1 | 0.9999 | 0.9975 | 0.9900 | 0.9775 | 0.9600 | 0.9375 | 0.9100 | 0.8775 | 0.8400 | 0.7975 | 0.7500 |
|   | 2 | 1.0000 | 1.0000 | 1.0000 | 1.0000 | 1.0000 | 1.0000 | 1.0000 | 1.0000 | 1.0000 | 1.0000 | 1.0000 |
| 3 | 0 | 0.97030 | 0.85738 | 0.729 | 0.61413 | 0.512 | 0.42187 | 0.343 | 0.27463 | 0.216 | 0.16638 | 0.125 |
|   | 1 | 0.99970 | 0.99275 | 0.972 | 0.93925 | 0.896 | 0.84375 | 0.784 | 0.71825 | 0.648 | 0.57475 | 0.500 |
|   | 2 | 1.00000 | 0.99988 | 0.999 | 0.99663 | 0.992 | 0.98437 | 0.973 | 0.95713 | 0.936 | 0.90887 | 0.875 |
|   | 3 | 1.00000 | 1.00000 | 1.000 | 1.00000 | 1.000 | 1.00000 | 1.000 | 1.00000 | 1.000 | 1.00000 | 1.000 |
| 4 | 0 | 0.96060 | 0.81451 | 0.6561 | 0.52201 | 0.4096 | 0.31641 | 0.2401 | 0.17851 | 0.1296 | 0.09151 | 0.0625 |
|   | 1 | 0.99941 | 0.98598 | 0.9477 | 0.89048 | 0.8192 | 0.73828 | 0.6517 | 0.56298 | 0.4752 | 0.39098 | 0.3125 |
|   | 2 | 1.00000 | 0.99952 | 0.9963 | 0.98802 | 0.9728 | 0.94922 | 0.9163 | 0.87352 | 0.8208 | 0.75852 | 0.6875 |
|   | 3 | 1.00000 | 0.99999 | 0.9999 | 0.99949 | 0.9984 | 0.99609 | 0.9919 | 0.98499 | 0.9744 | 0.95899 | 0.9375 |
|   | 4 | 1.00000 | 1.00000 | 1.0000 | 1.00000 | 1.0000 | 1.00000 | 1.0000 | 1.00000 | 1.0000 | 1.00000 | 1.0000 |
| 5 | 0 | 0.95099 | 0.77378 | 0.59049 | 0.44371 | 0.32768 | 0.23730 | 0.16807 | 0.11603 | 0.07776 | 0.05033 | 0.03125 |
|   | 1 | 0.99902 | 0.97741 | 0.91854 | 0.83521 | 0.73728 | 0.63281 | 0.52822 | 0.42842 | 0.33696 | 0.25622 | 0.18750 |
|   | 2 | 0.99999 | 0.99884 | 0.99144 | 0.97339 | 0.94208 | 0.89648 | 0.83692 | 0.76483 | 0.68256 | 0.59313 | 0.50000 |
|   | 3 | 1.00000 | 0.99997 | 0.99954 | 0.99777 | 0.99328 | 0.98437 | 0.96922 | 0.94598 | 0.91296 | 0.86878 | 0.81250 |
|   | 4 | 1.00000 | 1.00000 | 0.99999 | 0.99992 | 0.99968 | 0.99902 | 0.99757 | 0.99475 | 0.98976 | 0.98155 | 0.96875 |
|   | 5 | 1.00000 | 1.00000 | 1.00000 | 1.00000 | 1.00000 | 1.00000 | 1.00000 | 1.00000 | 1.00000 | 1.00000 | 1.00000 |
| 6 | 0 | 0.94148 | 0.73509 | 0.53144 | 0.37715 | 0.26214 | 0.17798 | 0.11765 | 0.07542 | 0.04666 | 0.02768 | 0.01563 |
|   | 1 | 0.99854 | 0.96723 | 0.88573 | 0.77648 | 0.65536 | 0.53394 | 0.42017 | 0.31908 | 0.23328 | 0.16357 | 0.10938 |
|   | 2 | 0.99998 | 0.99777 | 0.98415 | 0.95266 | 0.90112 | 0.83057 | 0.74431 | 0.64709 | 0.54432 | 0.44152 | 0.34375 |
|   | 3 | 1.00000 | 0.99991 | 0.99873 | 0.99411 | 0.98304 | 0.96240 | 0.92953 | 0.88258 | 0.82080 | 0.74474 | 0.65625 |
|   | 4 | 1.00000 | 1.00000 | 0.99994 | 0.99960 | 0.99840 | 0.99536 | 0.98906 | 0.97768 | 0.95904 | 0.93080 | 0.89062 |
|   | 5 | 1.00000 | 1.00000 | 1.00000 | 0.99999 | 0.99994 | 0.99976 | 0.99927 | 0.99816 | 0.99590 | 0.99170 | 0.98437 |
|   | 6 | 1.00000 | 1.00000 | 1.00000 | 1.00000 | 1.00000 | 1.00000 | 1.00000 | 1.00000 | 1.00000 | 1.00000 | 1.00000 |
| 7 | 0 | 0.93207 | 0.69834 | 0.47830 | 0.32058 | 0.20972 | 0.13348 | 0.08235 | 0.04902 | 0.02799 | 0.01522 | 0.00781 |
|   | 1 | 0.99797 | 0.95562 | 0.85031 | 0.71658 | 0.57672 | 0.44495 | 0.32942 | 0.23380 | 0.15863 | 0.10242 | 0.06250 |
|   | 2 | 0.99997 | 0.99624 | 0.97431 | 0.92623 | 0.85197 | 0.75641 | 0.64707 | 0.53228 | 0.41990 | 0.31644 | 0.22656 |
|   | 3 | 1.00000 | 0.99981 | 0.99727 | 0.98790 | 0.96666 | 0.92944 | 0.87396 | 0.80015 | 0.71021 | 0.60829 | 0.50000 |
|   | 4 | 1.00000 | 0.99999 | 0.99982 | 0.99878 | 0.99533 | 0.98712 | 0.97120 | 0.94439 | 0.90374 | 0.84707 | 0.77344 |
|   | 5 | 1.00000 | 1.00000 | 0.99999 | 0.99993 | 0.99963 | 0.99866 | 0.99621 | 0.99099 | 0.98116 | 0.96429 | 0.93750 |
|   | 6 | 1.00000 | 1.00000 | 1.00000 | 1.00000 | 0.99999 | 0.99994 | 0.99978 | 0.99936 | 0.99836 | 0.99626 | 0.99219 |
|   | 7 | 1.00000 | 1.00000 | 1.00000 | 1.00000 | 1.00000 | 1.00000 | 1.00000 | 1.00000 | 1.00000 | 1.00000 | 1.00000 |
| 8 | 0 | 0.92274 | 0.66342 | 0.43047 | 0.27249 | 0.16777 | 0.10011 | 0.05765 | 0.03186 | 0.01680 | 0.00837 | 0.00391 |
|   | 1 | 0.99731 | 0.94276 | 0.81310 | 0.65718 | 0.50332 | 0.36708 | 0.25530 | 0.16913 | 0.10638 | 0.06318 | 0.03516 |
|   | 2 | 0.99995 | 0.99421 | 0.96191 | 0.89479 | 0.79692 | 0.67854 | 0.55177 | 0.42781 | 0.31539 | 0.22013 | 0.14453 |
|   | 3 | 1.00000 | 0.99963 | 0.99498 | 0.97865 | 0.94372 | 0.88618 | 0.80590 | 0.70640 | 0.59409 | 0.47696 | 0.36328 |
|   | 4 | 1.00000 | 0.99998 | 0.99957 | 0.99715 | 0.98959 | 0.97270 | 0.94203 | 0.89391 | 0.82633 | 0.73962 | 0.63672 |
|   | 5 | 1.00000 | 1.00000 | 0.99998 | 0.99976 | 0.99877 | 0.99577 | 0.98871 | 0.97468 | 0.95019 | 0.91154 | 0.85547 |
|   | 6 | 1.00000 | 1.00000 | 1.00000 | 0.99999 | 0.99992 | 0.99962 | 0.99871 | 0.99643 | 0.99148 | 0.98188 | 0.96484 |
|   | 7 | 1.00000 | 1.00000 | 1.00000 | 1.00000 | 1.00000 | 0.99998 | 0.99993 | 0.99977 | 0.99934 | 0.99832 | 0.99609 |
|   | 8 | 1.00000 | 1.00000 | 1.00000 | 1.00000 | 1.00000 | 1.00000 | 1.00000 | 1.00000 | 1.00000 | 1.00000 | 1.00000 |

## Cumulative Binomial Distribution - 2

| n | x | .01 | .05 | .10 | .15 | .20 | p .25 | .30 | .35 | .40 | .45 | .50 |
|---|---|-----|-----|-----|-----|-----|-----|-----|-----|-----|-----|-----|
| 9 | 0 | 0.91352 | 0.63025 | 0.38742 | 0.23162 | 0.13422 | 0.07508 | 0.04035 | 0.02071 | 0.01008 | 0.00461 | 0.00195 |
|   | 1 | 0.99656 | 0.92879 | 0.77484 | 0.59948 | 0.43621 | 0.30034 | 0.19600 | 0.12109 | 0.07054 | 0.03852 | 0.01953 |
|   | 2 | 0.99992 | 0.99164 | 0.94703 | 0.85915 | 0.73820 | 0.60068 | 0.46283 | 0.33727 | 0.23179 | 0.14950 | 0.08984 |
|   | 3 | 1.00000 | 0.99936 | 0.99167 | 0.96607 | 0.91436 | 0.83427 | 0.72966 | 0.60889 | 0.48261 | 0.36138 | 0.25391 |
|   | 4 | 1.00000 | 0.99997 | 0.99911 | 0.99437 | 0.98042 | 0.95107 | 0.90119 | 0.82828 | 0.73343 | 0.62142 | 0.50000 |
|   | 5 | 1.00000 | 1.00000 | 0.99994 | 0.99937 | 0.99693 | 0.99001 | 0.97471 | 0.94641 | 0.90065 | 0.83418 | 0.74609 |
|   | 6 | 1.00000 | 1.00000 | 1.00000 | 0.99995 | 0.99969 | 0.99866 | 0.99571 | 0.98882 | 0.97497 | 0.95023 | 0.91016 |
|   | 7 | 1.00000 | 1.00000 | 1.00000 | 1.00000 | 0.99998 | 0.99989 | 0.99957 | 0.99860 | 0.99620 | 0.99092 | 0.98047 |
|   | 8 | 1.00000 | 1.00000 | 1.00000 | 1.00000 | 1.00000 | 1.00000 | 0.99998 | 0.99992 | 0.99974 | 0.99924 | 0.99805 |
|   | 9 | 1.00000 | 1.00000 | 1.00000 | 1.00000 | 1.00000 | 1.00000 | 1.00000 | 1.00000 | 1.00000 | 1.00000 | 1.00000 |
| 10 | 0 | 0.90438 | 0.59874 | 0.34868 | 0.19687 | 0.10737 | 0.05631 | 0.02825 | 0.01346 | 0.00605 | 0.00253 | 0.00098 |
|   | 1 | 0.99573 | 0.91386 | 0.73610 | 0.54430 | 0.37581 | 0.24403 | 0.14931 | 0.08595 | 0.04636 | 0.02326 | 0.01074 |
|   | 2 | 0.99989 | 0.98850 | 0.92981 | 0.82020 | 0.67780 | 0.52559 | 0.38278 | 0.26161 | 0.16729 | 0.09956 | 0.05469 |
|   | 3 | 1.00000 | 0.99897 | 0.98720 | 0.95003 | 0.87913 | 0.77588 | 0.64961 | 0.51383 | 0.38228 | 0.26604 | 0.17188 |
|   | 4 | 1.00000 | 0.99994 | 0.99837 | 0.99013 | 0.96721 | 0.92187 | 0.84973 | 0.75150 | 0.63310 | 0.50440 | 0.37695 |
|   | 5 | 1.00000 | 1.00000 | 0.99985 | 0.99862 | 0.99363 | 0.98027 | 0.95265 | 0.90507 | 0.83376 | 0.73844 | 0.62305 |
|   | 6 | 1.00000 | 1.00000 | 0.99999 | 0.99987 | 0.99914 | 0.99649 | 0.98941 | 0.97398 | 0.94524 | 0.89801 | 0.82812 |
|   | 7 | 1.00000 | 1.00000 | 1.00000 | 0.99999 | 0.99992 | 0.99958 | 0.99841 | 0.99518 | 0.98771 | 0.97261 | 0.94531 |
|   | 8 | 1.00000 | 1.00000 | 1.00000 | 1.00000 | 1.00000 | 0.99997 | 0.99986 | 0.99946 | 0.99832 | 0.99550 | 0.98926 |
|   | 9 | 1.00000 | 1.00000 | 1.00000 | 1.00000 | 1.00000 | 1.00000 | 0.99999 | 0.99997 | 0.99990 | 0.99966 | 0.99902 |
|   | 10 | 1.00000 | 1.00000 | 1.00000 | 1.00000 | 1.00000 | 1.00000 | 1.00000 | 1.00000 | 1.00000 | 1.00000 | 1.00000 |
| 11 | 0 | 0.89534 | 0.56880 | 0.31381 | 0.16734 | 0.08590 | 0.04224 | 0.01977 | 0.00875 | 0.00363 | 0.00139 | 0.00049 |
|   | 1 | 0.99482 | 0.89811 | 0.69736 | 0.49219 | 0.32212 | 0.19710 | 0.11299 | 0.06058 | 0.03023 | 0.01393 | 0.00586 |
|   | 2 | 0.99984 | 0.98476 | 0.91044 | 0.77881 | 0.61740 | 0.45520 | 0.31274 | 0.20013 | 0.11892 | 0.06522 | 0.03271 |
|   | 3 | 1.00000 | 0.99845 | 0.98147 | 0.93056 | 0.83886 | 0.71330 | 0.56956 | 0.42555 | 0.29628 | 0.19112 | 0.11328 |
|   | 4 | 1.00000 | 0.99989 | 0.99725 | 0.98411 | 0.94959 | 0.88537 | 0.78970 | 0.66831 | 0.53277 | 0.39714 | 0.27441 |
|   | 5 | 1.00000 | 0.99999 | 0.99970 | 0.99734 | 0.98835 | 0.96567 | 0.92178 | 0.85132 | 0.75350 | 0.63312 | 0.50000 |
|   | 6 | 1.00000 | 1.00000 | 0.99998 | 0.99968 | 0.99803 | 0.99244 | 0.97838 | 0.94986 | 0.90065 | 0.82620 | 0.72559 |
|   | 7 | 1.00000 | 1.00000 | 1.00000 | 0.99997 | 0.99976 | 0.99881 | 0.99571 | 0.98776 | 0.97072 | 0.93904 | 0.88672 |
|   | 8 | 1.00000 | 1.00000 | 1.00000 | 1.00000 | 0.99998 | 0.99987 | 0.99942 | 0.99796 | 0.99408 | 0.98520 | 0.96729 |
|   | 9 | 1.00000 | 1.00000 | 1.00000 | 1.00000 | 1.00000 | 0.99999 | 0.99995 | 0.99979 | 0.99927 | 0.99779 | 0.99414 |
|   | 10 | 1.00000 | 1.00000 | 1.00000 | 1.00000 | 1.00000 | 1.00000 | 1.00000 | 0.99999 | 0.99996 | 0.99985 | 0.99951 |
|   | 11 | 1.00000 | 1.00000 | 1.00000 | 1.00000 | 1.00000 | 1.00000 | 1.00000 | 1.00000 | 1.00000 | 1.00000 | 1.00000 |
| 12 | 0 | 0.88638 | 0.54036 | 0.28243 | 0.14224 | 0.06872 | 0.03168 | 0.01384 | 0.00569 | 0.00218 | 0.00077 | 0.00024 |
|   | 1 | 0.99383 | 0.88164 | 0.65900 | 0.44346 | 0.27488 | 0.15838 | 0.08503 | 0.04244 | 0.01959 | 0.00829 | 0.00317 |
|   | 2 | 0.99979 | 0.98043 | 0.88913 | 0.73582 | 0.55835 | 0.39068 | 0.25282 | 0.15129 | 0.08344 | 0.04214 | 0.01929 |
|   | 3 | 1.00000 | 0.99776 | 0.97436 | 0.90779 | 0.79457 | 0.64878 | 0.49252 | 0.34665 | 0.22534 | 0.13447 | 0.07300 |
|   | 4 | 1.00000 | 0.99982 | 0.99567 | 0.97608 | 0.92744 | 0.84236 | 0.72366 | 0.58335 | 0.43818 | 0.30443 | 0.19385 |
|   | 5 | 1.00000 | 0.99999 | 0.99946 | 0.99536 | 0.98059 | 0.94560 | 0.88215 | 0.78726 | 0.66521 | 0.52693 | 0.38721 |
|   | 6 | 1.00000 | 1.00000 | 0.99995 | 0.99933 | 0.99610 | 0.98575 | 0.96140 | 0.91537 | 0.84179 | 0.73931 | 0.61279 |
|   | 7 | 1.00000 | 1.00000 | 1.00000 | 0.99993 | 0.99942 | 0.99722 | 0.99051 | 0.97449 | 0.94269 | 0.88826 | 0.80615 |
|   | 8 | 1.00000 | 1.00000 | 1.00000 | 0.99999 | 0.99994 | 0.99961 | 0.99831 | 0.99439 | 0.98473 | 0.96443 | 0.92700 |

## Cumulative Binomial Distribution - 3

| n | x | .01 | .05 | .10 | .15 | .20 | p .25 | .30 | .35 | .40 | .45 | .50 |
|---|---|-----|-----|-----|-----|-----|-------|-----|-----|-----|-----|-----|
| 12 | 9 | 1.00000 | 1.00000 | 1.00000 | 1.00000 | 1.00000 | 0.99996 | 0.99979 | 0.99915 | 0.99719 | 0.99212 | 0.98071 |
| | 10 | 1.00000 | 1.00000 | 1.00000 | 1.00000 | 1.00000 | 1.00000 | 0.99998 | 0.99992 | 0.99968 | 0.99892 | 0.99683 |
| | 11 | 1.00000 | 1.00000 | 1.00000 | 1.00000 | 1.00000 | 1.00000 | 1.00000 | 1.00000 | 0.99998 | 0.99993 | 0.99976 |
| | 12 | 1.00000 | 1.00000 | 1.00000 | 1.00000 | 1.00000 | 1.00000 | 1.00000 | 1.00000 | 1.00000 | 1.00000 | 1.00000 |
| 13 | 0 | 0.87752 | 0.51334 | 0.25419 | 0.12091 | 0.05498 | 0.02376 | 0.00969 | 0.00370 | 0.00131 | 0.00042 | 0.00012 |
| | 1 | 0.99275 | 0.86458 | 0.62134 | 0.39828 | 0.23365 | 0.12671 | 0.06367 | 0.02958 | 0.01263 | 0.00490 | 0.00171 |
| | 2 | 0.99973 | 0.97549 | 0.86612 | 0.69196 | 0.50165 | 0.33260 | 0.20248 | 0.11319 | 0.05790 | 0.02691 | 0.01123 |
| | 3 | 0.99999 | 0.99690 | 0.96584 | 0.88200 | 0.74732 | 0.58425 | 0.42061 | 0.27827 | 0.16858 | 0.09292 | 0.04614 |
| | 4 | 1.00000 | 0.99971 | 0.99354 | 0.96584 | 0.90087 | 0.79396 | 0.65431 | 0.50050 | 0.35304 | 0.22795 | 0.13342 |
| | 5 | 1.00000 | 0.99998 | 0.99908 | 0.99247 | 0.96996 | 0.91979 | 0.83460 | 0.71589 | 0.57440 | 0.42681 | 0.29053 |
| | 6 | 1.00000 | 1.00000 | 0.99990 | 0.99873 | 0.99300 | 0.97571 | 0.93762 | 0.87053 | 0.77116 | 0.64374 | 0.50000 |
| | 7 | 1.00000 | 1.00000 | 0.99999 | 0.99984 | 0.99875 | 0.99435 | 0.98178 | 0.95380 | 0.90233 | 0.82123 | 0.70947 |
| | 8 | 1.00000 | 1.00000 | 1.00000 | 0.99998 | 0.99983 | 0.99901 | 0.99597 | 0.98743 | 0.96792 | 0.93015 | 0.86658 |
| | 9 | 1.00000 | 1.00000 | 1.00000 | 1.00000 | 0.99998 | 0.99987 | 0.99935 | 0.99749 | 0.99221 | 0.97966 | 0.95386 |
| | 10 | 1.00000 | 1.00000 | 1.00000 | 1.00000 | 1.00000 | 0.99999 | 0.99993 | 0.99965 | 0.99868 | 0.99586 | 0.98877 |
| | 11 | 1.00000 | 1.00000 | 1.00000 | 1.00000 | 1.00000 | 1.00000 | 0.99999 | 0.99997 | 0.99986 | 0.99948 | 0.99829 |
| | 12 | 1.00000 | 1.00000 | 1.00000 | 1.00000 | 1.00000 | 1.00000 | 1.00000 | 1.00000 | 0.99999 | 0.99997 | 0.99988 |
| | 13 | 1.00000 | 1.00000 | 1.00000 | 1.00000 | 1.00000 | 1.00000 | 1.00000 | 1.00000 | 1.00000 | 1.00000 | 1.00000 |
| 14 | 0 | 0.86875 | 0.48767 | 0.22877 | 0.10277 | 0.04398 | 0.01782 | 0.00678 | 0.00240 | 0.00078 | 0.00023 | 0.00006 |
| | 1 | 0.99160 | 0.84701 | 0.58463 | 0.35667 | 0.19791 | 0.10097 | 0.04748 | 0.02052 | 0.00810 | 0.00289 | 0.00092 |
| | 2 | 0.99966 | 0.96995 | 0.84164 | 0.64791 | 0.44805 | 0.28113 | 0.16084 | 0.08393 | 0.03979 | 0.01701 | 0.00647 |
| | 3 | 0.99999 | 0.99583 | 0.95587 | 0.85349 | 0.69819 | 0.52134 | 0.35517 | 0.22050 | 0.12431 | 0.06322 | 0.02869 |
| | 4 | 1.00000 | 0.99957 | 0.99077 | 0.95326 | 0.87016 | 0.74153 | 0.58420 | 0.42272 | 0.27926 | 0.16719 | 0.08978 |
| | 5 | 1.00000 | 0.99997 | 0.99853 | 0.98847 | 0.95615 | 0.88833 | 0.78052 | 0.64051 | 0.48585 | 0.33732 | 0.21198 |
| | 6 | 1.00000 | 1.00000 | 0.99982 | 0.99779 | 0.98839 | 0.96173 | 0.90672 | 0.81641 | 0.69245 | 0.54612 | 0.39526 |
| | 7 | 1.00000 | 1.00000 | 0.99998 | 0.99967 | 0.99760 | 0.98969 | 0.96853 | 0.92466 | 0.84986 | 0.74136 | 0.60474 |
| | 8 | 1.00000 | 1.00000 | 1.00000 | 0.99996 | 0.99962 | 0.99785 | 0.99171 | 0.97566 | 0.94168 | 0.88114 | 0.78802 |
| | 9 | 1.00000 | 1.00000 | 1.00000 | 1.00000 | 0.99995 | 0.99966 | 0.99833 | 0.99396 | 0.98249 | 0.95738 | 0.91022 |
| | 10 | 1.00000 | 1.00000 | 1.00000 | 1.00000 | 1.00000 | 0.99996 | 0.99975 | 0.99889 | 0.99609 | 0.98857 | 0.97131 |
| | 11 | 1.00000 | 1.00000 | 1.00000 | 1.00000 | 1.00000 | 1.00000 | 0.99997 | 0.99986 | 0.99939 | 0.99785 | 0.99353 |
| | 12 | 1.00000 | 1.00000 | 1.00000 | 1.00000 | 1.00000 | 1.00000 | 1.00000 | 0.99999 | 0.99994 | 0.99975 | 0.99908 |
| | 13 | 1.00000 | 1.00000 | 1.00000 | 1.00000 | 1.00000 | 1.00000 | 1.00000 | 1.00000 | 1.00000 | 0.99999 | 0.99994 |
| | 14 | 1.00000 | 1.00000 | 1.00000 | 1.00000 | 1.00000 | 1.00000 | 1.00000 | 1.00000 | 1.00000 | 1.00000 | 1.00000 |

## Cumulative Binomial Distribution - 4

| n | x | .01 | .05 | .10 | .15 | .20 | .25 | .30 | .35 | .40 | .45 | .50 |
|---|---|-----|-----|-----|-----|-----|-----|-----|-----|-----|-----|-----|
| 15 | 0 | 0.86006 | 0.46329 | 0.20589 | 0.08735 | 0.03518 | 0.01336 | 0.00475 | 0.00156 | 0.00047 | 0.00013 | 0.00003 |
| | 1 | 0.99037 | 0.82905 | 0.54904 | 0.31859 | 0.16713 | 0.08018 | 0.03527 | 0.01418 | 0.00517 | 0.00169 | 0.00049 |
| | 2 | 0.99958 | 0.96380 | 0.81594 | 0.60423 | 0.39802 | 0.23609 | 0.12683 | 0.06173 | 0.02711 | 0.01065 | 0.00369 |
| | 3 | 0.99999 | 0.99453 | 0.94444 | 0.82266 | 0.64816 | 0.46129 | 0.29687 | 0.17270 | 0.09050 | 0.04242 | 0.01758 |
| | 4 | 1.00000 | 0.99939 | 0.98728 | 0.93829 | 0.83577 | 0.68649 | 0.51549 | 0.35194 | 0.21728 | 0.12040 | 0.05923 |
| | 5 | 1.00000 | 0.99995 | 0.99775 | 0.98319 | 0.93895 | 0.85163 | 0.72162 | 0.56428 | 0.40322 | 0.26076 | 0.15088 |
| | 6 | 1.00000 | 1.00000 | 0.99969 | 0.99639 | 0.98194 | 0.94338 | 0.86886 | 0.75484 | 0.60981 | 0.45216 | 0.30362 |
| | 7 | 1.00000 | 1.00000 | 0.99997 | 0.99939 | 0.99576 | 0.98270 | 0.94999 | 0.88677 | 0.78690 | 0.65350 | 0.50000 |
| | 8 | 1.00000 | 1.00000 | 1.00000 | 0.99992 | 0.99922 | 0.99581 | 0.98476 | 0.95781 | 0.90495 | 0.81824 | 0.69638 |
| | 9 | 1.00000 | 1.00000 | 1.00000 | 0.99999 | 0.99989 | 0.99921 | 0.99635 | 0.98756 | 0.96617 | 0.92307 | 0.84912 |
| | 10 | 1.00000 | 1.00000 | 1.00000 | 1.00000 | 0.99999 | 0.99988 | 0.99933 | 0.99717 | 0.99065 | 0.97453 | 0.94077 |
| | 11 | 1.00000 | 1.00000 | 1.00000 | 1.00000 | 1.00000 | 0.99999 | 0.99991 | 0.99952 | 0.99807 | 0.99367 | 0.98242 |
| | 12 | 1.00000 | 1.00000 | 1.00000 | 1.00000 | 1.00000 | 1.00000 | 0.99999 | 0.99994 | 0.99972 | 0.99889 | 0.99631 |
| | 13 | 1.00000 | 1.00000 | 1.00000 | 1.00000 | 1.00000 | 1.00000 | 1.00000 | 1.00000 | 0.99997 | 0.99988 | 0.99951 |
| | 14 | 1.00000 | 1.00000 | 1.00000 | 1.00000 | 1.00000 | 1.00000 | 1.00000 | 1.00000 | 1.00000 | 0.99999 | 0.99997 |
| | 15 | 1.00000 | 1.00000 | 1.00000 | 1.00000 | 1.00000 | 1.00000 | 1.00000 | 1.00000 | 1.00000 | 1.00000 | 1.00000 |
| 20 | 0 | 0.81791 | 0.35849 | 0.12158 | 0.03876 | 0.01153 | 0.00317 | 0.00080 | 0.00018 | 0.00004 | 0.00001 | 0.00000 |
| | 1 | 0.98314 | 0.73584 | 0.39175 | 0.17556 | 0.06918 | 0.02431 | 0.00764 | 0.00213 | 0.00052 | 0.00011 | 0.00002 |
| | 2 | 0.99900 | 0.92452 | 0.67693 | 0.40490 | 0.20608 | 0.09126 | 0.03548 | 0.01212 | 0.00361 | 0.00093 | 0.00020 |
| | 3 | 0.99996 | 0.98410 | 0.86705 | 0.64773 | 0.41145 | 0.22516 | 0.10709 | 0.04438 | 0.01596 | 0.00493 | 0.00129 |
| | 4 | 1.00000 | 0.99743 | 0.95683 | 0.82985 | 0.62965 | 0.41484 | 0.23751 | 0.11820 | 0.05095 | 0.01886 | 0.00591 |
| | 5 | 1.00000 | 0.99967 | 0.98875 | 0.93269 | 0.80421 | 0.61717 | 0.41637 | 0.24540 | 0.12560 | 0.05533 | 0.02069 |
| | 6 | 1.00000 | 0.99997 | 0.99761 | 0.97806 | 0.91331 | 0.78578 | 0.60801 | 0.41663 | 0.25001 | 0.12993 | 0.05766 |
| | 7 | 1.00000 | 1.00000 | 0.99958 | 0.99408 | 0.96786 | 0.89819 | 0.77227 | 0.60103 | 0.41589 | 0.25201 | 0.13159 |
| | 8 | 1.00000 | 1.00000 | 0.99994 | 0.99867 | 0.99002 | 0.95907 | 0.88667 | 0.76238 | 0.59560 | 0.41431 | 0.25172 |
| | 9 | 1.00000 | 1.00000 | 0.99999 | 0.99975 | 0.99741 | 0.98614 | 0.95204 | 0.87822 | 0.75534 | 0.59136 | 0.41190 |
| | 10 | 1.00000 | 1.00000 | 1.00000 | 0.99996 | 0.99944 | 0.99606 | 0.98286 | 0.94683 | 0.87248 | 0.75071 | 0.58810 |
| | 11 | 1.00000 | 1.00000 | 1.00000 | 0.99999 | 0.99990 | 0.99906 | 0.99486 | 0.98042 | 0.94347 | 0.86923 | 0.74828 |
| | 12 | 1.00000 | 1.00000 | 1.00000 | 1.00000 | 0.99998 | 0.99982 | 0.99872 | 0.99398 | 0.97897 | 0.94197 | 0.86841 |
| | 13 | 1.00000 | 1.00000 | 1.00000 | 1.00000 | 1.00000 | 0.99997 | 0.99974 | 0.99848 | 0.99353 | 0.97859 | 0.94234 |
| | 14 | 1.00000 | 1.00000 | 1.00000 | 1.00000 | 1.00000 | 1.00000 | 0.99996 | 0.99969 | 0.99839 | 0.99357 | 0.97931 |
| | 15 | 1.00000 | 1.00000 | 1.00000 | 1.00000 | 1.00000 | 1.00000 | 0.99999 | 0.99995 | 0.99968 | 0.99847 | 0.99409 |
| | 16 | 1.00000 | 1.00000 | 1.00000 | 1.00000 | 1.00000 | 1.00000 | 1.00000 | 0.99999 | 0.99995 | 0.99972 | 0.99871 |
| | 17 | 1.00000 | 1.00000 | 1.00000 | 1.00000 | 1.00000 | 1.00000 | 1.00000 | 1.00000 | 0.99999 | 0.99996 | 0.99980 |
| | 18 | 1.00000 | 1.00000 | 1.00000 | 1.00000 | 1.00000 | 1.00000 | 1.00000 | 1.00000 | 1.00000 | 1.00000 | 0.99998 |
| | 19 | 1.00000 | 1.00000 | 1.00000 | 1.00000 | 1.00000 | 1.00000 | 1.00000 | 1.00000 | 1.00000 | 1.00000 | 1.00000 |
| | 20 | 1.00000 | 1.00000 | 1.00000 | 1.00000 | 1.00000 | 1.00000 | 1.00000 | 1.00000 | 1.00000 | 1.00000 | 1.00000 |

## Cumulative Binomial Distribution - 5

| n | x | .01 | .05 | .10 | .15 | .20 | .25 | .30 | .35 | .40 | .45 | .50 |
|---|---|-----|-----|-----|-----|-----|-----|-----|-----|-----|-----|-----|
| 25 | 0 | 0.77782 | 0.27739 | 0.07179 | 0.01720 | 0.00378 | 0.00075 | 0.00013 | 0.00002 | 0.00000 | 0.00000 | 0.00000 |
| | 1 | 0.97424 | 0.64238 | 0.27121 | 0.09307 | 0.02739 | 0.00702 | 0.00157 | 0.00030 | 0.00005 | 0.00001 | 0.00000 |
| | 2 | 0.99805 | 0.87289 | 0.53709 | 0.25374 | 0.09823 | 0.03211 | 0.00896 | 0.00213 | 0.00043 | 0.00007 | 0.00001 |
| | 3 | 0.99989 | 0.96591 | 0.76359 | 0.47112 | 0.23399 | 0.09621 | 0.03324 | 0.00968 | 0.00237 | 0.00048 | 0.00008 |
| | 4 | 1.00000 | 0.99284 | 0.90201 | 0.68211 | 0.42067 | 0.21374 | 0.09047 | 0.03205 | 0.00947 | 0.00231 | 0.00046 |
| | 5 | 1.00000 | 0.99879 | 0.96660 | 0.83848 | 0.61669 | 0.37828 | 0.19349 | 0.08262 | 0.02936 | 0.00860 | 0.00204 |
| | 6 | 1.00000 | 0.99983 | 0.99052 | 0.93047 | 0.78004 | 0.56110 | 0.34065 | 0.17340 | 0.07357 | 0.02575 | 0.00732 |
| | 7 | 1.00000 | 0.99998 | 0.99774 | 0.97453 | 0.89088 | 0.72651 | 0.51185 | 0.30608 | 0.15355 | 0.06385 | 0.02164 |
| | 8 | 1.00000 | 1.00000 | 0.99954 | 0.99203 | 0.95323 | 0.85056 | 0.67693 | 0.46682 | 0.27353 | 0.13398 | 0.05388 |
| | 9 | 1.00000 | 1.00000 | 0.99992 | 0.99786 | 0.98267 | 0.92867 | 0.81056 | 0.63031 | 0.42462 | 0.24237 | 0.11476 |
| | 10 | 1.00000 | 1.00000 | 0.99999 | 0.99951 | 0.99445 | 0.97033 | 0.90220 | 0.77116 | 0.58577 | 0.38426 | 0.21218 |
| | 11 | 1.00000 | 1.00000 | 1.00000 | 0.99990 | 0.99846 | 0.98927 | 0.95575 | 0.87458 | 0.73228 | 0.54257 | 0.34502 |
| | 12 | 1.00000 | 1.00000 | 1.00000 | 0.99998 | 0.99963 | 0.99663 | 0.98253 | 0.93956 | 0.84623 | 0.69368 | 0.50000 |
| | 13 | 1.00000 | 1.00000 | 1.00000 | 1.00000 | 0.99992 | 0.99908 | 0.99401 | 0.97454 | 0.92220 | 0.81731 | 0.65498 |
| | 14 | 1.00000 | 1.00000 | 1.00000 | 1.00000 | 0.99999 | 0.99979 | 0.99822 | 0.99069 | 0.96561 | 0.90402 | 0.78782 |
| | 15 | 1.00000 | 1.00000 | 1.00000 | 1.00000 | 1.00000 | 0.99996 | 0.99955 | 0.99706 | 0.98683 | 0.95604 | 0.88524 |
| | 16 | 1.00000 | 1.00000 | 1.00000 | 1.00000 | 1.00000 | 0.99999 | 0.99990 | 0.99921 | 0.99567 | 0.98264 | 0.94612 |
| | 17 | 1.00000 | 1.00000 | 1.00000 | 1.00000 | 1.00000 | 1.00000 | 0.99998 | 0.99982 | 0.99879 | 0.99417 | 0.97836 |
| | 18 | 1.00000 | 1.00000 | 1.00000 | 1.00000 | 1.00000 | 1.00000 | 1.00000 | 0.99997 | 0.99972 | 0.99836 | 0.99268 |
| | 19 | 1.00000 | 1.00000 | 1.00000 | 1.00000 | 1.00000 | 1.00000 | 1.00000 | 0.99999 | 0.99995 | 0.99962 | 0.99796 |
| | 20 | 1.00000 | 1.00000 | 1.00000 | 1.00000 | 1.00000 | 1.00000 | 1.00000 | 1.00000 | 0.99999 | 0.99993 | 0.99954 |
| | 21 | 1.00000 | 1.00000 | 1.00000 | 1.00000 | 1.00000 | 1.00000 | 1.00000 | 1.00000 | 1.00000 | 0.99999 | 0.99992 |
| | 22 | 1.00000 | 1.00000 | 1.00000 | 1.00000 | 1.00000 | 1.00000 | 1.00000 | 1.00000 | 1.00000 | 1.00000 | 0.99999 |
| | 23 | 1.00000 | 1.00000 | 1.00000 | 1.00000 | 1.00000 | 1.00000 | 1.00000 | 1.00000 | 1.00000 | 1.00000 | 1.00000 |
| | 24 | 1.00000 | 1.00000 | 1.00000 | 1.00000 | 1.00000 | 1.00000 | 1.00000 | 1.00000 | 1.00000 | 1.00000 | 1.00000 |
| | 25 | 1.00000 | 1.00000 | 1.00000 | 1.00000 | 1.00000 | 1.00000 | 1.00000 | 1.00000 | 1.00000 | 1.00000 | 1.00000 |
| 50 | 0 | 0.60501 | 0.07694 | 0.00515 | 0.00030 | 0.00001 | 0.00000 | 0.00000 | 0.00000 | 0.00000 | 0.00000 | 0.00000 |
| | 1 | 0.91056 | 0.27943 | 0.03379 | 0.00291 | 0.00019 | 0.00001 | 0.00000 | 0.00000 | 0.00000 | 0.00000 | 0.00000 |
| | 2 | 0.98618 | 0.54053 | 0.11173 | 0.01419 | 0.00129 | 0.00009 | 0.00000 | 0.00000 | 0.00000 | 0.00000 | 0.00000 |
| | 3 | 0.99840 | 0.76041 | 0.25029 | 0.04605 | 0.00566 | 0.00050 | 0.00003 | 0.00000 | 0.00000 | 0.00000 | 0.00000 |
| | 4 | 0.99985 | 0.89638 | 0.43120 | 0.11211 | 0.01850 | 0.00211 | 0.00017 | 0.00001 | 0.00000 | 0.00000 | 0.00000 |
| | 5 | 0.99999 | 0.96222 | 0.61612 | 0.21935 | 0.04803 | 0.00705 | 0.00072 | 0.00005 | 0.00000 | 0.00000 | 0.00000 |
| | 6 | 1.00000 | 0.98821 | 0.77023 | 0.36130 | 0.10340 | 0.01939 | 0.00249 | 0.00022 | 0.00001 | 0.00000 | 0.00000 |
| | 7 | 1.00000 | 0.99681 | 0.87785 | 0.51875 | 0.19041 | 0.04526 | 0.00726 | 0.00080 | 0.00006 | 0.00000 | 0.00000 |
| | 8 | 1.00000 | 0.99924 | 0.94213 | 0.66810 | 0.30733 | 0.09160 | 0.01825 | 0.00248 | 0.00023 | 0.00001 | 0.00000 |
| | 9 | 1.00000 | 0.99984 | 0.97546 | 0.79109 | 0.44374 | 0.16368 | 0.04023 | 0.00670 | 0.00076 | 0.00006 | 0.00000 |
| | 10 | 1.00000 | 0.99997 | 0.99065 | 0.88008 | 0.58356 | 0.26220 | 0.07885 | 0.01601 | 0.00220 | 0.00020 | 0.00001 |
| | 11 | 1.00000 | 1.00000 | 0.99678 | 0.93719 | 0.71067 | 0.38162 | 0.13904 | 0.03423 | 0.00569 | 0.00063 | 0.00005 |
| | 12 | 1.00000 | 1.00000 | 0.99900 | 0.96994 | 0.81394 | 0.51099 | 0.22287 | 0.06613 | 0.01325 | 0.00177 | 0.00015 |
| | 13 | 1.00000 | 1.00000 | 0.99971 | 0.98683 | 0.88941 | 0.63704 | 0.32788 | 0.11633 | 0.02799 | 0.00449 | 0.00047 |
| | 14 | 1.00000 | 1.00000 | 0.99993 | 0.99471 | 0.93928 | 0.74808 | 0.44683 | 0.18778 | 0.05395 | 0.01038 | 0.00130 |
| | 15 | 1.00000 | 1.00000 | 0.99998 | 0.99805 | 0.96920 | 0.83692 | 0.56918 | 0.28010 | 0.09550 | 0.02195 | 0.00330 |
| | 16 | 1.00000 | 1.00000 | 1.00000 | 0.99934 | 0.98556 | 0.90169 | 0.68388 | 0.38886 | 0.15609 | 0.04265 | 0.00767 |
| | 17 | 1.00000 | 1.00000 | 1.00000 | 0.99979 | 0.99374 | 0.94488 | 0.78219 | 0.50597 | 0.23688 | 0.07653 | 0.01642 |
| | 18 | 1.00000 | 1.00000 | 1.00000 | 0.99994 | 0.99749 | 0.97127 | 0.85944 | 0.62159 | 0.33561 | 0.12734 | 0.03245 |
| | 19 | 1.00000 | 1.00000 | 1.00000 | 0.99998 | 0.99907 | 0.98608 | 0.91520 | 0.72644 | 0.44648 | 0.19737 | 0.05946 |
| | 20 | 1.00000 | 1.00000 | 1.00000 | 1.00000 | 0.99968 | 0.99374 | 0.95224 | 0.81394 | 0.56103 | 0.28617 | 0.10132 |

## Cumulative Binomial Distribution - 6

| n | x | .01 | .05 | .10 | .15 | .20 | .25 | .30 | .35 | .40 | .45 | .50 |
|---|---|-----|-----|-----|-----|-----|-----|-----|-----|-----|-----|-----|
| 50 | 21 | 1.00000 | 1.00000 | 1.00000 | 1.00000 | 0.99990 | 0.99738 | 0.97491 | 0.88126 | 0.67014 | 0.38996 | 0.16112 |
| ctd | 22 | 1.00000 | 1.00000 | 1.00000 | 1.00000 | 0.99997 | 0.99898 | 0.98772 | 0.92904 | 0.76602 | 0.50191 | 0.23994 |
| | 23 | 1.00000 | 1.00000 | 1.00000 | 1.00000 | 0.99999 | 0.99963 | 0.99441 | 0.96036 | 0.84383 | 0.61341 | 0.33591 |
| | 24 | 1.00000 | 1.00000 | 1.00000 | 1.00000 | 1.00000 | 0.99988 | 0.99763 | 0.97933 | 0.90219 | 0.71604 | 0.44386 |
| | 25 | 1.00000 | 1.00000 | 1.00000 | 1.00000 | 1.00000 | 0.99996 | 0.99907 | 0.98996 | 0.94266 | 0.80337 | 0.55614 |
| | 26 | 1.00000 | 1.00000 | 1.00000 | 1.00000 | 1.00000 | 0.99999 | 0.99966 | 0.99546 | 0.96859 | 0.87207 | 0.66409 |
| | 27 | 1.00000 | 1.00000 | 1.00000 | 1.00000 | 1.00000 | 1.00000 | 0.99988 | 0.99809 | 0.98397 | 0.92204 | 0.76006 |
| | 28 | 1.00000 | 1.00000 | 1.00000 | 1.00000 | 1.00000 | 1.00000 | 0.99996 | 0.99925 | 0.99238 | 0.95562 | 0.83888 |
| | 29 | 1.00000 | 1.00000 | 1.00000 | 1.00000 | 1.00000 | 1.00000 | 0.99999 | 0.99973 | 0.99664 | 0.97646 | 0.89868 |
| | 30 | 1.00000 | 1.00000 | 1.00000 | 1.00000 | 1.00000 | 1.00000 | 1.00000 | 0.99991 | 0.99863 | 0.98840 | 0.94054 |
| | 31 | 1.00000 | 1.00000 | 1.00000 | 1.00000 | 1.00000 | 1.00000 | 1.00000 | 0.99997 | 0.99948 | 0.99470 | 0.96755 |
| | 32 | 1.00000 | 1.00000 | 1.00000 | 1.00000 | 1.00000 | 1.00000 | 1.00000 | 0.99999 | 0.99982 | 0.99776 | 0.98358 |
| | 33 | 1.00000 | 1.00000 | 1.00000 | 1.00000 | 1.00000 | 1.00000 | 1.00000 | 1.00000 | 0.99994 | 0.99913 | 0.99233 |
| | 34 | 1.00000 | 1.00000 | 1.00000 | 1.00000 | 1.00000 | 1.00000 | 1.00000 | 1.00000 | 0.99998 | 0.99969 | 0.99670 |
| | 35 | 1.00000 | 1.00000 | 1.00000 | 1.00000 | 1.00000 | 1.00000 | 1.00000 | 1.00000 | 1.00000 | 0.99990 | 0.99870 |
| | 36 | 1.00000 | 1.00000 | 1.00000 | 1.00000 | 1.00000 | 1.00000 | 1.00000 | 1.00000 | 1.00000 | 0.99997 | 0.99953 |
| | 37 | 1.00000 | 1.00000 | 1.00000 | 1.00000 | 1.00000 | 1.00000 | 1.00000 | 1.00000 | 1.00000 | 0.99999 | 0.99985 |
| | 38 | 1.00000 | 1.00000 | 1.00000 | 1.00000 | 1.00000 | 1.00000 | 1.00000 | 1.00000 | 1.00000 | 1.00000 | 0.99995 |
| | 39 | 1.00000 | 1.00000 | 1.00000 | 1.00000 | 1.00000 | 1.00000 | 1.00000 | 1.00000 | 1.00000 | 1.00000 | 0.99999 |
| | 40 | 1.00000 | 1.00000 | 1.00000 | 1.00000 | 1.00000 | 1.00000 | 1.00000 | 1.00000 | 1.00000 | 1.00000 | 1.00000 |
| | 41 | 1.00000 | 1.00000 | 1.00000 | 1.00000 | 1.00000 | 1.00000 | 1.00000 | 1.00000 | 1.00000 | 1.00000 | 1.00000 |
| | 42 | 1.00000 | 1.00000 | 1.00000 | 1.00000 | 1.00000 | 1.00000 | 1.00000 | 1.00000 | 1.00000 | 1.00000 | 1.00000 |
| | 43 | 1.00000 | 1.00000 | 1.00000 | 1.00000 | 1.00000 | 1.00000 | 1.00000 | 1.00000 | 1.00000 | 1.00000 | 1.00000 |
| | 44 | 1.00000 | 1.00000 | 1.00000 | 1.00000 | 1.00000 | 1.00000 | 1.00000 | 1.00000 | 1.00000 | 1.00000 | 1.00000 |
| | 45 | 1.00000 | 1.00000 | 1.00000 | 1.00000 | 1.00000 | 1.00000 | 1.00000 | 1.00000 | 1.00000 | 1.00000 | 1.00000 |
| | 46 | 1.00000 | 1.00000 | 1.00000 | 1.00000 | 1.00000 | 1.00000 | 1.00000 | 1.00000 | 1.00000 | 1.00000 | 1.00000 |
| | 47 | 1.00000 | 1.00000 | 1.00000 | 1.00000 | 1.00000 | 1.00000 | 1.00000 | 1.00000 | 1.00000 | 1.00000 | 1.00000 |
| | 48 | 1.00000 | 1.00000 | 1.00000 | 1.00000 | 1.00000 | 1.00000 | 1.00000 | 1.00000 | 1.00000 | 1.00000 | 1.00000 |
| | 49 | 1.00000 | 1.00000 | 1.00000 | 1.00000 | 1.00000 | 1.00000 | 1.00000 | 1.00000 | 1.00000 | 1.00000 | 1.00000 |
| | 50 | 1.00000 | 1.00000 | 1.00000 | 1.00000 | 1.00000 | 1.00000 | 1.00000 | 1.00000 | 1.00000 | 1.00000 | 1.00000 |
| 100 | 0 | 0.36603 | 0.00592 | 0.00003 | 0.00000 | 0.00000 | 0.00000 | 0.00000 | 0.00000 | 0.00000 | 0.00000 | 0.00000 |
| | 1 | 0.73576 | 0.03708 | 0.00032 | 0.00000 | 0.00000 | 0.00000 | 0.00000 | 0.00000 | 0.00000 | 0.00000 | 0.00000 |
| | 2 | 0.92063 | 0.11826 | 0.00194 | 0.00002 | 0.00000 | 0.00000 | 0.00000 | 0.00000 | 0.00000 | 0.00000 | 0.00000 |
| | 3 | 0.98163 | 0.25784 | 0.00784 | 0.00009 | 0.00000 | 0.00000 | 0.00000 | 0.00000 | 0.00000 | 0.00000 | 0.00000 |
| | 4 | 0.99657 | 0.43598 | 0.02371 | 0.00043 | 0.00000 | 0.00000 | 0.00000 | 0.00000 | 0.00000 | 0.00000 | 0.00000 |
| | 5 | 0.99947 | 0.61600 | 0.05758 | 0.00155 | 0.00002 | 0.00000 | 0.00000 | 0.00000 | 0.00000 | 0.00000 | 0.00000 |
| | 6 | 0.99993 | 0.76601 | 0.11716 | 0.00470 | 0.00008 | 0.00000 | 0.00000 | 0.00000 | 0.00000 | 0.00000 | 0.00000 |
| | 7 | 0.99999 | 0.87204 | 0.20605 | 0.01217 | 0.00028 | 0.00000 | 0.00000 | 0.00000 | 0.00000 | 0.00000 | 0.00000 |
| | 8 | 1.00000 | 0.93691 | 0.32087 | 0.02748 | 0.00086 | 0.00001 | 0.00000 | 0.00000 | 0.00000 | 0.00000 | 0.00000 |
| | 9 | 1.00000 | 0.97181 | 0.45129 | 0.05509 | 0.00233 | 0.00004 | 0.00000 | 0.00000 | 0.00000 | 0.00000 | 0.00000 |
| | 10 | 1.00000 | 0.98853 | 0.58316 | 0.09945 | 0.00570 | 0.00014 | 0.00000 | 0.00000 | 0.00000 | 0.00000 | 0.00000 |
| | 11 | 1.00000 | 0.99573 | 0.70303 | 0.16349 | 0.01257 | 0.00039 | 0.00001 | 0.00000 | 0.00000 | 0.00000 | 0.00000 |
| | 12 | 1.00000 | 0.99854 | 0.80182 | 0.24730 | 0.02533 | 0.00103 | 0.00002 | 0.00000 | 0.00000 | 0.00000 | 0.00000 |
| | 13 | 1.00000 | 0.99954 | 0.87612 | 0.34742 | 0.04691 | 0.00246 | 0.00006 | 0.00000 | 0.00000 | 0.00000 | 0.00000 |
| | 14 | 1.00000 | 0.99986 | 0.92743 | 0.45722 | 0.08044 | 0.00542 | 0.00016 | 0.00000 | 0.00000 | 0.00000 | 0.00000 |
| | 15 | 1.00000 | 0.99996 | 0.96011 | 0.56832 | 0.12851 | 0.01108 | 0.00040 | 0.00001 | 0.00000 | 0.00000 | 0.00000 |

## Cumulative Binomial Distribution - 7

| n | x | .01 | .05 | .10 | .15 | .20 | .25 | p .30 | .35 | .40 | .45 | .50 |
|---|---|-----|-----|-----|-----|-----|-----|-----|-----|-----|-----|-----|
| 100 | 16 | 1.00000 | 0.99999 | 0.97940 | 0.67246 | 0.19234 | 0.02111 | 0.00097 | 0.00002 | 0.00000 | 0.00000 | 0.00000 |
| ctd | 17 | 1.00000 | 1.00000 | 0.98999 | 0.76328 | 0.27119 | 0.03763 | 0.00216 | 0.00005 | 0.00000 | 0.00000 | 0.00000 |
|  | 18 | 1.00000 | 1.00000 | 0.99542 | 0.83717 | 0.36209 | 0.06301 | 0.00452 | 0.00014 | 0.00000 | 0.00000 | 0.00000 |
|  | 19 | 1.00000 | 1.00000 | 0.99802 | 0.89346 | 0.46016 | 0.09953 | 0.00889 | 0.00034 | 0.00001 | 0.00000 | 0.00000 |
|  | 20 | 1.00000 | 1.00000 | 0.99919 | 0.93368 | 0.55946 | 0.14883 | 0.01646 | 0.00078 | 0.00002 | 0.00000 | 0.00000 |
|  | 21 | 1.00000 | 1.00000 | 0.99969 | 0.96072 | 0.65403 | 0.21144 | 0.02883 | 0.00169 | 0.00004 | 0.00000 | 0.00000 |
|  | 22 | 1.00000 | 1.00000 | 0.99989 | 0.97786 | 0.73893 | 0.28637 | 0.04787 | 0.00343 | 0.00011 | 0.00000 | 0.00000 |
|  | 23 | 1.00000 | 1.00000 | 0.99996 | 0.98811 | 0.81091 | 0.37108 | 0.07553 | 0.00662 | 0.00025 | 0.00000 | 0.00000 |
|  | 24 | 1.00000 | 1.00000 | 0.99999 | 0.99392 | 0.86865 | 0.46167 | 0.11357 | 0.01213 | 0.00056 | 0.00001 | 0.00000 |
|  | 25 | 1.00000 | 1.00000 | 1.00000 | 0.99703 | 0.91252 | 0.55347 | 0.16313 | 0.02114 | 0.00119 | 0.00003 | 0.00000 |
|  | 26 | 1.00000 | 1.00000 | 1.00000 | 0.99862 | 0.94417 | 0.64174 | 0.22440 | 0.03514 | 0.00240 | 0.00007 | 0.00000 |
|  | 27 | 1.00000 | 1.00000 | 1.00000 | 0.99939 | 0.96585 | 0.72238 | 0.29637 | 0.05581 | 0.00460 | 0.00016 | 0.00000 |
|  | 28 | 1.00000 | 1.00000 | 1.00000 | 0.99974 | 0.97998 | 0.79246 | 0.37678 | 0.08482 | 0.00843 | 0.00036 | 0.00001 |
|  | 29 | 1.00000 | 1.00000 | 1.00000 | 0.99989 | 0.98875 | 0.85046 | 0.46234 | 0.12360 | 0.01478 | 0.00076 | 0.00002 |
|  | 30 | 1.00000 | 1.00000 | 1.00000 | 0.99996 | 0.99394 | 0.89621 | 0.54912 | 0.17302 | 0.02478 | 0.00154 | 0.00004 |
|  | 31 | 1.00000 | 1.00000 | 1.00000 | 0.99998 | 0.99687 | 0.93065 | 0.63311 | 0.23311 | 0.03985 | 0.00297 | 0.00009 |
|  | 32 | 1.00000 | 1.00000 | 1.00000 | 0.99999 | 0.99845 | 0.95540 | 0.71072 | 0.30288 | 0.06150 | 0.00550 | 0.00020 |
|  | 33 | 1.00000 | 1.00000 | 1.00000 | 1.00000 | 0.99926 | 0.97241 | 0.77926 | 0.38029 | 0.09125 | 0.00976 | 0.00044 |
|  | 34 | 1.00000 | 1.00000 | 1.00000 | 1.00000 | 0.99966 | 0.98357 | 0.83714 | 0.46243 | 0.13034 | 0.01663 | 0.00089 |
|  | 35 | 1.00000 | 1.00000 | 1.00000 | 1.00000 | 0.99985 | 0.99059 | 0.88392 | 0.54584 | 0.17947 | 0.02724 | 0.00176 |
|  | 36 | 1.00000 | 1.00000 | 1.00000 | 1.00000 | 0.99994 | 0.99482 | 0.92012 | 0.62692 | 0.23861 | 0.04290 | 0.00332 |
|  | 37 | 1.00000 | 1.00000 | 1.00000 | 1.00000 | 0.99998 | 0.99725 | 0.94695 | 0.70245 | 0.30681 | 0.06507 | 0.00602 |
|  | 38 | 1.00000 | 1.00000 | 1.00000 | 1.00000 | 0.99999 | 0.99860 | 0.96602 | 0.76987 | 0.38219 | 0.09514 | 0.01049 |
|  | 39 | 1.00000 | 1.00000 | 1.00000 | 1.00000 | 1.00000 | 0.99931 | 0.97901 | 0.82758 | 0.46208 | 0.13425 | 0.01760 |
|  | 40 | 1.00000 | 1.00000 | 1.00000 | 1.00000 | 1.00000 | 0.99968 | 0.98750 | 0.87498 | 0.54329 | 0.18306 | 0.02844 |
|  | 41 | 1.00000 | 1.00000 | 1.00000 | 1.00000 | 1.00000 | 0.99985 | 0.99283 | 0.91232 | 0.62253 | 0.24149 | 0.04431 |
|  | 42 | 1.00000 | 1.00000 | 1.00000 | 1.00000 | 1.00000 | 0.99994 | 0.99603 | 0.94057 | 0.69674 | 0.30865 | 0.06661 |
|  | 43 | 1.00000 | 1.00000 | 1.00000 | 1.00000 | 1.00000 | 0.99997 | 0.99789 | 0.96109 | 0.76347 | 0.38277 | 0.09667 |
|  | 44 | 1.00000 | 1.00000 | 1.00000 | 1.00000 | 1.00000 | 0.99999 | 0.99891 | 0.97540 | 0.82110 | 0.46133 | 0.13563 |
|  | 45 | 1.00000 | 1.00000 | 1.00000 | 1.00000 | 1.00000 | 1.00000 | 0.99946 | 0.98499 | 0.86891 | 0.54132 | 0.18410 |
|  | 46 | 1.00000 | 1.00000 | 1.00000 | 1.00000 | 1.00000 | 1.00000 | 0.99974 | 0.99116 | 0.90702 | 0.61956 | 0.24206 |
|  | 47 | 1.00000 | 1.00000 | 1.00000 | 1.00000 | 1.00000 | 1.00000 | 0.99988 | 0.99498 | 0.93621 | 0.69312 | 0.30865 |
|  | 48 | 1.00000 | 1.00000 | 1.00000 | 1.00000 | 1.00000 | 1.00000 | 0.99995 | 0.99725 | 0.95770 | 0.75957 | 0.38218 |
|  | 49 | 1.00000 | 1.00000 | 1.00000 | 1.00000 | 1.00000 | 1.00000 | 0.99998 | 0.99855 | 0.97290 | 0.81727 | 0.46020 |
|  | 50 | 1.00000 | 1.00000 | 1.00000 | 1.00000 | 1.00000 | 1.00000 | 0.99999 | 0.99926 | 0.98324 | 0.86542 | 0.53979 |
|  | 51 | 1.00000 | 1.00000 | 1.00000 | 1.00000 | 1.00000 | 1.00000 | 1.00000 | 0.99964 | 0.98999 | 0.90405 | 0.61782 |
|  | 52 | 1.00000 | 1.00000 | 1.00000 | 1.00000 | 1.00000 | 1.00000 | 1.00000 | 0.99983 | 0.99424 | 0.93383 | 0.69135 |
|  | 53 | 1.00000 | 1.00000 | 1.00000 | 1.00000 | 1.00000 | 1.00000 | 1.00000 | 0.99992 | 0.99680 | 0.95589 | 0.75794 |
|  | 54 | 1.00000 | 1.00000 | 1.00000 | 1.00000 | 1.00000 | 1.00000 | 1.00000 | 0.99997 | 0.99829 | 0.97161 | 0.81590 |
|  | 55 | 1.00000 | 1.00000 | 1.00000 | 1.00000 | 1.00000 | 1.00000 | 1.00000 | 0.99999 | 0.99912 | 0.98236 | 0.86437 |
|  | 56 | 1.00000 | 1.00000 | 1.00000 | 1.00000 | 1.00000 | 1.00000 | 1.00000 | 0.99999 | 0.99956 | 0.98943 | 0.90333 |
|  | 57 | 1.00000 | 1.00000 | 1.00000 | 1.00000 | 1.00000 | 1.00000 | 1.00000 | 1.00000 | 0.99979 | 0.99389 | 0.93339 |
|  | 58 | 1.00000 | 1.00000 | 1.00000 | 1.00000 | 1.00000 | 1.00000 | 1.00000 | 1.00000 | 0.99990 | 0.99660 | 0.95569 |
|  | 59 | 1.00000 | 1.00000 | 1.00000 | 1.00000 | 1.00000 | 1.00000 | 1.00000 | 1.00000 | 0.99996 | 0.99818 | 0.97156 |
|  | 60 | 1.00000 | 1.00000 | 1.00000 | 1.00000 | 1.00000 | 1.00000 | 1.00000 | 1.00000 | 0.99998 | 0.99906 | 0.98240 |
|  | 61 | 1.00000 | 1.00000 | 1.00000 | 1.00000 | 1.00000 | 1.00000 | 1.00000 | 1.00000 | 0.99999 | 0.99953 | 0.98951 |
|  | 62 | 1.00000 | 1.00000 | 1.00000 | 1.00000 | 1.00000 | 1.00000 | 1.00000 | 1.00000 | 1.00000 | 0.99978 | 0.99398 |
|  | 63 | 1.00000 | 1.00000 | 1.00000 | 1.00000 | 1.00000 | 1.00000 | 1.00000 | 1.00000 | 1.00000 | 0.99990 | 0.99668 |
|  | 64 | 1.00000 | 1.00000 | 1.00000 | 1.00000 | 1.00000 | 1.00000 | 1.00000 | 1.00000 | 1.00000 | 0.99996 | 0.99824 |
|  | 65 | 1.00000 | 1.00000 | 1.00000 | 1.00000 | 1.00000 | 1.00000 | 1.00000 | 1.00000 | 1.00000 | 0.99998 | 0.99911 |

## Cumulative Binomial Distribution - 8

| n | x | .01 | .05 | .10 | .15 | .20 | .25 | .30 | .35 | .40 | .45 | .50 |
|---|---|---|---|---|---|---|---|---|---|---|---|---|
| 100 | 66 | 1.00000 | 1.00000 | 1.00000 | 1.00000 | 1.00000 | 1.00000 | 1.00000 | 1.00000 | 1.00000 | 0.99999 | 0.99956 |
| ctd | 67 | 1.00000 | 1.00000 | 1.00000 | 1.00000 | 1.00000 | 1.00000 | 1.00000 | 1.00000 | 1.00000 | 1.00000 | 0.99980 |
| | 68 | 1.00000 | 1.00000 | 1.00000 | 1.00000 | 1.00000 | 1.00000 | 1.00000 | 1.00000 | 1.00000 | 1.00000 | 0.99991 |
| | 69 | 1.00000 | 1.00000 | 1.00000 | 1.00000 | 1.00000 | 1.00000 | 1.00000 | 1.00000 | 1.00000 | 1.00000 | 0.99996 |
| | 70 | 1.00000 | 1.00000 | 1.00000 | 1.00000 | 1.00000 | 1.00000 | 1.00000 | 1.00000 | 1.00000 | 1.00000 | 0.99998 |
| | 71 | 1.00000 | 1.00000 | 1.00000 | 1.00000 | 1.00000 | 1.00000 | 1.00000 | 1.00000 | 1.00000 | 1.00000 | 0.99999 |
| | 72 | 1.00000 | 1.00000 | 1.00000 | 1.00000 | 1.00000 | 1.00000 | 1.00000 | 1.00000 | 1.00000 | 1.00000 | 1.00000 |
| | 73 | 1.00000 | 1.00000 | 1.00000 | 1.00000 | 1.00000 | 1.00000 | 1.00000 | 1.00000 | 1.00000 | 1.00000 | 1.00000 |
| | 74 | 1.00000 | 1.00000 | 1.00000 | 1.00000 | 1.00000 | 1.00000 | 1.00000 | 1.00000 | 1.00000 | 1.00000 | 1.00000 |
| | 75 | 1.00000 | 1.00000 | 1.00000 | 1.00000 | 1.00000 | 1.00000 | 1.00000 | 1.00000 | 1.00000 | 1.00000 | 1.00000 |
| | 76 | 1.00000 | 1.00000 | 1.00000 | 1.00000 | 1.00000 | 1.00000 | 1.00000 | 1.00000 | 1.00000 | 1.00000 | 1.00000 |
| | 77 | 1.00000 | 1.00000 | 1.00000 | 1.00000 | 1.00000 | 1.00000 | 1.00000 | 1.00000 | 1.00000 | 1.00000 | 1.00000 |
| | 78 | 1.00000 | 1.00000 | 1.00000 | 1.00000 | 1.00000 | 1.00000 | 1.00000 | 1.00000 | 1.00000 | 1.00000 | 1.00000 |
| | 79 | 1.00000 | 1.00000 | 1.00000 | 1.00000 | 1.00000 | 1.00000 | 1.00000 | 1.00000 | 1.00000 | 1.00000 | 1.00000 |
| | 80 | 1.00000 | 1.00000 | 1.00000 | 1.00000 | 1.00000 | 1.00000 | 1.00000 | 1.00000 | 1.00000 | 1.00000 | 1.00000 |
| | 81 | 1.00000 | 1.00000 | 1.00000 | 1.00000 | 1.00000 | 1.00000 | 1.00000 | 1.00000 | 1.00000 | 1.00000 | 1.00000 |
| | 82 | 1.00000 | 1.00000 | 1.00000 | 1.00000 | 1.00000 | 1.00000 | 1.00000 | 1.00000 | 1.00000 | 1.00000 | 1.00000 |
| | 83 | 1.00000 | 1.00000 | 1.00000 | 1.00000 | 1.00000 | 1.00000 | 1.00000 | 1.00000 | 1.00000 | 1.00000 | 1.00000 |
| | 84 | 1.00000 | 1.00000 | 1.00000 | 1.00000 | 1.00000 | 1.00000 | 1.00000 | 1.00000 | 1.00000 | 1.00000 | 1.00000 |
| | 85 | 1.00000 | 1.00000 | 1.00000 | 1.00000 | 1.00000 | 1.00000 | 1.00000 | 1.00000 | 1.00000 | 1.00000 | 1.00000 |
| | 86 | 1.00000 | 1.00000 | 1.00000 | 1.00000 | 1.00000 | 1.00000 | 1.00000 | 1.00000 | 1.00000 | 1.00000 | 1.00000 |
| | 87 | 1.00000 | 1.00000 | 1.00000 | 1.00000 | 1.00000 | 1.00000 | 1.00000 | 1.00000 | 1.00000 | 1.00000 | 1.00000 |
| | 88 | 1.00000 | 1.00000 | 1.00000 | 1.00000 | 1.00000 | 1.00000 | 1.00000 | 1.00000 | 1.00000 | 1.00000 | 1.00000 |
| | 89 | 1.00000 | 1.00000 | 1.00000 | 1.00000 | 1.00000 | 1.00000 | 1.00000 | 1.00000 | 1.00000 | 1.00000 | 1.00000 |
| | 90 | 1.00000 | 1.00000 | 1.00000 | 1.00000 | 1.00000 | 1.00000 | 1.00000 | 1.00000 | 1.00000 | 1.00000 | 1.00000 |
| | 91 | 1.00000 | 1.00000 | 1.00000 | 1.00000 | 1.00000 | 1.00000 | 1.00000 | 1.00000 | 1.00000 | 1.00000 | 1.00000 |
| | 92 | 1.00000 | 1.00000 | 1.00000 | 1.00000 | 1.00000 | 1.00000 | 1.00000 | 1.00000 | 1.00000 | 1.00000 | 1.00000 |
| | 93 | 1.00000 | 1.00000 | 1.00000 | 1.00000 | 1.00000 | 1.00000 | 1.00000 | 1.00000 | 1.00000 | 1.00000 | 1.00000 |
| | 94 | 1.00000 | 1.00000 | 1.00000 | 1.00000 | 1.00000 | 1.00000 | 1.00000 | 1.00000 | 1.00000 | 1.00000 | 1.00000 |
| | 95 | 1.00000 | 1.00000 | 1.00000 | 1.00000 | 1.00000 | 1.00000 | 1.00000 | 1.00000 | 1.00000 | 1.00000 | 1.00000 |
| | 96 | 1.00000 | 1.00000 | 1.00000 | 1.00000 | 1.00000 | 1.00000 | 1.00000 | 1.00000 | 1.00000 | 1.00000 | 1.00000 |
| | 97 | 1.00000 | 1.00000 | 1.00000 | 1.00000 | 1.00000 | 1.00000 | 1.00000 | 1.00000 | 1.00000 | 1.00000 | 1.00000 |
| | 98 | 1.00000 | 1.00000 | 1.00000 | 1.00000 | 1.00000 | 1.00000 | 1.00000 | 1.00000 | 1.00000 | 1.00000 | 1.00000 |
| | 99 | 1.00000 | 1.00000 | 1.00000 | 1.00000 | 1.00000 | 1.00000 | 1.00000 | 1.00000 | 1.00000 | 1.00000 | 1.00000 |
| | 100 | 1.00000 | 1.00000 | 1.00000 | 1.00000 | 1.00000 | 1.00000 | 1.00000 | 1.00000 | 1.00000 | 1.00000 | 1.00000 |

# Bibliography

[1] Robert I. Kobacoff, *R in Action: Data Analysis and Graphics with R*, 2nd ed., Manning Publications, 2015.

[2] http://www.businessdictionary.com/definition/sampling-distribution.html

[3] https://www.emathzone.com/tutorials/basic-statistics/simple-random-sampling.html#ixzz5EhfEhbLUhttps://www.emathzone.com/tutorials/basic-statistics/simple-random-sampling.html#ixzz5EhaygQsf

[4] https://www.britannica.com/science/statistics/Sample-survey-methods#ref367539

[5] https://www.intmath.com/counting-probability/13-poisson-probability-distribution.php#mean_

[6] https://www.umass.edu/wsp/resources/poisson/#end_

[7] https://www.isixsigma.com/tools-templates/control-charts/a-guide-to-control-charts/

[8] https://businessjargons.com/chi-square-distribution.html

[9] https://www.statisticshowto.datasciencecentral.com/probability-and-statistics/chi-square/

# Author's Biography

## MUSTAPHA AKINKUNMI

**Dr. Mustapha Akinkunmi** is a Financial Economist and Technology Strategist. He has over 25 years of experience in estimation, planning, and forecasting using statistical and econometric methods, with particular expertise in risk, expected utility, discounting, binomial-tree valuation methods, financial econometrics models, Monte Carlo simulations, macroeconomics, and exchange rate modeling. Dr. Akinkunmi has performed extensive software development for quantitative analysis of capital markets, revenue and payment gateway, predictive analytics, data science, and credit risk management.

He has a record of success in identifying and implementing change management programs and institutional development initiatives in both public and private sector organizations. He has been in high profile positions as a Consultant, Financial Advisor, Project Manager, and Business Strategist to AT&T, Salomon Brothers, Goldman Sachs, Phibro Energy, First Boston (Credit Suisse First Boston), World Bank, and Central Bank of Nigeria. He is an internationally recognized co-author (*Introduction to Strategic Financial Management*, May 2013) and leader in demand analysis, specializing in working with very large databases. Furthermore, he has conducted teaching and applied research in areas that include analyses of expenditure patterns, inflation and exchange rate modeling for Manhattan College, Riverdale, NY, Fordham University, New York, NY, University of Lagos, Lagos, Nigeria, State University of New York-FIT, New York, NY, Montclair State University, Montclair, NJ, and American University, Yola, Nigeria.

In 1990, he founded Technology Solutions Incorporated (TSI) in New York, which focused on data science and software application development for clients including major financial services institutions. After ten years of successful operations and rapid growth under Dr. Akinkunmi's leadership, TSI was acquired by a publicly traded technology company based in the U.S. in a value-creating transaction. Dr. Akinkunmi was the former Honorable Commissioner for Finance, Lagos State, Nigeria. He is now an Associate Professor of Finance and Chair of the Accounting and Finance Department at the American University of Nigeria, Yola, Nigeria.

著名数学家 A. Battersby 曾指出:

　　没有数学语言的帮助,具有复杂组织的商业就会延缓发展,甚至停止发展.在管理科学中也同其他科学一样,数学成为进步的条件.

　　在商业与工业生产中统计学是被用到最多的一个数学分支,尽管学数学的人认为它太简单,不够深刻,但毕竟有用才是硬道理.

　　本书是一部英文原版的统计学著作,中文书名可译为《R 统计学概论》.本书的作者为穆斯塔法・阿金昆米(Mustapha Akinkunmi),他是尼日利亚人.穆斯塔法・阿金昆米博士现在是尼日利亚约拉的尼日利亚美国大学金融学副教授、会计与金融系主任,他是一位金融经济学家和技术战略家,他在使用统计和计量经济学方法进行估计、规划和预测方面拥有超过25 年的经验,尤其在风险、预期效用、贴现、二叉树估值方法、金融计量经济学模型、蒙特卡洛模拟、宏观经济学和汇率建模方面拥有丰富的经验.穆斯塔法・阿金昆米博士为资本市场、收入和支付网关、预测分析、数据科学和信用风险管理的定量分析进行了广泛的软件开发工作.

　　作者在前言中介绍:

　　第 1 章:统计分析介绍

　　本章可以帮助那些对统计学中的不同度量尺度知之甚少或一无所知的读者.它有助于读者理解数据的概念、数据收集,以及掌握如何呈现所收集数据的方法.此外,本章还帮助读者理解不同类别的数据分组,探索数据分析和可视化.

編
輯
手
記

第 2 章:R 软件介绍

本章重点介绍如何在计算机系统上下载和安装 R 包,给出了使用 R 的原因,并详细说明安装 R 所涉及的步骤.本章通过示例向读者介绍 R 中的基本功能.本章介绍 R 中的基本操作、内置函数(数值、统计概率)以及 R 中的其他有用的函数.本章概述了如何导入包以及如何更改用于读取和写入本地平面文件的目录.它有助于解释如何使用 R 命令连接到数据库,演示了通过 R 中的可视化进行的数据探索,并绘制了所需的图表.

第 3 章:描述数据

本章提供了不同类型的统计方法来分析与业务相关的数据.本章重点讨论了集中趋势和分散的度量,并给出了集中趋势和分散度量的特点.本章中提到的每个描述性统计数据都给出了实际示例,以及简短的解释性 R 脚本.本章还通过说明性示例解释了分布的形状.

第 4 章:基本的概率概念

本章给出了一些概率术语的意义——实验、样本空间、基本事件、互补事件、互斥事件、包含事件、韦恩图、独立和非独立事件,将概率公理与概率的基本属性一起进行了处理.本章将引导读者了解概率以及条件概率的加性与乘性规则.本章展示了如何使用 R 来生成和计算概率.

第 5 章:离散概率分布

本章解释了离散概率分布、概率质量函数、期望值和离散概率分布的方差的概念.给出了离散概率的例子,并着重讨论了二项概率分布,其中一个小节专门展示如何推导二项分布的期望值和方差.本章教读者如何从二项分布中生成随机样本.本章中给出的所有示例也是用 R 语言编写的,以使读者熟悉该软件.

第 6 章:连续概率分布

除了前面章节解释的离散概率分布之外,读者也需要了解连续概率分布.本章重点介绍其他章节中提到的其他连续概率分布中的正态分布.读者可以清晰地区分离散概率分布和连续概率分布.用清晰的例子解释正态曲线,并说明了正态分布的性质.另外,读者可以使用标准正态分数($z$—分数)去解决商业问题.本章向读者展示了如何使用正态近似来解决二项式问题.许多工作实例以及 R 代码均以正态概率给出,以使读者对其在商业中的应用更加敏感.

第 7 章:其他连续概率分布

本章是第 6 章的扩展.本章解释了在假设检验中很重要的常用分布.这些分布是 Student-$t$、卡方检验和 F 分布,以及它们的性质和用途.本章帮助读者熟悉上述每个分布用于假设检验时的条件.本章的主要目的是让读者能够知道何时可以使用每个分布,并获得分布的相应表值,甚至使用 R 命令去完成上述操作.

第 8 章:抽样与抽样分布

本章概述了抽样技术及其优缺点.本章将抽样分为概率抽样和非概率抽样.均值的抽样分布是通过对数据进行替换的和不替换的简单随机抽样来建立的.本书的这一部分通过实例介绍了中心极限定理及其意义.

第 9 章:单总体均值与比例的置信区间

本章通过示例说明如何构建均值和比例的置信区间.在给出置信水平和误差范围时,它更清楚地说明了如何计算样本量.本章给出了决定误差幅度的主要因素.读者应该使用适当的测试统计来构建置信界限.

第 10 章:单总体均值与比例的假设检验

这一章是关于决策过程的,它解释了如何形成和验证假设.它为读者准备了进行假设检验和解释结果的步骤.本章帮助读者使用现有数据得出有效结论.

第 11 章:回归分析与相关分析

两个或者更多变量之间存在的关系会在本章中进行讨论.读者将会理解并区分回归分析与相关分析.本章解释了简单线性回归和多元线性回归的用途和假设.本章帮助读者了解了回归模型的阐释,以及怎样在做出预测时使用回归分析.还借助图表讨论了变量之间的关联程度;这将使读者直观地了解回归分析和相关分析.文中给出了许多例子来扩大读者对该主题的理解范围.

第 12 章:泊松分布

本章处理了计数数据.给出了统计的定义和泊松分布的实际例子.通过不同的泊松分布图来展示作为其参数增加的特征.本章推导并证明泊松分布的均值和方差是相同的.本章还解释了泊松分布在生活中各个方面的应用.而且,该部分还通过一些工作实例证明了泊松是如何近似为二项分布的.

第 13 章:均匀分布

本章的主要目标是让读者能够识别均匀分布,以及它的使用和应用.本章借助图表和使用均匀分布的条件来解释均匀分布.还展示了如何导出一个均匀分布的均值和方差.

本书目录为:

要理解概率与统计,先要理解随机性.

　　研究气体的性质知道,由于气体是由数目众多的分子构成,这些分子以很快的速度进行剧烈的运动,在运动的过程中相互碰撞而改变其动量和方向,因而每个分子的运动是随机现象,而大量的分子运动呈现出的总体现象——温度、压强却满足波义耳定律.

　　曾经有人认为,之所以会出现事前不可预言的偶然现象,是因为我们对一个现象出现的原因还缺乏全面的知识,有人认为随着科学的发展和人类认识的深化,总有一天将不再存在不可预言的随机现象.

　　诚然,增加条件组的条件来减少随机性是可能的.例如,人的高度按不同的年龄、地区、性别是有差异的,若限定在同一地区,在一定年龄范围内选取同性别的人来测量高度,可能会得到比一般任意选取时较均匀的结果,但随机因素的影响总是不可避免的,很多现象初始条件的稍微改变,其产生的后果却差别很大,在实际中即使人们有可能把条件组的条件绝对控制到每次都一样,但影响的因素还是大量

的,且互相作用错综复杂,例如在关于气体分子运动的例子中,即使我们把一立方
厘米气体中的 $2.683 \times 10^{18}$ 个分子的运动方程和初始条件都列出来,且不说我们要
求出这组联立方程的解也是很困难的,更应注意这里在建立方程和确定初始条件
时已是忽略了许多次要的,但往往是随机的因素.

再一个是统计量(Statistic)的概念.样本的已知函数,其作用是把样本中有关总体的信
息汇集起来,是数理统计学中的一个重要的基本概念,常用的统计量有样本矩、次序统计量、
$U$ 统计量和秩统计量等.

客观地说,本书的数学抽象度是较低的,如概率论中曾经指出,概率是指一个事件发生
的可能性大小的度量,而事件是指"事情".一般数学专业会先用样本空间的观点讲述事件,
进而介绍概率的公理化定义①.


## 一、样本空间

在概率论中,随机试验是指在一定条件下出现的结果带有随机性的试验.我们
用 $E$ 表示随机试验.随机试验的所有可能出现的结果构成一个集合,而把每一个可
能出现的试验结果称为一个基本事件.随机试验 $E$ 的所有基本事件构成所谓样本
空间.下面举几个实际例子.

**例 1**  掷一枚分币.出现"正面""反面"都是基本事件.这两个基本事件构成一
个样本空间.

**例 2**  掷一颗骰子.分别出现"1 点""2 点""3 点""4 点""5 点""6 点"都是基本
事件,这六个基本事件构成一个样本空间.

**例 3**  向实数轴的 $(0,1)$ 区间上随意地投掷一个点.在 $(0,1)$ 区间中的每一个点
是一个基本事件,而所有点的集合(即 $(0,1)$ 区间)构成一个样本空间.

抽象地说,样本空间是一个点的集合,此集合中每个点都称为样本点.样本空
间记为 $\Omega=(\omega)$,其中 $\omega$ 表示样本点.这里小括号表示所有样本点构成的集合.

样本空间的某些子集称为事件.从数学观点看,要求事件(样本点的集合)之间
有一定的联系,亦即对事件需加一些约束.

**定义**  设样本空间 $\Omega=(\omega)$ 的某些子集构成的集合记为 $\mathcal{F}$,如果 $\mathcal{F}$ 满足下列性
质:

(1) $\Omega \in \mathcal{F}$;

---

① 摘自《随机过程》,汪荣鑫编,西安交通大学出版社,2013.

(2)若 $A\in\mathscr{F}$,则 $\overline{A}=\Omega-A\in\mathscr{F}$;

(3)若 $A_k\in\mathscr{F},k=1,2,\cdots,$则 $\bigcup_{k=1}^{\infty}A_k\in\mathscr{F}$,

那么称 $\mathscr{F}$ 是一个波雷尔(Borel)事件域,或 $\sigma$ 事件域.波雷尔事件域中每一个样本空间 $\Omega$ 的子集称为一个事件.

特别指出,样本空间 $\Omega$ 称为必然事件,而空集 $\varnothing$ 称为不可能事件.

在上面三个样本空间的例子中,每一个样本点都是基本事件.但是,一般并不要求样本点必须是基本事件.

在例 1 中共有两个样本点:"正面""反面".作 $\mathscr{F}=($正面或反面,正面,反面,空集$)$,它构成一个波雷尔事件域,其中每一个元素都是一个事件.需要说明,$\mathscr{F}$ 表达式中的花括号,是指事件的集合.

在例 2 中共有六个样本点,记 $\omega_i$ 为出现"$i$ 点"的样本点,$i=1,2,3,4,5,6.$ 作 $\mathscr{F}=\{\omega_1,\omega_2,\cdots,\omega_6,(\omega_1,\omega_2),(\omega_1,\omega_3),\cdots,(\omega_5,\omega_6),(\omega_1,\omega_2,\omega_3),\cdots,(\omega_4,\omega_5,\omega_6),(\omega_1,\omega_2,\omega_3,\omega_4),\cdots,(\omega_3,\omega_4,\omega_5,\omega_6),(\omega_1,\omega_2,\omega_3,\omega_4,\omega_5),\cdots,(\omega_2,\omega_3,\omega_4,\omega_5,\omega_6),(\omega_1,\omega_2,\omega_3,\omega_4,\omega_5,\omega_6)\},$它构成一个波雷尔事件域.这里每一对小括号表示它所包含的样本点的集合.$\mathscr{F}$ 中每一元素(即 $\omega_1,\omega_2,\cdots,\omega_6$ 或每一对小括号表示的样本点集合)是一个事件.

在例 3 中,作 $\mathscr{F}_1=\{(0,1)$ 区间中任意子集$\}.\mathscr{F}_1$ 构成一个波雷尔事件域,其中每一个元素是一个事件.再构造另一个波雷尔事件域.若取 $G=\{\bigcup_{k=1}^{n}(a_k,b_k]:0<a_k<b_k<1,k=1,2,\cdots,n,n\geqslant1\},$即 $G$ 是 $(0,1)$ 区间中所有的左开右闭区间有限和集构成的集类.集类是指以点集作为元素的集合.显然 $G$ 不具有波雷尔事件域的第三条性质,这是因为 $G$ 中可列无限个元素之和,也可以是无限多个左开右闭区间之和,这种和不再是 $G$ 中的元素,因而 $G$ 不是波雷尔事件域.记 $\mathscr{F}_2$ 是包含 $G$ 的最小的波雷尔事件域.数学上可以证明 $\mathscr{F}_2$ 与 $\mathscr{F}_1$ 并不重合,而 $\mathscr{F}_2$ 中的元素比 $\mathscr{F}_1$ 少.波雷尔事件域 $\mathscr{F}_2$ 中的每一个元素都是事件.

需要指出,在上面的三个例子中,四个 $\mathscr{F}$ 有三个取为样本空间 $\Omega$ 中任意子集全体构成的波雷尔域,因而样本空间的任意一个子集都是事件.但是,$\mathscr{F}$ 还可以选 $\Omega$ 的一部分子集构成一个波雷尔事件域,如例 3 中的 $\mathscr{F}_2$.又如在例 1 中取 $\mathscr{F}=\{\Omega,\varnothing\}$,这种 $\mathscr{F}$ 也构成波雷尔事件域.此时只有两个事件,但这样取 $\mathscr{F}$ 的实际意义不大.

## 二、概率的公理化定义

在概率论中曾提及概率的统计定义和古典概率定义.概率的统计定义与大量

重复试验相联系. 古典概率定义要求样本空间由 $N$ 个等可能性的基本事件构成, 具有一定的局限性. 现在介绍一种概率的抽象的数学定义——公理化定义. 这种定义是从一些具体的概率定义(如概率的统计定义,古典概率定义等)抽象出来的, 同时又保留了具体概率定义中的一些特征. 事件的概率对应于波雷尔事件域 $\mathscr{F}$ 中每一个 $\Omega$ 的子集的一个数, 即可以看成集合函数.

**概率的公理化定义**　设 $P(A)$ 是定义在样本空间 $\Omega$ 中波雷尔事件域 $\mathscr{F}$ 上的集合函数. 如果 $P(A)$ 满足:

(1) 对任一 $A \in \mathscr{F}$, 有 $0 \leqslant P(A) \leqslant 1$;

(2) $P(\Omega) = 1, P(\varnothing) = 0$;

(3) 若 $A_1, A_2, \cdots$ 两两不相交, 即 $A_k A_j = \varnothing, k \neq j$, 且 $A_k \in \mathscr{F}, k = 1, 2, \cdots$, 则

$$P(\bigcup_{k=1}^{\infty} A_k) = \sum_{k=1}^{\infty} P(A_k)$$

那么称 $P$ 是波雷尔事件域上的概率.

在例 1 中定义 $P(A) = \dfrac{k}{2}$, 其中 $k$ 是事件 $A$ 包含的样本点数, $k = 0, 1, 2$, 那么 $P$ 是概率. 另外, 如果定义 $P(\text{正面}) = \dfrac{11}{20}, P(\text{反面}) = \dfrac{9}{20}, P(\text{正面或反面}) = 1, P(\text{空集}) = 0$, 这样定义的 $P$ 也是概率.

在例 2 中定义 $P(A) = \dfrac{k}{6}$, 其中 $k$ 是事件 $A$ 包含的样本点数, $k = 0, 1, 2, 3, 4, 5, 6$, 那么 $P$ 是概率.

在例 3 中考虑波雷尔事件域 $\mathscr{F}_2$, 数学上可以证明在 $\mathscr{F}_2$ 上存在一个集合函数 $P$, 满足概率公理化定义中的三个条件, 且对 $A = \bigcup\limits_{k=1}^{\infty} (a_k, b_k]$, 有 $P(A) = \sum\limits_{k=1}^{n} (b_k - a_k)$, 其中 $(a_k, b_k]$ 两两不相交(显然 $A$ 是 $G$ 中元素), 所以这个 $\mathscr{F}_2$ 上的集合函数 $P$ 是概率. 此概率表示 $(0, 1)$ 区间上的均匀分布. 特别指出, $\mathscr{F}_1$ 是由 $(0, 1)$ 区间上任意子集构成的波雷尔事件域, 数学上已经证明并不存在 $\mathscr{F}_1$ 上的集合函数 $P$, 对上述事件 $A$ 有 $P(A) = \sum\limits_{k=1}^{n} (b_k - a_k)$, 且满足概率公理化定义中的三个条件.

对随机试验 $E$ 而言, 样本空间 $\Omega$ 给出它的所有可能的试验结果, $\mathscr{F}$ 给出了由这些可能结果组成的各种各样的事件, 而 $P$ 给出每一事件发生的概率. $(\Omega, \mathscr{F}, P)$ 称为概率空间.

统计的实用非常广泛,例如有一种叫统计决策理论①.

　　要完整地描述一个统计问题,除了其统计模型——样本空间与样本分布族外,还必须明确以下两点:①需要解决什么问题,即所得结论采取怎样的形式.②用怎样的准则去判定不同的解法的优劣.Wald 于 1950 年创立的统计决策(又称统计判决)提供了阐释这些问题的一种方便的框架.

　　按 Wald 理论的观点,一个统计问题的完整描述,包含三个要素,其一就是样本空间和样本分布族,另外两个则分别针对我们刚才提出的两个问题,它们是:

　　1. 行动空间,或称决策空间,即对所提问题所有可能做出的结论或答案的总和 $A$. 例如,问题是通过对一批产品进行抽样检验以决定是否接收该批产品,可能的结论有两个:$a_0$——接收,$a_1$——拒收,于是 $A=\{a_0,a_1\}$,即行动空间仅由两个元素构成,不论 $a_0$ 或 $a_1$ 都代表人们采取的一种决策或行动,因此在本例中,"行动空间"或"决策空间"的用词都甚属自然,在有些例子中,所作结论或答案不一定立即牵涉具体的行动,但我们不必拘泥于这一点.

　　如果我们的问题是要通过从该批产品中抽样以估计其不合格品率,那么行动空间 $A$ 可取为闭区间 $[0,1]$(点估计),或 $[0,1]$ 区间的一切子区间之集(区间估计).对前者而言,$A$ 中的一元 $a$ 表示"用 $a$ 去估计该批产品的不合格率"这个行动或决策,对后者有类似的解释,又如,有 $r$ 批产品,要通过抽样检验来对其不合格品率的高低定出一个次序,则行动空间 $A$ 包含 $r!$ 个元,每个元都是 $(1,2,\cdots,r)$ 的某一置换.例如,$(i_1,i_2,\cdots,i_r)$ 表示这样一个结论:第 $i_1$ 批产品不合格品率最高,其次是第 $i_2$ 批,等等.

　　大多数常见的统计问题,其行动空间 $A$ 不外乎这三种情况:①$A$ 包含两个元素.这种情况一般可解释或归结为有关参数 $\theta$ 的假设检验问题.如在上例中,是否接收该批产品,取决于其不合格品率 $\theta$ 的值,可以指定这样一个值 $\theta_0$,当 $\theta\leqslant\theta_0$ 时认为不合格品率足够小,以至认为接收该批产品有利.若 $\theta>\theta_0$,则相反.于是,是否接收该批产品的问题归结为检验二项分布 $B(n,\theta)$ 中有关 $\theta$ 的假设 $\theta\leqslant\theta_0$ 的问题.②$A$ 是欧氏空间中的一个区域.这种情况一般可解释为有关参数 $\theta$ 的点或区间估计问题.③$A$ 中包含有限个元,其数目大于 2.这种情况照理说在应用上出现很多很重要,且往往在提法上比假设检验的提法更合理更自然,但这种情况(称为多判决问题)在目前数理统计学中研究得比前两种情况少得多,大概是由于其在数学上不易处理因而难于得出深入的结果.

---

① 　摘自《高等数理统计学习》,陈希孺著,中国科学技术大学出版社,1999.

2.损失函数.针对每一具体情况(即参数 $\theta$ 的具体值),各种可能的行动或决策,其优劣有差别,如在上例中,真实的不合格品率为 $\theta$,而我们采取 $a$ 这个"行动",即用 $a$ 去估计 $\theta$,显然,$a=\theta$ 这个行动最好,$a$ 离 $\theta$ 越远就越差,Wald 引进一个定义于 $\Theta \times A$ 上的非负函数 $L(\theta,a)$,以从数量上来刻画这个优劣程度,注意 $L$ 是代表因采取行动 $a$ 而带来的损失,故 $L(\theta,a)$ 越小,行动 $a$ 就越好.如在前例中,针对 $A=\{a_0,a_1\}$ 和 $A=[0,1]$ 这两种情况,损失函数可分别取为

$$L(\theta,a)=\begin{cases}0, & \text{当 } \theta \leqslant \theta_0,a=a_0,\text{或 } \theta>\theta_0,a=a_1 \\ 1, & \text{当 } \theta \leqslant \theta_0,a=a_1,\text{或 } \theta>\theta_0,a=a_0\end{cases}$$

$$L(\theta,a)=(\theta-a)^2$$

前一个取法体现了假设检验中的两类错误并认为这两类错误的后果一样,后者是著名的平方损失函数,在点估计的理论中用得很多.

行动空间及损失函数,连同样本空间与样本分布族,就构成一个统计决策问题的完整提法(在 Bayes 统计中还需要规定 $\theta$ 的先验分布,以后再讨论这个问题).

(统计)决策函数及其风险函数.定义于样本空间 $\mathcal{X}$ 上而取值于行动空间上的函数 $\delta$,称为是该统计决策问题的一个决策函数或称判决函数.一旦根据某种考虑选定了这样一个决策函数 $\delta$,则每当有了样本 $x$ 时,算出 $\delta(x)$,它是 $A$ 的一元,就用它作为我们所采取的行动或决策.因此在 Wald 的理论中,解决一个统计问题,就是要选取一个适当的决策函数.

当真正的参数值为 $\theta$,选用决策函数 $\delta$,则当样本为 $x$ 时,所蒙受的损失为 $L(\theta,\delta(x))$.此值越小,$\delta$ 也就越好,但这个损失依赖于参数真值 $\theta$ 和样本 $x$,前者未知而后者为随机的,故需要寻找某种综合性指标以作为比较的标准.目前在统计决策理论中惯用的指标是损失函数 $L(\theta,\delta(x))$ 的期望值

$$R(\theta,\delta)=E_\theta(L(\theta,\delta(X)))=\int_{\mathcal{X}} L(\theta,\delta(x))\mathrm{d}P_\theta(x)$$

这里的记号 $E_\theta,P_\theta$ 都是为了强调:计算期望和概率是在参数值为 $\theta$ 的条件下进行的.$R(\theta,\delta)$ 称为决策函数 $\delta$ 的风险函数,它就是当参数值为 $\theta$ 时,采用决策函数 $\delta$ 的平均损失,风险越小,决策函数就越好,设 $\delta_0$ 和 $\delta$ 为两个决策函数,如果

$$R(\theta,\delta_0) \leqslant R(\theta,\delta), \theta \in \Theta \tag{1}$$

那么称 $\delta_0$ 一致地优于 $\delta$.如果至少对一个 $\theta$ 上式成立严格的不等号,那么称 $\delta_0$ 严格地一致优于 $\delta$.这时,从风险尽可能小的角度看,就没有理由采用 $\delta$,因为用 $\delta_0$ 有更好的效果(当然,在应用上也还有别的考虑,如计算上的方便,直观上是否易于为应用者接受等,损失函数的选择及采用综合指标 $R(\theta,\delta)$ 的合理性也可能受到质疑),假定存在这样一个决策函数 $\delta_0$,使对任意的决策函数都成立式(1),则称 $\delta_0$ 为一致最优的.假如这种 $\delta_0$ 真正存在,则在风险尽可能小的原则下,它是最好的选择,可

惜的是,在任何有意义的统计决策问题中,这样的 $\delta_0$ 绝不可能存在.因此,为了通过风险函数去比较决策函数的优劣,还须建立较为松弛的比较准则,这个问题在以后有机会讨论.

为定义风险函数,需要积分 $\int_{\mathscr{X}} L(\theta,\delta(x))\mathrm{d}P_\theta(x)$ 有意义.这需对 $L$ 及 $\delta$ 加上一些可测性条件,例如:

(1)在行动空间中引进 $\sigma$ 域 $\mathscr{B}_A$,$L(\theta,a)$ 作为 $a$ 的函数,为 $\mathscr{B}_A$ 可测.

(2)$\delta(x)$ 为 $\mathscr{B}_x$ 可测.

这两条,加上 $L$ 非负的事实,保证了上述积分有意义.

下面来介绍两个与风险函数的比较有关的重要概念.

1.容许性.一个决策函数 $\delta$,如果存在着一个决策函数 $\delta^*$,其风险函数严格地一致优于 $\delta$,则称 $\delta$ 是不可容许的,否则就是可容许的.这个名称的来由显然:若把"风险尽可能小"作为选择决策函数的唯一标准,则自然舍 $\delta$ 而用 $\delta^*$,不过,在现实中没有这么简单.决策函数在直观上看的合理性,易于为实用者接受与否,计算上的难易等,都可与取舍有关,还有损失定得是否合理,及风险(它是平均损失)作为衡量优良性的指标的合理性等,都可受到质疑.

在数理统计学中,讨论两类容许性问题:一是证明特定的决策函数为容许或否,二是寻求在一特定问题中全部可容许决策函数.这是理论统计学中最困难的方面之一,至今进展有限并主要限于几类简单的参数估计模型中.

2.(决策函数的)完全类与本质完全类.设 $J$ 为一类决策函数,$J_1 \subset J$.若对任何 $\delta \in J - J_1$,必存在 $\delta_1 \in J_1$ 严格地一致优于 $\delta$,则称 $J_1$ 为($J$ 的)完全子类,如果 $J$ 就是全体决策函数的类,那么 $J_1$ 常称为完全类,若在前面将"严格地"一词删去,则 $J_1$ 称为本质完全子类.Wald 决策理论的一个中心问题,就是在一定条件下,确定某种特定的决策函数类为完全或本质完全的.

本书完全是一本以应用为主的著作.说到数学的应用,笔者几年前曾看到一个段子说:在评价诗人时,数学也是有用的.比如喝酒,我们知道,中国诗人除了苏东坡之外,大诗人的酒量都非常大,李白和杜甫都喜欢喝酒.诗人郭沫若说,李白喜欢喝酒,好!为什么呢?因为李白喜欢喝酒,就说明他跟劳动人民打成一片.光从逻辑上推理的话,剥削阶级也喝酒,为什么说喝酒就是和劳动人民打成一片?他是这样论证的,他说,盛唐以后,凡是小酒店,酒店外面挂一块布,上面写着几个字——"太白遗风",小酒店一般是穷苦人去喝酒的,老百姓一看"太白遗风",就进去喝上一杯,他们认可李白的传统,说明李白跟劳动人民打成一片.杜甫也喜欢喝酒.郭沫若却说,杜甫终生嗜酒如命,是一种典型的剥削阶级的生活形态.但如果用数学手段来评判一下,可能恰恰结论相反.我们从他们所喝酒的酒价上来计算一下,李白喝的是好酒,他有诗云:"金樽美酒斗十千",一斗酒要十千钱来买,而杜甫在长安时则很穷困,偶然得到一点钱请朋友喝酒,"速宜相就饮一斗,恰有三百青铜钱".杜甫喝的酒的价钱是一斗酒三百钱,李白是一斗酒一万钱,一比较我们知道,价格相差 33.33 倍,如果用今天的酒来做例子,李白喝的是茅台、五粮液,而杜甫喝的是二锅头,为什么说喝茅台的李白和劳动人民打成一片,而喝二锅头的杜甫是剥削阶级呢? 这当然是不对的.

刘培杰

2023 年 1 月 10 日

于哈工大

# 刘培杰数学工作室
## 已出版(即将出版)图书目录——原版影印

| 书　名 | 出版时间 | 定　价 | 编号 |
|---|---|---|---|
| 数学物理大百科全书.第1卷(英文) | 2016—01 | 418.00 | 508 |
| 数学物理大百科全书.第2卷(英文) | 2016—01 | 408.00 | 509 |
| 数学物理大百科全书.第3卷(英文) | 2016—01 | 396.00 | 510 |
| 数学物理大百科全书.第4卷(英文) | 2016—01 | 408.00 | 511 |
| 数学物理大百科全书.第5卷(英文) | 2016—01 | 368.00 | 512 |
| zeta函数,q-zeta函数,相伴级数与积分(英文) | 2015—08 | 88.00 | 513 |
| 微分形式:理论与练习(英文) | 2015—08 | 58.00 | 514 |
| 离散与微分包含的逼近和优化(英文) | 2015—08 | 58.00 | 515 |
| 艾伦·图灵:他的工作与影响(英文) | 2016—01 | 98.00 | 560 |
| 测度理论概率导论,第2版(英文) | 2016—01 | 88.00 | 561 |
| 带有潜在故障恢复系统的半马尔柯夫模型控制(英文) | 2016—01 | 98.00 | 562 |
| 数学分析原理(英文) | 2016—01 | 88.00 | 563 |
| 随机偏微分方程的有效动力学(英文) | 2016—01 | 88.00 | 564 |
| 图的谱半径(英文) | 2016—01 | 58.00 | 565 |
| 量子机器学习中数据挖掘的量子计算方法(英文) | 2016—01 | 98.00 | 566 |
| 量子物理的非常规方法(英文) | 2016—01 | 118.00 | 567 |
| 运输过程的统一非局部理论:广义波尔兹曼物理动力学,第2版(英文) | 2016—01 | 198.00 | 568 |
| 量子力学与经典力学之间的联系在原子、分子及电动力学系统建模中的应用(英文) | 2016—01 | 58.00 | 569 |
| 算术域(英文) | 2018—01 | 158.00 | 821 |
| 高等数学竞赛:1962—1991年的米洛克斯·史怀哲竞赛(英文) | 2018—01 | 128.00 | 822 |
| 用数学奥林匹克精神解决数论问题(英文) | 2018—01 | 108.00 | 823 |
| 代数几何(德文) | 2018—04 | 68.00 | 824 |
| 丢番图逼近论(英文) | 2018—01 | 78.00 | 825 |
| 代数几何学基础教程(英文) | 2018—01 | 98.00 | 826 |
| 解析数论入门课程(英文) | 2018—01 | 78.00 | 827 |
| 数论中的丢番图问题(英文) | 2018—01 | 78.00 | 829 |
| 数论(梦幻之旅):第五届中日数论研讨会演讲集(英文) | 2018—01 | 68.00 | 830 |
| 数论新应用(英文) | 2018—01 | 68.00 | 831 |
| 数论(英文) | 2018—01 | 78.00 | 832 |

# 刘培杰数学工作室
# 已出版(即将出版)图书目录——原版影印

| 书　名 | 出版时间 | 定　价 | 编号 |
|---|---|---|---|
| 湍流十讲(英文) | 2018－04 | 108.00 | 886 |
| 无穷维李代数:第3版(英文) | 2018－04 | 98.00 | 887 |
| 等值、不变量和对称性(英文) | 2018－04 | 78.00 | 888 |
| 解析数论(英文) | 2018－09 | 78.00 | 889 |
| 《数学原理》的演化:伯特兰·罗素撰写第二版时的手稿与笔记(英文) | 2018－04 | 108.00 | 890 |
| 哈密尔顿数学论文集(第4卷):几何学、分析学、天文学、概率和有限差分等(英文) | 2019－05 | 108.00 | 891 |
| 偏微分方程全局吸引子的特性(英文) | 2018－09 | 108.00 | 979 |
| 整函数与下调和函数(英文) | 2018－09 | 118.00 | 980 |
| 幂等分析(英文) | 2018－09 | 118.00 | 981 |
| 李群、离散子群与不变量理论(英文) | 2018－09 | 108.00 | 982 |
| 动力系统与统计力学(英文) | 2018－09 | 118.00 | 983 |
| 表示论与动力系统(英文) | 2018－09 | 118.00 | 984 |
| 分析学练习.第1部分(英文) | 2021－01 | 88.00 | 1247 |
| 分析学练习.第2部分,非线性分析(英文) | 2021－01 | 88.00 | 1248 |
| 初级统计学:循序渐进的方法:第10版(英文) | 2019－05 | 68.00 | 1067 |
| 工程师与科学家微分方程用书:第4版(英文) | 2019－07 | 58.00 | 1068 |
| 大学代数与三角学(英文) | 2019－06 | 78.00 | 1069 |
| 培养数学能力的途径(英文) | 2019－07 | 38.00 | 1070 |
| 工程师与科学家统计学:第4版(英文) | 2019－06 | 58.00 | 1071 |
| 贸易与经济中的应用统计学:第6版(英文) | 2019－06 | 58.00 | 1072 |
| 傅立叶级数和边值问题:第8版(英文) | 2019－05 | 48.00 | 1073 |
| 通往天文学的途径:第5版(英文) | 2019－05 | 58.00 | 1074 |
| 拉马努金笔记.第1卷(英文) | 2019－06 | 165.00 | 1078 |
| 拉马努金笔记.第2卷(英文) | 2019－06 | 165.00 | 1079 |
| 拉马努金笔记.第3卷(英文) | 2019－06 | 165.00 | 1080 |
| 拉马努金笔记.第4卷(英文) | 2019－06 | 165.00 | 1081 |
| 拉马努金笔记.第5卷(英文) | 2019－06 | 165.00 | 1082 |
| 拉马努金遗失笔记.第1卷(英文) | 2019－06 | 109.00 | 1083 |
| 拉马努金遗失笔记.第2卷(英文) | 2019－06 | 109.00 | 1084 |
| 拉马努金遗失笔记.第3卷(英文) | 2019－06 | 109.00 | 1085 |
| 拉马努金遗失笔记.第4卷(英文) | 2019－06 | 109.00 | 1086 |
| 数论:1976年纽约洛克菲勒大学数论会议记录(英文) | 2020－06 | 68.00 | 1145 |
| 数论:卡本代尔1979:1979年在南伊利诺伊卡本代尔大学举行的数论会议记录(英文) | 2020－06 | 78.00 | 1146 |
| 数论:诺德韦克豪特1983:1983年在诺德韦克豪特举行的Journees Arithmetiques数论大会会议记录(英文) | 2020－06 | 68.00 | 1147 |
| 数论:1985－1988年在纽约城市大学研究生院和大学中心举办的研讨会(英文) | 2020－06 | 68.00 | 1148 |

# 刘培杰数学工作室
# 已出版(即将出版)图书目录——原版影印

| 书　名 | 出版时间 | 定　价 | 编号 |
|---|---|---|---|
| 数论:1987 年在乌尔姆举行的 Journees Arithmetiques 数论大会会议记录(英文) | 2020—06 | 68.00 | 1149 |
| 数论:马德拉斯 1987:1987 年在马德拉斯安娜大学举行的国际拉马努金百年纪念大会会议记录(英文) | 2020—06 | 68.00 | 1150 |
| 解析数论:1988 年在东京举行的日法研讨会会议记录(英文) | 2020—06 | 68.00 | 1151 |
| 解析数论:2002 年在意大利切特拉罗举行的 C. I. M. E. 暑期班演讲集(英文) | 2020—06 | 68.00 | 1152 |
| 量子世界中的蝴蝶:最迷人的量子分形故事(英文) | 2020—06 | 118.00 | 1157 |
| 走进量子力学(英文) | 2020—06 | 118.00 | 1158 |
| 计算物理学概论(英文) | 2020—06 | 48.00 | 1159 |
| 物质,空间和时间的理论:量子理论(英文) | 2020—10 | 48.00 | 1160 |
| 物质,空间和时间的理论:经典理论(英文) | 2020—10 | 48.00 | 1161 |
| 量子场理论:解释世界的神秘背景(英文) | 2020—07 | 38.00 | 1162 |
| 计算物理学概论(英文) | 2020—06 | 48.00 | 1163 |
| 行星状星云(英文) | 2020—10 | 38.00 | 1164 |
| 基本宇宙学:从亚里士多德的宇宙到大爆炸(英文) | 2020—08 | 58.00 | 1165 |
| 数学磁流体力学(英文) | 2020—07 | 58.00 | 1166 |
| 计算科学:第 1 卷,计算的科学(日文) | 2020—07 | 88.00 | 1167 |
| 计算科学:第 2 卷,计算与宇宙(日文) | 2020—07 | 88.00 | 1168 |
| 计算科学:第 3 卷,计算与物质(日文) | 2020—07 | 88.00 | 1169 |
| 计算科学:第 4 卷,计算与生命(日文) | 2020—07 | 88.00 | 1170 |
| 计算科学:第 5 卷,计算与地球环境(日文) | 2020—07 | 88.00 | 1171 |
| 计算科学:第 6 卷,计算与社会(日文) | 2020—07 | 88.00 | 1172 |
| 计算科学.别卷,超级计算机(日文) | 2020—07 | 88.00 | 1173 |
| 多复变函数论(日文) | 2022—06 | 78.00 | 1518 |
| 复变函数入门(日文) | 2022—06 | 78.00 | 1523 |
| 代数与数论:综合方法(英文) | 2020—10 | 78.00 | 1185 |
| 复分析:现代函数理论第一课(英文) | 2020—07 | 58.00 | 1186 |
| 斐波那契数列和卡特兰数:导论(英文) | 2020—10 | 68.00 | 1187 |
| 组合推理:计数艺术介绍(英文) | 2020—07 | 88.00 | 1188 |
| 二次互反律的傅里叶分析证明(英文) | 2020—07 | 48.00 | 1189 |
| 旋瓦兹分布的希尔伯特变换与应用(英文) | 2020—07 | 58.00 | 1190 |
| 泛函分析:巴拿赫空间理论入门(英文) | 2020—07 | 48.00 | 1191 |
| 卡塔兰数入门(英文) | 2019—05 | 68.00 | 1060 |
| 测度与积分(英文) | 2019—04 | 68.00 | 1059 |
| 组合学手册.第一卷(英文) | 2020—06 | 128.00 | 1153 |
| ＊—代数、局部紧群和巴拿赫＊—代数丛的表示.第一卷,群和代数的基本表示理论(英文) | 2020—05 | 148.00 | 1154 |
| 电磁理论(英文) | 2020—08 | 48.00 | 1193 |
| 连续介质力学中的非线性问题(英文) | 2020—09 | 78.00 | 1195 |
| 多变量数学入门(英文) | 2021—05 | 68.00 | 1317 |
| 偏微分方程入门(英文) | 2021—05 | 88.00 | 1318 |
| 若尔当典范性:理论与实践(英文) | 2021—07 | 68.00 | 1366 |
| 伽罗瓦理论.第 4 版(英文) | 2021—08 | 88.00 | 1408 |
| R 统计学概论 | 2023—03 | 88.00 | 1614 |
| 基于不确定静态和动态问题解的仿射算术(英文) | 2023—03 | 38.00 | 1618 |

# 刘培杰数学工作室
# 已出版(即将出版)图书目录——原版影印

| 书　　名 | 出版时间 | 定　价 | 编号 |
|---|---|---|---|
| 典型群,错排与素数(英文) | 2020—11 | 58.00 | 1204 |
| 李代数的表示:通过 gln 进行介绍(英文) | 2020—10 | 38.00 | 1205 |
| 实分析演讲集(英文) | 2020—10 | 38.00 | 1206 |
| 现代分析及其应用的课程(英文) | 2020—10 | 58.00 | 1207 |
| 运动中的抛射物数学(英文) | 2020—10 | 38.00 | 1208 |
| 2—纽结与它们的群(英文) | 2020—10 | 38.00 | 1209 |
| 概率,策略和选择:博弈与选举中的数学(英文) | 2020—11 | 58.00 | 1210 |
| 分析学引论(英文) | 2020—11 | 58.00 | 1211 |
| 量子群:通往流代数的路径(英文) | 2020—11 | 38.00 | 1212 |
| 集合论入门(英文) | 2020—10 | 48.00 | 1213 |
| 酉反射群(英文) | 2020—11 | 58.00 | 1214 |
| 探索数学:吸引人的证明方式(英文) | 2020—11 | 58.00 | 1215 |
| 微分拓扑短期课程(英文) | 2020—10 | 48.00 | 1216 |
| 抽象凸分析(英文) | 2020—11 | 68.00 | 1222 |
| 费马大定理笔记(英文) | 2021—03 | 48.00 | 1223 |
| 高斯与雅可比和(英文) | 2021—03 | 78.00 | 1224 |
| π 与算术几何平均:关于解析数论和计算复杂性的研究(英文) | 2021—01 | 58.00 | 1225 |
| 复分析入门(英文) | 2021—03 | 48.00 | 1226 |
| 爱德华·卢卡斯与素性测定(英文) | 2021—03 | 78.00 | 1227 |
| 通往凸分析及其应用的简单路径(英文) | 2021—01 | 68.00 | 1229 |
| 微分几何的各个方面.第一卷(英文) | 2021—01 | 58.00 | 1230 |
| 微分几何的各个方面.第二卷(英文) | 2020—12 | 58.00 | 1231 |
| 微分几何的各个方面.第三卷(英文) | 2020—12 | 58.00 | 1232 |
| 沃克流形几何学(英文) | 2020—11 | 58.00 | 1233 |
| 彷射和韦尔几何应用(英文) | 2020—12 | 58.00 | 1234 |
| 双曲几何学的旋转向量空间方法(英文) | 2021—02 | 58.00 | 1235 |
| 积分:分析学的关键(英文) | 2020—12 | 48.00 | 1236 |
| 为有天分的新生准备的分析学基础教材(英文) | 2020—11 | 48.00 | 1237 |
| 数学不等式.第一卷.对称多项式不等式(英文) | 2021—03 | 108.00 | 1273 |
| 数学不等式.第二卷.对称有理不等式与对称无理不等式(英文) | 2021—03 | 108.00 | 1274 |
| 数学不等式.第三卷.循环不等式与非循环不等式(英文) | 2021—03 | 108.00 | 1275 |
| 数学不等式.第四卷.Jensen 不等式的扩展与加细(英文) | 2021—03 | 108.00 | 1276 |
| 数学不等式.第五卷.创建不等式与解不等式的其他方法(英文) | 2021—04 | 108.00 | 1277 |

# 刘培杰数学工作室
# 已出版(即将出版)图书目录——原版影印

| 书　　名 | 出版时间 | 定　价 | 编号 |
|---|---|---|---|
| 冯·诺依曼代数中的谱位移函数:半有限冯·诺依曼代数中的谱位移函数与谱流(英文) | 2021-06 | 98.00 | 1308 |
| 链接结构:关于嵌入完全图的直线中链接单形的组合结构(英文) | 2021-05 | 58.00 | 1309 |
| 代数几何方法.第1卷(英文) | 2021-06 | 68.00 | 1310 |
| 代数几何方法.第2卷(英文) | 2021-06 | 68.00 | 1311 |
| 代数几何方法.第3卷(英文) | 2021-06 | 58.00 | 1312 |

| 书　　名 | 出版时间 | 定　价 | 编号 |
|---|---|---|---|
| 代数、生物信息和机器人技术的算法问题.第四卷,独立恒等式系统(俄文) | 2020-08 | 118.00 | 1199 |
| 代数、生物信息和机器人技术的算法问题.第五卷,相对覆盖性和独立可拆分恒等式系统(俄文) | 2020-08 | 118.00 | 1200 |
| 代数、生物信息和机器人技术的算法问题.第六卷,恒等式和准恒等式的相等问题、可推导性和可实现性(俄文) | 2020-08 | 128.00 | 1201 |
| 分数阶微积分的应用:非局部动态过程,分数阶导热系数(俄文) | 2021-01 | 68.00 | 1241 |
| 泛函分析问题与练习:第2版(俄文) | 2021-01 | 98.00 | 1242 |
| 集合论、数学逻辑和算法论问题:第5版(俄文) | 2021-01 | 98.00 | 1243 |
| 微分几何和拓扑短期课程(俄文) | 2021-01 | 98.00 | 1244 |
| 素数规律(俄文) | 2021-01 | 88.00 | 1245 |
| 无穷边值问题解的递减:无界域中的拟线性椭圆和抛物方程(俄文) | 2021-01 | 48.00 | 1246 |
| 微分几何讲义(俄文) | 2020-12 | 98.00 | 1253 |
| 二次型和矩阵(俄文) | 2021-01 | 98.00 | 1255 |
| 积分和级数.第2卷,特殊函数(俄文) | 2021-01 | 168.00 | 1258 |
| 积分和级数.第3卷,特殊函数补充:第2版(俄文) | 2021-01 | 178.00 | 1264 |
| 几何图上的微分方程(俄文) | 2021-01 | 138.00 | 1259 |
| 数论教程:第2版(俄文) | 2021-01 | 98.00 | 1260 |
| 非阿基米德分析及其应用(俄文) | 2021-03 | 98.00 | 1261 |
| 古典群和量子群的压缩(俄文) | 2021-03 | 98.00 | 1263 |
| 数学分析习题集.第3卷,多元函数:第3版(俄文) | 2021-03 | 98.00 | 1266 |
| 数学习题:乌拉尔国立大学数学力学系大学生奥林匹克(俄文) | 2021-03 | 98.00 | 1267 |
| 柯西定理和微分方程的特解(俄文) | 2021-03 | 98.00 | 1268 |
| 组合极值问题及其应用:第3版(俄文) | 2021-03 | 98.00 | 1269 |
| 数学词典(俄文) | 2021-01 | 98.00 | 1271 |
| 确定性混沌分析模型(俄文) | 2021-06 | 168.00 | 1307 |
| 精选初等数学习题和定理.立体几何.第3版(俄文) | 2021-03 | 68.00 | 1316 |
| 微分几何习题:第3版(俄文) | 2021-05 | 98.00 | 1336 |
| 精选初等数学习题和定理.平面几何.第4版(俄文) | 2021-05 | 68.00 | 1335 |
| 曲面理论在欧氏空间 $E_n$ 中的直接表示(俄文) | 2022-01 | 68.00 | 1444 |
| 维纳—霍普夫离散算子和托普利兹算子:某些可数赋范空间中的诺特性和可逆性(俄文) | 2022-03 | 108.00 | 1496 |
| Maple 中的数论:数论中的计算机计算(俄文) | 2022-03 | 88.00 | 1497 |
| 贝尔曼和克努特问题及其概括:加法运算的复杂性(俄文) | 2022-03 | 138.00 | 1498 |

# 刘培杰数学工作室
## 已出版(即将出版)图书目录——原版影印

| 书　名 | 出版时间 | 定　价 | 编号 |
|---|---|---|---|
| 复分析:共形映射(俄文) | 2022—07 | 48.00 | 1542 |
| 微积分代数样条和多项式及其在数值方法中的应用(俄文) | 2022—08 | 128.00 | 1543 |
| 蒙特卡罗方法中的随机过程和场模型:算法和应用(俄文) | 2022—08 | 88.00 | 1544 |
| 线性椭圆型方程组:论二阶椭圆型方程的迪利克雷问题(俄文) | 2022—08 | 98.00 | 1561 |
| 动态系统解的增长特性:估值、稳定性、应用(俄文) | 2022—08 | 118.00 | 1565 |
| 群的自由积分解:建立和应用(俄文) | 2022—08 | 78.00 | 1570 |
| 混合方程和偏差自变数方程问题:解的存在和唯一性(俄文) | 2023—01 | 78.00 | 1582 |
| 拟度量空间分析:存在和逼近定理(俄文) | 2023—01 | 108.00 | 1583 |
| 二维和三维流形上函数的拓扑性质:函数的拓扑分类(俄文) | 2023—03 | 68.00 | 1584 |
| 齐次马尔科夫过程建模的矩阵方法:此类方法能够用于不同目上的的复杂系统研究、设计和完善(俄文) | 2023—03 | 68.00 | 1594 |
| 周期函数的近似方法和特性:特殊课程(俄文) | 2023—04 | 158.00 | 1622 |
| 扩散方程解的矩函数:变分法(俄文) | 2023—03 | 58.00 | 1623 |
| 多赋范空间和广义函数:理论及应用(俄文) | 2023—03 | 98.00 | 1632 |
| 分析中的多值映射:部分应用(俄文) | 2023—06 | 98.00 | 1634 |
| 数学物理问题(俄文) | 2023—03 | 78.00 | 1636 |

| 书　名 | 出版时间 | 定　价 | 编号 |
|---|---|---|---|
| 狭义相对论与广义相对论:时空与引力导论(英文) | 2021—07 | 88.00 | 1319 |
| 束流物理学和粒子加速器的实践介绍:第2版(英文) | 2021—07 | 88.00 | 1320 |
| 凝聚态物理中的拓扑和微分几何简介(英文) | 2021—05 | 88.00 | 1321 |
| 混沌映射:动力学、分形学和快速涨落(英文) | 2021—05 | 128.00 | 1322 |
| 广义相对论:黑洞、引力波和宇宙学介绍(英文) | 2021—06 | 68.00 | 1323 |
| 现代分析电磁均质化(英文) | 2021—06 | 68.00 | 1324 |
| 为科学家提供的基本流体动力学(英文) | 2021—06 | 88.00 | 1325 |
| 视觉天文学:理解夜空的指南(英文) | 2021—06 | 68.00 | 1326 |
| 物理学中的计算方法(英文) | 2021—06 | 68.00 | 1327 |
| 单星的结构与演化:导论(英文) | 2021—06 | 108.00 | 1328 |
| 超越居里:1903年至1963年物理界四位女性及其著名发现(英文) | 2021—06 | 68.00 | 1329 |
| 范德瓦尔斯流体热力学的进展(英文) | 2021—06 | 68.00 | 1330 |
| 先进的托卡马克稳定性理论(英文) | 2021—06 | 88.00 | 1331 |
| 经典场论导论:基本相互作用的过程(英文) | 2021—07 | 88.00 | 1332 |
| 光致电离量子动力学方法原理(英文) | 2021—07 | 108.00 | 1333 |
| 经典域论和应力:能量张量(英文) | 2021—05 | 88.00 | 1334 |
| 非线性太赫兹光谱的概念与应用(英文) | 2021—06 | 68.00 | 1337 |
| 电磁学中的无穷空间并矢格林函数(英文) | 2021—06 | 88.00 | 1338 |
| 物理科学基础数学.第1卷,齐次边值问题、傅里叶方法和特殊函数(英文) | 2021—07 | 108.00 | 1339 |
| 离散量子力学(英文) | 2021—07 | 68.00 | 1340 |
| 核磁共振的物理学和数学(英文) | 2021—07 | 108.00 | 1341 |
| 分子水平的静电学(英文) | 2021—08 | 68.00 | 1342 |
| 非线性波:理论、计算机模拟、实验(英文) | 2021—06 | 108.00 | 1343 |
| 石墨烯光学:经典问题的电解解决方案(英文) | 2021—06 | 68.00 | 1344 |
| 超材料多元宇宙(英文) | 2021—07 | 68.00 | 1345 |
| 银河系外的天体物理学(英文) | 2021—07 | 68.00 | 1346 |
| 原子物理学(英文) | 2021—07 | 68.00 | 1347 |
| 将光打结:将拓扑学应用于光学(英文) | 2021—07 | 68.00 | 1348 |
| 电磁学:问题与解法(英文) | 2021—07 | 88.00 | 1364 |
| 海浪的原理:介绍量子力学的技巧与应用(英文) | 2021—07 | 108.00 | 1365 |

# 刘培杰数学工作室
# 已出版(即将出版)图书目录——原版影印

| 书 名 | 出版时间 | 定 价 | 编号 |
|---|---|---|---|
| 多孔介质中的流体:输运与相变(英文) | 2021—07 | 68.00 | 1372 |
| 洛伦兹群的物理学(英文) | 2021—08 | 68.00 | 1373 |
| 物理导论的数学方法和解决方法手册(英文) | 2021—08 | 68.00 | 1374 |
| 非线性波数学物理学入门(英文) | 2021—08 | 88.00 | 1376 |
| 波:基本原理和动力学(英文) | 2021—07 | 68.00 | 1377 |
| 光电子量子计量学.第1卷,基础(英文) | 2021—07 | 88.00 | 1383 |
| 光电子量子计量学.第2卷,应用与进展(英文) | 2021—07 | 68.00 | 1384 |
| 复杂流的格子玻尔兹曼建模的工程应用(英文) | 2021—08 | 68.00 | 1393 |
| 电偶极矩挑战(英文) | 2021—08 | 108.00 | 1394 |
| 电动力学:问题与解法(英文) | 2021—09 | 68.00 | 1395 |
| 自由电子激光的经典理论(英文) | 2021—08 | 68.00 | 1397 |
| 曼哈顿计划——核武器物理学简介(英文) | 2021—09 | 68.00 | 1401 |
| 粒子物理学(英文) | 2021—09 | 68.00 | 1402 |
| 引力场中的量子信息(英文) | 2021—09 | 128.00 | 1403 |
| 器件物理学的基本经典力学(英文) | 2021—09 | 68.00 | 1404 |
| 等离子体物理及其空间应用导论.第1卷,基本原理和初步过程(英文) | 2021—09 | 68.00 | 1405 |
| 磁约束聚变等离子体物理:理想MHD理论(英文) | 2023—03 | 68.00 | 1613 |
| 相对论量子场论.第1卷,典范形式体系(英文) | 2023—03 | 38.00 | 1615 |
| 相对论量子场论.第2卷,路径积分形式(英文) | 2023—06 | 38.00 | 1616 |
| 相对论量子场论.第3卷,量子场论的应用(英文) | 2023—06 | 38.00 | 1617 |
| 涌现的物理学(英文) | 2023—05 | 58.00 | 1619 |
| 量子化旋涡:一本拓扑激发手册(英文) | 2023—04 | 68.00 | 1620 |
| 非线性动力学:实践的介绍性调查(英文) | 2023—05 | 68.00 | 1621 |
| 静电加速器:一个多功能工具(英文) | 2023—06 | 58.00 | 1625 |
| 相对论多体理论与统计力学(英文) | 2023—06 | 58.00 | 1626 |
| 经典力学.第1卷,工具与向量(英文) | 2023—04 | 38.00 | 1627 |
| 经典力学.第2卷,运动学和匀加速运动(英文) | 2023—04 | 58.00 | 1628 |
| 经典力学.第3卷,牛顿定律和匀速圆周运动(英文) | 2023—04 | 58.00 | 1629 |
| 经典力学.第4卷,万有引力定律(英文) | 2023—04 | 38.00 | 1630 |
| 经典力学.第5卷,守恒定律与旋转运动(英文) | 2023—04 | 38.00 | 1631 |
| 对称问题:纳维尔-斯托克斯问题(英文) | 2023—04 | 38.00 | 1638 |
| 摄影的物理和艺术.第1卷,几何与光的本质(英文) | 2023—04 | 78.00 | 1639 |
| 摄影的物理和艺术.第2卷,能量与色彩(英文) | 2023—04 | 78.00 | 1640 |
| 摄影的物理和艺术.第3卷,探测器与数码的意义(英文) | 2023—04 | 78.00 | 1641 |
| | | | |
| 拓扑与超弦理论焦点问题(英文) | 2021—07 | 58.00 | 1349 |
| 应用数学:理论、方法与实践(英文) | 2021—07 | 78.00 | 1350 |
| 非线性特征值问题:牛顿型方法与非线性瑞利函数(英文) | 2021—07 | 58.00 | 1351 |
| 广义膨胀和齐性:利用齐性构造齐次系统的李雅普诺夫函数和控制律(英文) | 2021—06 | 48.00 | 1352 |
| 解析数论焦点问题(英文) | 2021—07 | 58.00 | 1353 |
| 随机微分方程:动态系统方法(英文) | 2021—07 | 58.00 | 1354 |
| 经典力学与微分几何(英文) | 2021—07 | 58.00 | 1355 |
| 负定相交形式流形上的瞬子模空间几何(英文) | 2021—07 | 68.00 | 1356 |
| | | | |
| 广义卡塔兰轨道分析:广义卡塔兰轨道计算数字的方法(英文) | 2021—07 | 48.00 | 1367 |
| 洛伦兹方法的变分:二维与三维洛伦兹方法(英文) | 2021—08 | 38.00 | 1378 |
| 几何、分析和数论精编(英文) | 2021—08 | 68.00 | 1380 |
| 从一个新角度看数论:通过遗传方法引入现实的概念(英文) | 2021—07 | 58.00 | 1387 |
| 动力系统:短期课程(英文) | 2021—08 | 68.00 | 1382 |
| 几何路径:理论与实践(英文) | 2021—08 | 48.00 | 1385 |

| 书　名 | 出版时间 | 定　价 | 编号 |
|---|---|---|---|
| 论天体力学中某些问题的不可积性(英文) | 2021—07 | 88.00 | 1396 |
| 广义斐波那契数列及其性质(英文) | 2021—08 | 38.00 | 1386 |
| 对称函数和麦克唐纳多项式:余代数结构与 Kawanaka 恒等式(英文) | 2021—09 | 38.00 | 1400 |
| 杰弗里·英格拉姆·泰勒科学论文集:第 1 卷.固体力学(英文) | 2021—05 | 78.00 | 1360 |
| 杰弗里·英格拉姆·泰勒科学论文集:第 2 卷.气象学、海洋学和湍流(英文) | 2021—05 | 68.00 | 1361 |
| 杰弗里·英格拉姆·泰勒科学论文集:第 3 卷.空气动力学以及落弹数和爆炸的力学(英文) | 2021—05 | 68.00 | 1362 |
| 杰弗里·英格拉姆·泰勒科学论文集:第 4 卷.有关流体力学(英文) | 2021—05 | 58.00 | 1363 |
| 非局域泛函演化方程:积分与分数阶(英文) | 2021—08 | 48.00 | 1390 |
| 理论工作者的高等微分几何:纤维丛、射流流形和拉格朗日理论(英文) | 2021—08 | 68.00 | 1391 |
| 半线性退化椭圆微分方程:局部定理与整体定理(英文) | 2021—07 | 48.00 | 1392 |
| 非交换几何、规范理论和重整化:一般简介与非交换量子场论的重整化(英文) | 2021—09 | 78.00 | 1406 |
| 数论论文集:拉普拉斯变换和带有数论系数的幂级数(俄文) | 2021—09 | 48.00 | 1407 |
| 挠理论专题:相对极大值,单射与扩充模(英文) | 2021—09 | 88.00 | 1410 |
| 强正则图与欧几里得若尔当代数:非通常关系中的启示(英文) | 2021—10 | 48.00 | 1411 |
| 拉格朗日几何和哈密顿几何:力学的应用(英文) | 2021—10 | 48.00 | 1412 |
| 时滞微分方程与差分方程的振动理论:二阶与三阶(英文) | 2021—10 | 98.00 | 1417 |
| 卷积结构与几何函数理论:用以研究特定几何函数理论方向的分数阶微积分算子与卷积结构(英文) | 2021—10 | 48.00 | 1418 |
| 经典数学物理的历史发展(英文) | 2021—10 | 78.00 | 1419 |
| 扩展线性丢番图问题(英文) | 2021—10 | 38.00 | 1420 |
| 一类混沌动力系统的分歧分析与控制:分歧分析与控制(英文) | 2021—11 | 38.00 | 1421 |
| 伽利略空间和伪伽利略空间中一些特殊曲线的几何性质(英文) | 2022—01 | 68.00 | 1422 |
| 一阶偏微分方程:哈密尔顿—雅可比理论(英文) | 2021—11 | 48.00 | 1424 |
| 各向异性黎曼多面体的反问题:分段光滑的各向异性黎曼多面体反边界谱问题:唯一性(英文) | 2021—11 | 33.00 | 1425 |
| 项目反应理论手册.第一卷,模型(英文) | 2021—11 | 138.00 | 1431 |
| 项目反应理论手册.第二卷,统计工具(英文) | 2021—11 | 118.00 | 1432 |
| 项目反应理论手册.第三卷,应用(英文) | 2021—11 | 138.00 | 1433 |
| 二次无理数:经典数论入门(英文) | 2022—05 | 138.00 | 1434 |

# 刘培杰数学工作室
## 已出版(即将出版)图书目录——原版影印

| 书　名 | 出版时间 | 定　价 | 编号 |
|---|---|---|---|
| 数,形与对称性:数论,几何和群论导论(英文) | 2022—05 | 128.00 | 1435 |
| 有限域手册(英文) | 2021—11 | 178.00 | 1436 |
| 计算数论(英文) | 2021—11 | 148.00 | 1437 |
| 拟群与其表示简介(英文) | 2021—11 | 88.00 | 1438 |
| 数论与密码学导论:第二版(英文) | 2022—01 | 148.00 | 1423 |
| 几何分析中的柯西变换与黎兹变换:解析调和容量和李普希兹调和容量、变化和振荡以及一致可求长性(英文) | 2021—12 | 38.00 | 1465 |
| 近似不动点定理及其应用(英文) | 2022—05 | 28.00 | 1466 |
| 局部域的相关内容解析:对局部域的扩展及其伽罗瓦群的研究(英文) | 2022—01 | 38.00 | 1467 |
| 反问题的二进制恢复方法(英文) | 2022—03 | 28.00 | 1468 |
| 对几何函数中某些类的各个方面的研究:复变量理论(英文) | 2022—01 | 38.00 | 1469 |
| 覆盖、对应和非交换几何(英文) | 2022—01 | 28.00 | 1470 |
| 最优控制理论中的随机线性调节器问题:随机最优线性调节器问题(英文) | 2022—01 | 38.00 | 1473 |
| 正交分解法:涡流流体动力学应用的正交分解法(英文) | 2022—01 | 38.00 | 1475 |
| 芬斯勒几何的某些问题(英文) | 2022—03 | 38.00 | 1476 |
| 受限三体问题(英文) | 2022—05 | 38.00 | 1477 |
| 利用马利亚万微积分进行 Greeks 的计算:连续过程、跳跃过程中的马利亚万微积分和金融领域中的 Greeks(英文) | 2022—05 | 48.00 | 1478 |
| 经典分析和泛函分析的应用:分析学的应用(英文) | 2022—03 | 38.00 | 1479 |
| 特殊芬斯勒空间的探究(英文) | 2022—03 | 48.00 | 1480 |
| 某些图形的施泰纳距离的细谷多项式:细谷多项式与图的维纳指数(英文) | 2022—05 | 38.00 | 1481 |
| 图论问题的遗传算法:在新鲜与模糊的环境中(英文) | 2022—05 | 48.00 | 1482 |
| 多项式映射的渐近簇(英文) | 2022—05 | 38.00 | 1483 |
| 一维系统中的混沌:符号动力学,映射序列,一致收敛和沙可夫斯基定理(英文) | 2022—05 | 38.00 | 1509 |
| 多维边界层流动与传热分析:粘性流体流动的数学建模与分析(英文) | 2022—05 | 38.00 | 1510 |
| 演绎理论物理学的原理:一种基于量子力学波函数的逐次置信估计的一般理论的提议(英文) | 2022—05 | 38.00 | 1511 |
| $R^2$ 和 $R^3$ 中的仿射弹性曲线:概念和方法(英文) | 2022—08 | 38.00 | 1512 |
| 算术数列中除数函数的分布:基本内容、调查、方法、第二矩、新结果(英文) | 2022—05 | 28.00 | 1513 |
| 抛物型狄拉克算子和薛定谔方程:不定常薛定谔方程的抛物型狄拉克算子及其应用(英文) | 2022—07 | 28.00 | 1514 |
| 黎曼-希尔伯特问题与量子场论:可积重正化、戴森-施温格方程(英文) | 2022—08 | 38.00 | 1515 |
| 代数结构和几何结构的形变理论(英文) | 2022—08 | 48.00 | 1516 |
| 概率结构和模糊结构上的不动点:概率结构和直觉模糊度量空间的不动点定理(英文) | 2022—08 | 38.00 | 1517 |

# 刘培杰数学工作室
## 已出版(即将出版)图书目录——原版影印

| 书 名 | 出版时间 | 定 价 | 编号 |
|---|---|---|---|
| 反若尔当对:简单反若尔当对的自同构(英文) | 2022—07 | 28.00 | 1533 |
| 对某些黎曼—芬斯勒空间变换的研究:芬斯勒几何中的某些变换(英文) | 2022—07 | 38.00 | 1534 |
| 内诣零流形映射的尼尔森数的阿诺索夫关系(英文) | 2023—01 | 38.00 | 1535 |
| 与广义积分变换有关的分数次演算:对分数次演算的研究(英文) | 2023—01 | 48.00 | 1536 |
| 强子的芬斯勒几何和吕拉几何(宇宙学方面):强子结构的芬斯勒几何和吕拉几何(拓扑缺陷)(英文) | 2022—08 | 38.00 | 1537 |
| 一种基于混沌的非线性最优化问题:作业调度问题(英文) | 2023—03 | 38.00 | 1538 |
| 广义概率论发展前景:关于趣味数学与置信函数实际应用的一些原创观点(英文) | 2023—03 | 48.00 | 1539 |
| 纽结与物理学:第二版(英文) | 2022—09 | 118.00 | 1547 |
| 正交多项式和q—级数的前沿(英文) | 2022—09 | 98.00 | 1548 |
| 算子理论问题集(英文) | 2022—09 | 108.00 | 1549 |
| 抽象代数:群、环与域的应用导论:第二版(英文) | 2023—01 | 98.00 | 1550 |
| 菲尔兹奖得主演讲集:第三版(英文) | 2023—01 | 138.00 | 1551 |
| 多元实函数教程(英文) | 2022—09 | 118.00 | 1552 |
| 球面空间形式群的几何学:第二版(英文) | 2022—09 | 98.00 | 1566 |
| 对称群的表示论(英文) | 2023—01 | 98.00 | 1585 |
| 纽结理论:第二版(英文) | 2023—01 | 88.00 | 1586 |
| 拟群理论的基础与应用(英文) | 2023—01 | 88.00 | 1587 |
| 组合学:第二版(英文) | 2023—01 | 98.00 | 1588 |
| 加性组合学:研究问题手册(英文) | 2023—01 | 68.00 | 1589 |
| 扭曲、平铺与镶嵌:几何折纸中的数学方法(英文) | 2023—01 | 98.00 | 1590 |
| 离散与计算几何手册:第三版(英文) | 2023—01 | 248.00 | 1591 |
| 离散与组合数学手册:第二版(英文) | 2023—01 | 248.00 | 1592 |
| 分析学教程.第1卷,一元实变量函数的微积分分析学介绍(英文) | 2023—01 | 118.00 | 1595 |
| 分析学教程.第2卷,多元函数的微分和积分,向量微积分(英文) | 2023—01 | 118.00 | 1596 |
| 分析学教程.第3卷,测度与积分理论,复变量的复值函数(英文) | 2023—01 | 118.00 | 1597 |
| 分析学教程.第4卷,傅里叶分析,常微分方程,变分法(英文) | 2023—01 | 118.00 | 1598 |
| 沃尔夫数学奖.第1卷 | 2023—05 | 118.00 | 1644 |
| 沃尔夫数学奖.第2卷 | 2023—05 | 138.00 | 1645 |
| 沃尔夫数学奖.第3卷 | 2023—05 | 108.00 | 1646 |
| 沃尔夫数学奖.第4卷 | 2023—05 | 108.00 | 1647 |

# 刘培杰数学工作室
## 已出版(即将出版)图书目录——原版影印

| 书　　名 | 出版时间 | 定　价 | 编号 |
|---|---|---|---|
| 共形映射及其应用手册(英文) | 2023—07 | 158.00 | 1674 |
| 广义三角函数与双曲函数(英文) | 2023—07 | 78.00 | 1675 |
| 振动与波:概论:第二版(英文) | 2023—07 | 88.00 | 1676 |
| 几何约束系统原理手册(英文) | 2023—07 | 120.00 | 1677 |
| 微分方程与包含的拓扑方法(英文) | 即将出版 | | 1678 |
| 数学分析中的前沿话题(英文) | 即将出版 | | 1679 |
| 流体力学建模:不稳定性与湍流(英文) | 即将出版 | | 1680 |

**联系地址**:哈尔滨市南岗区复华四道街 10 号　哈尔滨工业大学出版社刘培杰数学工作室
**网　　址**:http://lpj.hit.edu.cn/
**邮　　编**:150006
**联系电话**:0451—86281378　　13904613167
E-mail:lpj1378@163.com